RINGLINGVILLE USA

RINGLINGVILLE
USA

THE STUPENDOUS STORY OF SEVEN SIBLINGS AND THEIR STUNNING CIRCUS SUCCESS

JERRY APPS

FOREWORD BY FRED DAHLINGER JR.

WISCONSIN HISTORICAL SOCIETY PRESS

Madison, Wisconsin

Published by the Wisconsin Historical Society Press

Publication of this book was made possible in part by a grant from the John C. Geilfuss fellowship fund.

All images courtesy of the Wisconsin Historical Society's Circus World Museum, Baraboo, Wisconsin, unless otherwise indicated. All Circus World images are identified as CWM.

Publications of the Wisconsin Historical Society Press are available at quantity discounts for promotions, fund raising, and educational use. Write to the above address for more information.

Printed in the United States of America

Designed by Jane Tenenbaum

09 08 07 06 05   5 4 3 2 1

Library of Congress Cataloging-in-Publication Data

Apps, Jerold W., 1934–

  Ringlingville USA: the stupendous story of seven siblings and their stunning circus success / Jerry Apps ; foreword by Fred Dahlinger Jr.

      p. cm.

  Includes bibliographical references and index.

  ISBN 0-87020-354-1 (hardcover: alk. paper)—ISBN 0-87020-355-X (pbk.: alk. paper)

  1. Ringling Brothers—History. 2. Ringling Brothers Barnum and Bailey Combined Shows—History. 3. Circus performers—United States—Biography. 4. Circus—United States. I. Title.

GV1821.R5A66 2005

791.3—dc22

                                                                              2004007086

For Fred Dahlinger Jr.
and Circus World Museum,
national treasures.

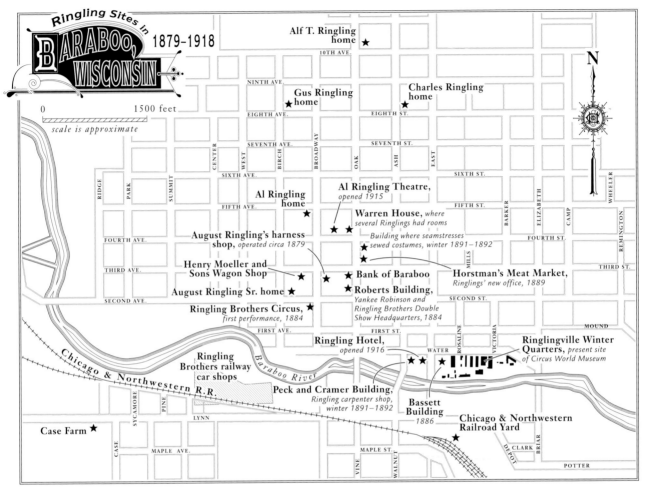

Ringling Sites in
BARABOO, WISCONSIN
1879–1918

0   1500 feet
scale is approximate

N

Alf T. Ringling home ★

Gus Ringling ★ home

Charles Ringling home ★

Al Ringling home ★

Al Ringling Theatre, *opened 1915*

Warren House, *where several Ringlings had rooms*

August Ringling's harness shop, *operated circa 1879*

Building where seamstresses ★ sewed costumes, winter 1891–1892

Henry Moeller and Sons Wagon Shop ★

★ Bank of Baraboo

Horstman's Meat Market, *Ringlings' new office, 1889*

August Ringling Sr. home ★

★ Roberts Building, *Yankee Robinson and Ringling Brothers Double Show Headquarters, 1884*

Ringling Brothers Circus, *first performance, 1884* ★

Ringling Hotel, *opened 1916*

Ringlingville Winter Quarters, *present site of Circus World Museum*

Chicago & Northwestern R.R.

Ringling Brothers railway car shops

Baraboo River

Peck and Cramer Building, *Ringling carpenter shop, winter 1891–1892*

Bassett Building *1886*

Chicago & Northwestern Railroad Yard ★

Case Farm ★

MAP BY AMELIA JANES

Contents

Foreword

The Ringling story is one that typifies what was and is possible in America. Seven sons born to recent immigrants were propelled by a childhood dream to escape their poverty through hard work. They chose a path for which they had no experience or capital, only their self-discipline and determination. The business they selected was one of the riskiest in the world: the circus. It required everything of its people: the full measure of time, energy, and money, along with knowledge of public performance, technology and transportation, marketing, creative artistry in several forms, and a broad awareness of the national economy in all of its many ramifications.

The Ringling Brothers succeeded in their quest, far beyond their wildest dreams. The secret of their achievements was teamwork, facilitated by their personal bonds. It was their mutual respect and trust, not a piece of paper, that empowered them to rise above all competitors. Each had his assigned area of responsibility, but their capability in working together was greater than the sum of the parts because of their awesome allegiance to each other.

The Ringlings and their circus were last studied in depth more than four decades ago. A significant amount of new archival material has subsequently become available to justify an entirely new appraisal of the Ringlings as people, their circus, and the winter quarters where they organized their show efforts for each annual tour. For the first time, the circus's financial records, along with the personal correspondence that passed among the brothers as they planned and managed their circus empire, are available for review and analysis. Jerry Apps has woven that information together with local documentation in newspapers, circus ephemera, and photography to re-create the time of the Baraboo boys and their circus. Placed in the context of the America of their time, the work brings about a broader perspective of the importance of their accomplishments and contributions.

The Ringling circuses were marvels of business enterprise, enthusiastically admired as much for their logistical expertise, technological innovations, and educational value as for their tented presentations. But their rise was probably fueled equally by the Brothers' genuine appreciation for their guests. Their philosophy of "The New School of American Showmen" set the stage. Their circus was a quality enterprise, safe and wholesome for the entire family, devoid of anything that anyone might have judged, in that time, offensive in the slightest degree.

Initially, the Ringlings were "Baraboo's Boys" and "Wisconsin's own" adopted sons, owners of an upstart circus that was prospering largely by efforts that took them outside of the Badger State. Their payroll pumped dollars into the pockets of local merchants during the winter, and their deposits enhanced the status of the Bank of Baraboo. Their good fortune, however, did not translate into recognized community support. The Ringlings' only charitable giving that was publicly noted during their residency was a contribution toward a local church's pipe organ.

The Brothers may have expressed their charitable demeanor by continuing to personally manage their circuses long after they could have sold them and retired as wealthy men. They felt an obligation to the well-chosen, dedicated men and women who served them diligently for many years. The Brothers continued on with the road shows until they died in harness. Anyone seeking financial improvement could have taken a job with the Ringlings and worked hard, as the Brothers did in the beginning to earn their security. And thousands did so.

Eventually, like the prophet, the one place where the Ringlings did not have honor was in their hometown. When the Brothers offered the Al Ringling Theatre as a gift to the city, Baraboo rebuffed the offer. The reaction was a hallmark of the local perspective. Taxes were another sore point, and the Brothers kept them at bay through constant leaks of "plans" to relocate elsewhere. The failure of the circus to return home following the 1918 tour caused hardly a ripple in the city that had served as its winter quarters for over three decades. The rift that was first felt years before was complete.

In 1919, long after the Ringling Brothers had risen to the top of the circus world, John Ringling admitted, "The psychology of the circus is really simple: Our appeal is to elemental instincts, to the child that is in every man. What they call 'the lure of the circus' is merely the great, unexpressed yearning of every human being to be young again." The Brothers' quest to make their valued guests feel young again suggests that they sought to relive their own childhood, one marked by poverty but also by imagination that knew no bounds.

Fred Dahlinger Jr.
Former Director of Historic Resources and Facilities
Circus World Museum, Baraboo, Wisconsin

Preface

When I started this project I knew almost nothing about the circus or the Ringlings. As a kid, I had never attended a circus, had never been in a Big Top tent, and had never seen a circus menagerie or a sideshow display. I had heard about the Ringling Brothers, of course, but I didn't even know how many brothers there were.

A few years ago, when I was working on a presentation about barns, I contacted Circus World Museum about photographing some of the old winter quarters barns that I knew were there. I drove up to Baraboo and met curator Fred Dahlinger, who showed me through the buildings. As we crawled up ladders and looked into dusty corners, Fred began sharing his vast knowledge of these structures that the Ringlings had built to house everything from elephants, horses, and giraffes to pythons, panthers, and zebras.

"Any interest in writing about what's here?" Fred asked when I returned a second time for more information. I answered no, that I was immersed in another book project. But his invitation intrigued me, and a couple of months later I was back in Baraboo, and Fred was showing me the vast collection of materials in Circus World's Robert L. Parkinson Library and Research Center. Soon I was making weekly visits to the library, reading old newspapers, paging through route books (the day-to-day records of each season's shows), glancing at account ledgers, looking at circus posters, examining circus records, and before long becoming thoroughly confused and overwhelmed. But I was more than a little intrigued with what I was learning and felt compelled to continue the research. It also became evident that I was facing a book-length project.

One summer day, Fred called and said that a couple of circus historians were coming to Baraboo. Would I like to have lunch with them? The four of us gathered at a little coffee shop in downtown Baraboo and talked circus—I should say, I listened and asked questions while Fred, Richard Reynolds III, and Fred Pfening III, talked. Before we finished coffee, both men had agreed to help me with the project. Some months later, I had lunch with Stuart Thayer, circus historian and author of several circus histories, and I learned even more. Thayer, an expert on pre–Civil War circus history, helped me begin to put the Ringling story into a broader historical perspective.

I read *The Circus Kings* (1960) by Henry Ringling North and Alden Hatch for an overview of the Brothers and their circus and for some perspective on the project I was undertaking.[1] But I purposely did not read other books about the Ringlings until later because I did not want anything that had been written earlier to effect the approach I might take to the work.

By this time I had decided that the book I was attempting to write had to include not only the Baraboo story but also the history of the Ringling Brothers: how they got started and how they created the largest and most prosperous circus in the world.

I spent a week in Columbus, Ohio, at Fred Pfening's invitation. There I pored over Ringling account books, photocopied original correspondence, and became acquainted with Pfening's vast collection of Ringling material. To have unlimited access to original letters and spend uninterrupted hours paging through business records is the kind of situation any historian hopes for. These materials had been largely unexamined, especially the financial and employee records, which provided new insights into the Ringlings' circus operations.

After a news article about the book project appeared in the Baraboo paper, several people contacted me and offered to share stories about the Ringlings in Baraboo. Often the stories were part of oral family histories as people shared anecdotes told to them by their grandparents. I twice interviewed Chappie Fox, longtime director of Circus World Museum and a font of Ringling stories, some that have become legends. (Chappie Fox died on September 12, 2003.) Such stories put a human face on history, and for me they are essential to historical writing.

My wife and I spent several days in McGregor, Iowa, guests of Iowa historians Elmer and Carol Marting, to get the flavor of the town where the Ringling Brothers grew up and first developed their ideas for a circus. I read old Iowa newspapers, dug through the archives in the library, and interviewed locals who had Ringling stories.

By this time I had accumulated boxes of research materials—audiotapes of interviews, photocopies of newspaper articles, correspondence—and I hadn't written a word. In the writing workshops I teach I tell my students that once they have done some research, they should listen to the material and it will tell them how it wants to be organized and presented. My six file boxes of material stood mute.

Faced with a contract deadline, I began writing without knowing where I was headed. But quickly, the words began coming, pages of words. The story was taking shape. Occasionally as I wrote, I discovered that I needed to do more research. Along the way, as happens in most historical research, I encountered contradictions. When circus records contradicted newspaper accounts, I relied on the circus records. Some stories of the Ringlings, especially those from oral histories, have likely been embellished as the years have passed. I have tried to point out which stories may not be entirely true—but I kept the stories.

After several months of writing, and even more rewriting, the Ringling story began to take shape. It is one of the most interesting, intriguing, and sometimes baffling stories I have ever encountered.

Acknowledgments

Fred Dahlinger Jr., former Director of Historic Resources and Facilities at Circus World Museum in Baraboo, Wisconsin, convinced me to work on this project and helped me every step of the way. When I couldn't find what I needed at Circus World Museum's Robert L. Parkinson Library and Research Center, Fred pointed me in the direction to look. John F. Polacsek (Detroit, Michigan) provided access to his vast newspaper clipping files at Circus World Museum. The late Bob Brisendine (Atlanta, Georgia) did the same with his notes and files, also at Circus World Museum. Meg Allen, former Parkinson library assistant, and Erin Foley, former Circus World Museum archivist, were of great help in finding and photocopying materials from the library.

Circus historian Fred D. Pfening III (Columbus, Ohio) made his collection of Ringling materials available and spent untold hours computing Ringling 1890s circus income for me. He also read and commented on the entire manuscript. Fred's father, Fred D. Pfening Jr., also a circus historian, shared his materials collections as well. Circus historian Richard J. Reynolds III (Atlanta, Georgia) read the manuscript page by page, suggesting additions and spotting errors. Stuart LeR. Thayer (Seattle, Washington), author of several circus history books, met with me, read the manuscript, and offered many useful comments.

My never-tiring wife, Ruth, read the manuscript several times, correcting errors. My son, Steve, a professional photographer and journalist, offered many suggestions for improvement and took several photographs for the book. Susan Apps Horman, my daughter, read early drafts of the material and helped me decide on a structure for the work.

Others who helped with research include Carol and Elmer Marting, Monona, Iowa; Michelle Pettit, head librarian, McGregor Public Library; Sally Veitt Scarff, McGregor, Iowa; Peter Shrake and Mary Farrell-Stieve, Sauk County Historical Society Library; Paul Wolter, president of the Sauk County Historical Society; the late C. P. "Chappie" Fox, longtime director of Circus World Museum; Walter Gollmar Jr., Evansville, Wisconsin; Jorge and Lou Ann Jacob Barreda, elephant trainers; Paul Ringling (grandson of Alf T. Ringling), Miles City, Montana; Merlin E. Zitzner, president, Baraboo National Bank; Robert Barnes, Madison; Allen Paschen, Baraboo; Verne Albert, Baraboo; John and George Isenberg (direct descendents of the Ringling contractor); Marge Krohn,

Madison; Donald Heflin, Naples, Florida; John Dresser, Marshalltown, Iowa; Steve Swenson, Aldo Leopold Foundation, Baraboo; and Jan and Duane Neuman, Baraboo.

I have likely overlooked several people who have helped me with this project. I thank you for your kindness and apologize for the oversight. A book of this magnitude requires the assistance of many. I so much appreciate everyone's contributions.

Introduction

In the late nineteenth century the Midwest was still a frontier, with immigrants and other settlers continuing to arrive by the thousands. Most people lived on farms and in small towns. Winters were miserably cold, summers were humid and hot, and life was hard, with little opportunity for entertainment. The circus, with its exotic performers, beautiful horses, wild animals, and low admission cost—fifty cents for adults, twenty-five cents for children—was the major entertainment in many communities, especially rural towns.

Modern-day circuses have their beginnings in the late eighteenth century in England, and the first known circus in the United States showed in 1793 in Philadelphia. These early circuses did not travel, had but one show ring, and performed inside a building. It wasn't until 1825 that a New York circus man, J. Purdy Brown, had a tent sewn that would cover a circus ring and provide shelter for a few hundred customers. With tents as shelters, circuses began traveling on horse-drawn wagons and later moved by riverboat and rail.

The first circus to show in Wisconsin was Samuel Nichols's tented circus, which appeared in Racine on August 11, 1843. At least one circus visited Wisconsin each year thereafter, playing in Milwaukee, Kenosha, Racine, Beloit, Janesville, and Watertown. These cities had major population concentrations at the time, as did the lead-mining region of southwestern Wisconsin, where by 1850 circuses had also visited Dodgeville, Mineral Point, Platteville, and Hazel Green.

The Samuel Nichols tented circus was the first circus to appear in Wisconsin Territory. It opened in Racine on August 2, 1843, five years before Wisconsin became a state. RACINE ADVOCATE, AUGUST 2, 1843. WHS MICROFILM P28649

In 1847 circus owners Edmund and Jeremiah Mabie, originally from New York State, arrived in Delavan in southeastern Wisconsin. Edmund Mabie bought four hundred acres on Delavan Lake with pastureland for horses, plentiful water, and a location that allowed him to take his Grand Olympic Arena and United States Circus to midwestern states before his East Coast competitors. Several circuses eventually followed suit and settled in Wisconsin for the same reasons.

Delavan was a growing city in the heart of what had become the nation's new frontier. This little city, still with fewer than one thousand inhabitants, was a trading center for settlers who were moving in and clearing the rich southern Wisconsin land. Delavan already boasted blacksmiths, wagon makers, a general store, and a grain mill.

In 1847 circus owners Edmund and Jeremiah Mabie arrived in Delavan and bought property near Delavan Lake. Several other circuses soon followed the Mabies to Delavan, which became a major circus center. WHS MAP H GX9028 W24 1857 R

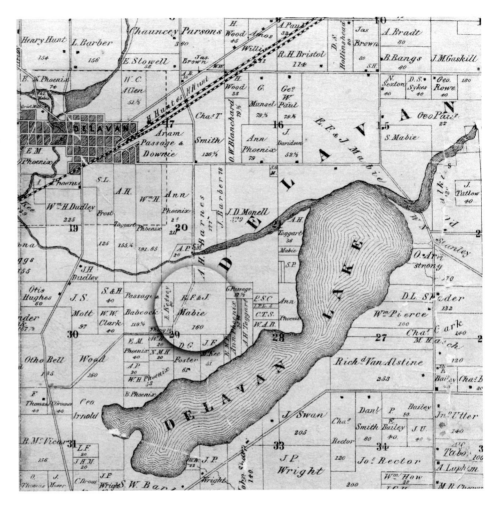

The Mabies attracted circus performers and workers to Delavan, eventually forming a substantial circus colony there. In 1847 Matthew Buckley, a performer with the Mabie Circus, became one of the first circus performers to move to Delavan. In 1856 Buckley's son, Harry, a skilled rider, organized the first circus to originate in Wisconsin—twenty-eight years before the Ringlings put their show on the road. Between 1847 and 1894, some twenty-six circuses had winter quarters in Delavan.

P. T. Barnum, founder of the American Museum in Manhattan in 1841, entered the circus business in late 1870 with partners William C. Coup (from Delavan) and Dan Castello (a longtime circus man from Racine, Wisconsin). This was the beginning of the famous Barnum & Bailey Circus, with headquarters in Bridgeport, Connecticut.

The Ringling Brothers organized their first overland circus in 1884—by which time

A Ringling Brothers circus herald for 1884, their first year. It was the only year that the Ringlings allowed someone else's name to precede theirs in the billing. PRINT COLLECTION, CWM

circuses had been in the United States for nearly one hundred years and were well established in Wisconsin and the rest of the Midwest. In some ways the Ringlings were late in coming to the circus business, and they may well have benefited by not being pioneers in the business. By the time their circus began touring, the circus world was a rich environment for growth and success. This likely was one reason they were able to flourish and eventually become the largest circus in the world.

The story of the Ringling Brothers' Circus is the story of seven brothers. They began in the most modest of circumstances and, through perseverance, hard work, careful attention to detail, tremendous business savvy, and some luck, created the greatest circus in the world. The Ringling Brothers became very wealthy men, one fifty-cent ticket at a time.[2]

The Circus Comes to Town

The circus train's first section, the Flying Squadron, arrives in the still dark hour before sunup. The engineer carefully eases the circus cars onto a sidetrack for unloading while many town residents stand nearby, having risen early from their beds to witness the remarkable events.

For six days of the week during the show season, the circus staff unloaded the train each morning, held two performances, and then loaded the train again to travel through the night to the next town on the route. PRINT COLLECTION, CWM

The circus's advance agent, called a twenty-four-hour man, had arrived the previous day to make sure everything was in order at both at the rail yard and the show site. He checked the streets the circus wagons would travel and called on local businesses that had contracts for feed and other supplies to remind them of their commitments. Now he meets the Flying Squadron and shows the early arrivals the way to the show lot.

At the train site, workmen begin unloading the horses, which wore their harnesses on the train. Other men immediately begin unloading circus wagons from the railcars using two long gangplanks made of wood and iron that are attached to the end of the last flatcar. Two men called polers grab a wagon tongue and guide the wagon as a team of horses on a long rope slowly pull it forward. Other men place flat pieces of steel called crossover plates between the flatcars that allow the horses to pull each wagon from one flatcar to the next until it reaches the runway at the end.

Before running the wagon down the ramp, workers attach a rope with a metal hook and wind it around an iron bar fastened to the railroad car. The burly men hold the rope with all their might, preventing the wagon from running down the ramp too fast. Just before the wagon reaches the bottom of the ramp, the men ease off on the rope, leaving the wagon enough momentum to roll out of the way so the next wagon can be unloaded.

Percheron horses in teams of four, six, and eight are quickly hitched to the wagons and begin pulling them to the show lot, some distance from the rail yard. Quickly, efficiently, the workers finish unloading the first section of the train just as the second section arrives; the engineer switches the train into position, and workers continue the unloading. Horses, wagons, and men are everywhere. Lions roar; elephants trumpet. Exotic sights

The Circus Comes to Town

and sounds saturate the early morning air. Already the circus is astounding to observers, especially these rural people who have never seen anything like it. The smells of dust, horse sweat, and manure hang in the air as the teams lean into their harnesses and pull the heavy wagons toward the circus grounds.

The boss canvasman—the man in charge of erecting tents—arrives at the show grounds ahead of the others and begins spotting the location for each of the eighteen or so tents that make up the circus. He carries with him a sketch of what should go where, a part of the contract the circus had negotiated with the host city. If the lot contains trees, low spots, rocks, or other features that might cause problems, he relocates tents and driveways accordingly. He instructs employees to set the hundreds of small, two- to three-foot-long iron pins that will define where each tent is to be placed.

Canvasmen locate the Big Top's center poles, mark the spots with metal stakes with small white ribbons attached, and string tape lines from the center poles, measuring the outside reach of the tent. Then they place pins marked with red ribbons to show where the main guy ropes are to go and pins with blue ribbons to indicate the position for each stake.

The Big Top and other large tents, called round tops, can be made even larger by lacing in middle pieces between the two giant half-circles. At its largest, the Big Top tent, where the major performances are held, is 440

The trip from the rail yard to the show lot was sometimes more than a mile. Here an eight-horse team is pulling the extremely heavy center-pole wagon. Photo by H. W. Pelton; Print Collection, CWM

feet long and about 190 feet wide and seats more than ten thousand people, with ample room for three rings and a hippodrome racetrack.

While the boss canvasman continues laying out the show lot, other men hurriedly assemble the cooking department, including the kitchen, refrigerator, water wagons (which had been filled the previous night), and cook and dining tents. Workers quickly erect the cook tent and start fires in the kitchen stoves. Steaks and chops, prepared the night before, and potatoes and eggs are soon sizzling. Other workers draw water from the water

(continued on page xx)

The Circus Comes to Town

(continued from page xix)

wagon and pour it into giant black kettles that sit above crackling open fires outside the cook tent. In minutes coffee is boiling. The cook staff erect the dining tents, spread tablecloths, and place dishes in position. Usually by six a.m., waiters dressed in white will be ready to serve breakfast to the hungry crew.

The pole wagons and horse tent wagons arrive. Men unload the huge center poles near where they will be raised, while others erect the horse tents and canvas mangers. Seven horse tents go up, each forty by eight-

Pounding the tent stakes was a difficult job, requiring both strength and timing. As seen in this 1902 image, several men took turns hitting the same stake. RICHARD E. AND ALBERT CONOVER COLLECTION, CWM

Black kettles steam over a campfire; in minutes coffee will be ready for the circus staff. RICHARD E. AND ALBERT CONOVER COLLECTION, CWM

four feet. As soon as the horses are cooled from their early morning work, they are fed and watered.

Six-man crews of stake drivers take their positions around four-foot-long, two- to three-inch-thick wooden stakes that will hold the great tents in place. One by one the muscular men strike the stake with a huge seventeen-pound sledgehammer. These human stake drivers are rhythm in motion, filling the air with an even "bang, bang, bang." When one stake is in place, the crew moves on to the next. In about forty-five minutes some thirty stake drivers pound in as many as one thousand stakes.[1]

Next, twenty to thirty men, with the help of many horses, raise the center poles for the Big Top tent. While

Waiters dressed in formal white attire await hundreds of hungry circus workers. The tables and seats came apart, making them highly portable. RICHARD E. AND ALBERT CONOVER COLLECTION, CWM

The Circus Comes to Town

the center poles are going up, other workers spread the canvas on the ground and lace together the center pieces. Then they raise the side poles, shove them into the pockets at the eaves, attach the sidewall canvas, and loosely tie ropes from each side pole to the stakes.

Men gather at the middle of the tent and, with ropes and pulleys, begin raising the tent up the center poles. They tie ropes to the metal bale rings attached to the canvas and slide the rings up the poles. After they have raised the tent a few feet, they hitch a team of horses to the ropes and quickly pull the tent to its full height. Finally, workers lift the quarter poles into place and tighten the guy ropes.

With the Big Top in position, the workers move on to the three show rings, the bleacher seats, the rigging for the aerial acts, and hundreds of other details, readying the big tent for its thousands of visitors. Tents for the menagerie, dressing room, sideshow, wardrobe, harness and repair, blacksmith shop, and barber are soon in place. Throughout the morning local dray wagons of various sizes and shapes arrive to deliver vegetables, groceries, meats, ice, water, milk, hay, and grain.

With the Big Top up, workers file into the dining

Putting up the Big Top center poles, using both man- and horsepower. The center poles were as long as fifty feet. PHOTO BY STEVE ALBASING; ALBASING COLLECTION, CWM

Workers lace together the canvas pieces in preparation for raising the Big Top. RICHARD E. ALBERT CONOVER COLLECTION, CWM

Spreading the Big Top canvas was a difficult task requiring a large team of workers. The canvas crew was the largest of all the circus crews. RICHARD E. AND ALBERT CONOVER COLLECTION, CWM

tents with appetites sharpened by several hours of hard work. When they are finished eating, the performers and workmen begin to prepare for the circus parade that will wind its way along the town streets later in the morning

(continued on page xxii)

The Circus Comes to Town

(continued from page xxi)

to attract audiences for the day's two Big Top shows, at 2:00 and 8:00 p.m.

Before the tent shows, visitors take in an hour-long band concert in the Big Top or tour the circus menagerie, all part of the fifty-cent admission price. With a blast from the ringmaster's whistle, the first Big Top show starts promptly at 2:00 p.m. The ringmaster welcomes children of all ages and introduces the first event—a colorful parade of animals and performers, a hint of the spectacle to come. For two hours awestruck visitors behold high-wire aerialists swinging from the high wires; jugglers, bareback riders, horses, elephants performing; and of course, clowns by the dozens, all accompanied by a live orchestra. When the afternoon show is completed, workers and performers have a few short hours to rest and eat their evening meal before the evening crowds arrive and another show begins promptly at 8:00 p.m.

Even before the evening Big Top performance starts, workers are dismantling the horse tents and smaller tents and are loading the circus train for its journey to the next stop. They lower the sideshow tent about 8:00 p.m. and close the menagerie and move the animals to the train promptly at 9:00 p.m. By the end of the performance all that remain standing are the Big Top and the dressing room tent. Audience members who bought tickets for the after-show program move to their reserved seats, where they hear musical selections and perhaps see a juggler perform or enjoy some acrobatic acts. The staff remove the bleacher seats and get into position to take down the Big Top when the show ends.

The boss canvasman blows his whistle. Despite the long day of toil, the workers quickly and adeptly take down the sidewalls and roll the canvas into huge bundles. They lower the gaslights and loosen the ropes that held the canvas to the center pole. The big tent slowly

The Big Top is up, the three rings are in place, and the seats await the next crowd of eager circus customers. PRINT COLLECTION, CWM

eases to the ground, like a giant animal preparing for sleep.

The men unlace the tent pieces, roll the huge sections of canvas into bundles called bales, and load them into wagons. They lower the center poles and yank the hundreds of stakes out of the ground with a stake puller, a device that includes an axle and two low wheels with a tongue and a chain. The chain is wrapped around a stake, several men push down on the tongue, and the stake practically jumps out of the ground. Soon the last stake is loaded and the remaining wagons lumber off to the rail yard to catch the last section of the train. Two other train sections have already left about a half-hour apart.

The next day, and the day after that, and every day except Sunday from April to November, these traveling circus workers will repeat this same fascinating routine.

NOTES

1. Fred Dahlinger Jr., "The Circus Stake Driver: The Best, Simplest, and Most Economical Machine Ever Invented," *Bandwagon*, January–February 1999, p. 6.

Ringlingville USA

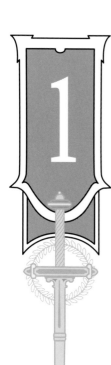

The Idea for a Circus: 1848–1881

"A. Ringling, half way up Main Street, is turning out some of the handsomest as well as the most substantial harness that McGregor citizens or visitors ever looked upon or used."[1]

It was while they were growing up in McGregor, Iowa, and Prairie du Chien, Wisconsin, that the Ringling Brothers developed both the enthusiasm and the essential skills for operating a circus. In those early years they also learned about frugality and perseverance from their father, who spent most of his adult years struggling to earn a living for his large family.

August Frederich Rungeling was twenty-two when he arrived in Milwaukee in 1848, the year Wisconsin achieved statehood. Rungeling had been living in Canada, having arrived there from Hanover, Germany, in 1847.[2] A harness maker by trade, he quickly found a job in the collar-making department of a company that manufactured horse harnesses, saddles, and related leather equipment in this bustling port city nestled against Lake Michigan.

Not long after his arrival in Milwaukee, Rungeling's father, Frederich, his mother, Rosina, and his sister, Wilhelmina, joined him there. The harness-making business prospered. Horses were everywhere, and each one needed a collar and a harness.

Young August learned English quickly, and after a year he could read English well and speak it with scarcely an accent. He changed the family name from Rungeling to Ringling to make it easier to spell and pronounce.[3]

August Ringling advanced rapidly in his work, becoming a foreman at the harness factory. Then cholera struck, claiming his father in the early 1850s. August's mother, heartbroken and in frail health, died a few months later.

August married Salome Marie Juliar on February 16, 1852. The Juliars had arrived from Ostheim, France, in 1844 and lived on a farm near Milwaukee. Salome's sister and

Right: August Frederich Rungeling (later Ringling) (1826–1898), father of the Ringling Brothers of circus fame, was born in Hanover, Germany. PRINT COLLECTION, CWM

Far right: The Ringling boys' mother, Salome Marie Juliar (1833–1907), was born in Ostheim, Alsace, France. She married August Ringling on February 16, 1852, in Milwaukee, where both she and August were living at the time. PRINT COLLECTION, CWM

brother-in-law, the Gollmars, were living in Chicago, and August and Salome soon joined them there.[4]

The Ringlings' first child, Albert (called Al), was born December 13, 1852, in Chicago. The Ringlings moved back to Milwaukee in 1853, and August claimed his old job as a harness maker. A second son, August Albert (called Gus), was born in Milwaukee on July 20, 1854.

Meanwhile, the Gollmars moved to Baraboo, Wisconsin, where Gottlieb Gollmar established a wagon-making shop. No doubt with the Gollmars' encouragement, the Ringlings followed them to Baraboo in 1855.

When the Ringlings arrived in Baraboo in 1855, August immediately established what he called a "One Horse [small] Harness Shop." In an ad that ran in the *Baraboo Republic* in 1855 and 1856, Ringling wrote that he had saddles, bridles, trunks, valises, whips, and whip lashes for sale. He also advertised stirrups, curry combs, and brushes. With a bit of exaggeration—a hint of his sons' later gift for hyperbole—he wrote: "His motto is to accommodate all who will buy of him and those who will not will suffer a loss. All are invited to come immediately for there is danger of them being gone in a short time. Now if any are desirous to know where these cheap things stay they will crowd their way to the shop of the undersigned nearly opposite the Sumner House. A. Ringling."[5]

Business was good for August Ringling until 1857, when an economic downturn forced tax sales and mortgage foreclosures for many. Wisconsin suffered more deeply and longer from the Panic of 1857 than most other states.[6] Banks had restricted their lending to Wisconsin merchants and manufacturers, and farmers had little money to pay their bills.

The depression deepened in 1858. With no alternative in sight, August Ringling sold many of his goods at bargain rates. He even began selling groceries "at hard time prices."[7]

In June 1858 the third Ringling son, William Henry (called Otto), was born. Otto was the only Ringling child born in Baraboo. Wisconsin didn't substantially recover from the 1857 depression for three more years—too late for the Ringlings' Baraboo harness shop. With three children and a wife to support, August Ringling was once more on the move. Sometime in 1860 the family moved to McGregor, Iowa, across the Mississippi River from Prairie du Chien, Wisconsin.

When the Ringlings arrived in McGregor, the need for harness makers was great. In December 1862 the *North Iowa Times* mentioned August Ringling's harness shop: "A. Ringling advertises his harness shop which had been removed from his old stand on Arnold's corner, to the new building two doors east of Walter Bros. He is an excellent workman."[8]

Four more sons were born to the Ringlings in McGregor: Alfred Theodore (called Alf T.) in 1863, Carl Edward (called Charles) in 1864, John Nicholas in 1866, and Henry William George in 1868.

Baraboo in the 1850s

In the 1850s Baraboo was a small, isolated farm community located north of Madison in the hill country referred to as the Baraboo Bluffs. It was county seat of Sauk County, and its post office had opened on March 8, 1847. In 1855 one of the largest enterprises in town was the Bassett and Sanford flour mill, which ground up to twenty thousand barrels of wheat flour each year. Like the local woolen mill and sawmill, it was water powered by a dam on the Baraboo River.[1]

Many of the recent arrivals in Sauk County were farmers looking for land and a future in this new region. Sauk County saw phenomenal growth, from 102 persons in 1840 to 4,372 in 1850.

NOTES

1. Bob Dewel, "Baraboo Always Was a Good Dam Town," *Baraboo (Wisconsin) Sun*, March 26, 1998.

The August Ringling family lived in McGregor, Iowa, from 1860 to 1872. At one time they lived in this modest house. Four of the boys (Alf T., Charles, John, and Henry) were born in McGregor. HOWARD GUSLER COLLECTION, CWM

The Civil War depressed the demand for fancy handmade harnesses. By 1863 August Ringling had sold his harness shop and was working at William Koss's large harness shop in McGregor.[9]

After the war, demand for harnesses again increased, and in 1867 August once again opened his own harness shop. An 1867 newspaper ad stated: "A. Ringling, half way up Main Street, is turning out some of the handsomest as well as the most substantial harness that McGregor citizens or visitors ever looked upon or used. . . . Harness, collars, saddles, bridles and repairing of all kinds. Go to A. Ringling, nearly opposite Murray House.[10]

In 1870 Al and Gus worked in their father's shop, learning the trade of harness making. A newspaper ad from that year indicated that August Ringling's harness shop was now "Opposite Walter Bros., McGregor."[11] But even with the two oldest sons' labors, the harness shop did not provide enough money for the family to make a decent living, and the Ringling family was having a tough time making ends meet. In an oral history, Gretchen Daubenberger, a longtime McGregor resident, recalled an incident when McGregor's practical nurse and midwife called on Daubenberger's mother. The nurse mentioned that "the Ringlings up the Hollow have just had another baby. There isn't a second sheet for the mother's bed, nor a stitch of clothing for the new babe. It is a pitiful state of affairs." Daubenberger's mother gave the nurse used baby clothes, some fresh bed linens, and much of her morning bakery to be delivered to the Ringling family.[12] Living in such dire poverty no doubt had a great influence on the Ringling Brothers later in life.

Before and after the Civil War, circuses traveled mainly by horse-drawn wagons; a few traveled by rail, and several traveled by steamboat on the Ohio and Mississippi Rivers. The steamboat shows visited most towns along the Mississippi between New Orleans and St. Paul, Minnesota, and McGregor was a popular stopping place.

During the summer of 1866 three circuses visited McGregor.[13] In 1867 four circuses visited the town.[14] The seven Ringling boys thus had ample opportunity to see circuses loading and unloading, setting up tents, and preparing for their shows—sights that surely captured their active imaginations. On May 23, 1870, the Sensation Circus, advertised as "The Great Show of the Period," came to McGregor. George W. De Haven was owner and manager. There were horse acts and acrobats, "three great clowns," a "fully educated horse," and a balloon ascension that was scheduled just ahead of the afternoon show. Unfortunately, disaster struck the balloon ascension; the wind blew the balloon into the river, and the performer drowned.[15]

In *Life Story of the Ringling Brothers* (published in 1900), Alf T. Ringling included four chapters about the brothers' adventures in McGregor. He described a circus boat coming to McGregor in the 1860s with its elephant and circus performers. "It was a great day in the lives of these boys, who for two weeks had read and reread the crude posters on the walls of McGregor, which announced that on this particular morning a circus was coming to town."[16]

Several researchers have tried to determine which circus it was that Alf T. remembered. Circus historian Stuart Thayer concluded that Alf T. must have combined his memories of Dan Rice's riverboat circus, which visited McGregor on June 21, 1869, with John Stowe and Company's Great Western Circus, a wagon show that arrived in McGregor on September 7, 1869.[17] Apparently, the boys had gotten free tickets for the Stowe show because their harness-maker father had repaired some equipment for the "Cannonball Juggler," one of the performers.[18]

The Ringling boys soon began putting on their own "circuses" on Saturdays. They charged ten straight pins and, later, a penny for admission. Other boys and girls have attended the circus and have afterward "played circus," but few did so with the earnestness of the Ringling boys, especially Al, the oldest. They attempted to re-create many of the things they had seen in the professional circuses: "An old, neglected white horse belonging to a man who lived nearby was the favorite with the Ringling boys, and it was on its sway back they attempted their first 'bareback' riding."[19]

In an oral history, Clara Curtis Otis, formerly of McGregor, recalled stories she had heard about the Ringling boys' early circuses in McGregor:

[There] was a parade down Main Street and over to a barn. [The Brothers] had an outside animal show before admittance to the performance. The animal show consisted of cats, dogs, several rabbits, two tiny kittens with a sign "from Timbuctoo"; a monster bull frog with a sign "captured at great risk from the depths of a far-away swamp from which no other frog-collector ever emerged alive"; a crowing rooster with tail feathers colored a bright red; a bantam pullet which laid an egg while the neighbors were seeing the animals; some tadpoles swimming in a glass container, in which, to the amazement of the boys, some tiny frogs emerged in time for the show; a white hen and rooster, "the only ones in captivity"; some English sparrows, "imported from an unnamed Pacific Island"; and Mrs. Ringling's canary, "the head of the great dynasty." The boys performed on swings and walked across a long beam. The dogs set up a great barking, the cats became frightened, and pandemonium seemed about to break loose when the elder Ringling boy fed them with some meat, which he was supposed to bring home for supper.[20]

The Ringling boys enjoyed acrobatics and practiced often. Sally Veit Scarff, a McGregor historian, recalled a story she heard from her father, Charles L. Viet Sr., about the Ringling boys: "The boys ran a wire from Marquette peak [formerly North McGregor, now Marquette] to the Berry Hotel, and proceeded to walk down it. Everyone watched intently, certain they would kill themselves, but they emerged at the bottom, unscathed and smiling."[21]

Although the harness-making business appeared brisk, trouble once again loomed. Factory-made harnesses and horse collars cheaper than those made by hand were arriving on the market. By 1871 August was out of the harness-making business, and in 1872 he moved his family to Prairie du Chien, Wisconsin.

Gus, then eighteen, stayed behind in McGregor to work in another harness shop. This was the first time the family was separated.

In Prairie du Chien August and oldest son Al worked as carriage trimmers for the

RINGLING BROTHERS' FIRST PARADE.

The Ringling boys truly were only boys when they put on their first "parades." ALF T. RINGLING, **BENEATH WHITE TENTS: ROUTE BOOK OF RINGLING BROTHERS**, 1894 SEASON, CWM

newly formed Traner Carriage Works, doing specialty leather work for carriages that could not be done with machines.

Unfortunately, a fire destroyed the Traner factory. That, combined with the depression of 1873, again left the Ringlings without work. The Prairie du Chien years became most difficult for the family. They moved from their rather spacious house north of town to a log house in a nearby coulee (a valley without an outlet). They had one horse and a large vegetable garden. August worked part time for a Prairie du Chien harness maker and at one time made seventy-five leather fire buckets for the local fire department. The buckets were described as "perfect gems of workmanship."[22] Still, the family struggled to make ends meet. Despite hard times, Al never gave up his interest in the circus. He continued honing his skills as a balancer and juggler in his free time, practicing walking a tightrope and juggling everything he could get his hands on. In 1873 Al Ringling left home and found work in a Brodhead, Wisconsin, carriage, wagon, and blacksmith shop owned by Antone Durner and Sebastian Laube.[23] It was reported that on Saturday afternoons, he would string a rope across the street from two tall buildings and walk across on it. Some even said that he carried a small stove with him and cooked a meal while balancing on the rope.[24]

McGregor, Iowa, 1860–1872

Many circuses traveled the Mississippi River after the Civil War, showing in river towns such as McGregor, Iowa, where the Ringlings grew up. The Brothers were so enthralled with the circuses they saw there that they were soon offering circus "performances" for their childhood friends. PH 1006

McGregor was a bustling place the year before the Civil War, with nearly two thousand residents. Its location on the Mississippi made it an entry point for settlers and others going west. The town was also a shipping center for wheat that was barged south on the river. Fortunes were made as this river town stored wheat for river shipment from as far as 150 miles to the west.

In the 1860s McGregor had from twenty-eight to thirty-two saloons scattered from one end of town to the other. Along with the saloons, McGregor "had its share of 'shady' characters and because of this could be imagined to have the usual brawls and arguments."[1]

The McGregor Brewery, owned by J. F. Hagensick, was four stories high and brewed ten thousand barrels of beer a year, probably enough to meet the needs of the local saloons.

McGregor also had six churches. August Ringling was one of the charter members of the German Lutheran Church, organized in 1862.

NOTES

1. Lucy Rodenberg Holst, *Echoes of McGregor's Past*, vol. 2, (McGregor, Iowa: Stone Balloon Books, 1994), p. 27.

Al also dazzled onlookers by balancing a breaking plow on his chin. The plow—there were many sizes and shapes available by this time—had a wooden frame and weighed no more than seventy pounds. Historian Alvin Harlow explained how he did it: "Al would seize the plow by the handles, swing it into the air above his head, then lower it until a chalk mark in the middle of the brace was centered as nearly as possible on his chin—moving it a little this way and that to get a perfect balance—then let go the handles for a few moments. It fairly took the onlookers' breath away, and well it might."[25]

In February 1874 August and his wife welcomed a daughter, Ida Lorina Wilhemina,

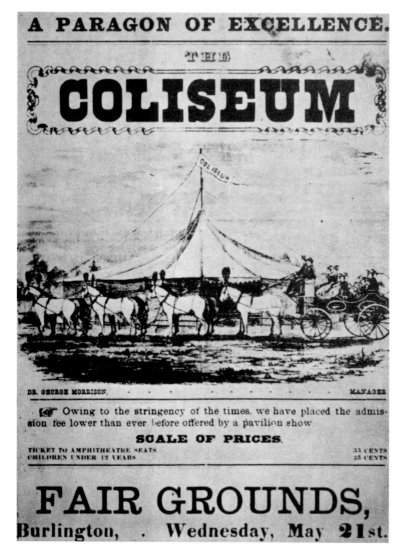

A PARAGON OF EXCELLENCE.

THE

COLISEUM

DR. GEORGE MORRISON. · · · · · · · · · · · · MANAGER

☞ Owing to the stringency of the times, we have placed the admission fee lower than ever before offered by a pavilion show

SCALE OF PRICES.

TICKET TO AMPHITHEATRE SEATS   35 CENTS
CHILDREN UNDER 12 YEARS   25 CENTS

FAIR GROUNDS,
Burlington, . Wednesday, May 21st.

In 1879 Al Ringling and his thirteen-year-old brother, John, performed with Dr. Morrison's Coliseum Show. GIFT FROM GORDON YADON; HANDBILL COLLECTION, CWM

to their family. There were now eight children in the family, with six living at home. Three other babies had died in infancy.

The next year August and his family moved to Stillwater, Minnesota.[26] August couldn't find a job in Stillwater, however, and he quickly moved the family back to Baraboo and began working for his brother-in-law, Henry Moeller Sr., a wagon maker, who had a shop on Fourth Street.[27] Henry Moeller had also married one of the Juliar sisters, and now the three sisters were once more together in the same town.

August Ringling worked about a year with Henry Moeller before again opening his own harness-making shop, this one on the corner of Third and Broadway. An ad for his establishment declared, "A. Ringling, manufacturer and dealer in harnesses, collars, trunks, valises, robes, blankets, whips, etc. Carriage trimming a specialty. Sign of the big collar."[28] Also in 1876, son Otto, now eighteen, was working in Racine at a wagon and carriage company.

Two years later a fire destroyed nearly an entire city block in Baraboo and leveled August's harness shop. He moved his business to another site and was soon winning prizes at the Sauk County Fair for his high-quality harnesses.[29] By this time Charles and Alf T. were both old enough to work alongside their father.

In 1880 logging continued in the northern reaches of the state, and farming in southern and central Wisconsin had begun to shift from growing wheat to dairying and cheese making.[30] Three of the Ringling boys, Al, Gus, and Otto, had left home. Al continued his strong interest in the circus, and Alf T. and Charles, no doubt with their mother's strong encouragement, discovered that they had musical talent and began following those interests, taking up horns and the violin.

From 1879 to 1883 Al Ringling performed with several circuses, including Parson and Roy's Great Palace Show, which headquartered in Darlington, Wisconsin.
WAUKESHA COUNTY DEMOCRAT, AUGUST 6, 1881

Al hired out to several different circuses between 1879 and 1883. In 1879 Al and his brother John, who was only thirteen, appeared with Dr. Morrison's Coliseum Show. "With his show Al Ringling was the strong man and juggler, and John Ringling is said to have been the black-face comedian."[31]

The many challenges the Ringling family faced as August's harness-making business alternately thrived and faltered brought the family close together. They learned how to depend on each other and to work together. They knew what it was like to not have enough to eat and to have little clothing to wear. The boys learned to save what little money they had for future contingencies. All these skills would later prove invaluable as they built and maintained their circus empire.

Although the Ringling boys knew harness making and knew it well, they had seen the struggles their father faced as he moved the family from town to town trying to eke out a living. Show business couldn't be any harder than harness making, or so it seemed to Al, John, Alf T., and Charles as they considered starting a traveling hall show and organizing a circus.

Hall Shows and an Overland Circus: 1882–1884

"The Ringling 'Classic and Comic' Concert Company which exhibited here Wednesday evening of last week, failed by a large majority of satisfying their audience."[1]

While Al and young John Ringling were gaining valuable experience with several circuses, brothers Alf T. and Charles were honing their musical skills back in Baraboo; Charles was becoming an excellent violinist, and Alf T. had learned to play several brass instruments. But along with know-how and experience, it takes money to run a circus. The Brothers soon decided that one way to start earning money—and gain more experience as well—was to organize a hall show, a traveling indoor performance that included music and acting. By the summer of 1882, Al Ringling was in Baraboo organizing a musical road company to include his brothers Alf T., who was then nineteen, and Charles, who would be eighteen in December.[2]

Show business, then as now, was risky business. Preachers commonly railed about actors and their loose morals and about performances motivated by the devil himself. An actor's pay was paltry. Farmers and town businessmen in the late nineteenth century earned little money, but they never went hungry. Actors, especially those who were just breaking into the business, often couldn't find their next meal.

The Ringling Brothers set out to do something so different from harness making that it was difficult to comprehend. But the times were right. East Coast urban areas were developing rapidly in the late 1880s, but the Midwest was still pioneer country. People were settling the land in much of northern Wisconsin, in Minnesota, and in the western states. The population would soon be booming: Wisconsin's population increased from 1.31 million in 1880 to 1.69 million by 1890 and 2.07 million by 1900. In 1880 about 76 percent of Wisconsin's people lived on farms and in small towns.[3]

Local newspapers—a necessary advertising medium for any out-of-town show—

This early handbill, circa 1881 and never before reprinted, announced Al Ringling's "Double Specialty Show," including his "New Comic Play, *The Dude.*" HANDBILL COLLECTION, CWM

were on the increase as the Ringlings prepared to mount their hall show. In 1873 Wisconsin had about 175 newspapers; by 1891 the state had approximately 490 papers, of which 49 were dailies.[4]

Every adult was expected to work ten or more hours a day, six days a week, and most work was back-breaking physical labor—for farm people, it lasted from before daybreak until after dark. What little recreation and entertainment people had was usually homemade and was provided through the country schools and churches by way of church choirs, Christmas programs, and other celebrations. Midwesterners thirsted for a break from the grueling task of making a living. They welcomed an opportunity to spend an evening with a group of entertainers, even rank amateurs. Those who lived in towns served by railroads had better opportunities to see outside entertainment, as professional show people traveled from town to town by rail.

Al, Alf T., and Charles called their first hall show effort the "Ringling Bros. Classic and Comic Concert Company." They invited Edward Kimball, a Baraboo musician and actor, and three other actor-musicians to join the troupe. John Ringling, just sixteen, joined in mid-December, when the group had already been on the road for several weeks. Otto, who was working in Minneapolis, was convinced to join the group the following year, in 1883. (That year Gus was working as a carriage trimmer in Minneapolis, and Henry was only fifteen years old.) Little did anyone know that in a few short years, this ragtag troupe of would-be performers would become the famous five of circus fame.

The Ringlings mounted their first hall show on Monday, November 27, 1882, in Mazomanie, Wisconsin, a farming town located about thirty-five miles west of Madison. Alf T. later described their preparations: "It was a cold November morning when the boys left their parent's home to give their first show as professionals. A light snow had fallen during the night, and the morning air was crisp and clear."[5] The boys loaded their trunks and instruments on wagons and set out for Sauk City, where they boarded the train to Mazomanie. Anxious about their new endeavor, the boys intended to travel far enough from Baraboo so no one would recognize them.

But they were not at all bashful in proclaiming the virtues of their efforts. The show program stated: "Do not fail to see the many attractions presented by this company. See our Priseworthy and Unequalled Program."

Alf T. later wrote: "We had about a thirteen-dollar house, but the fifty-nine people composing the audience looked bigger to me than an audience of fifteen thousand under our tents does today. It seemed as if every individual knew our history, and was aware that this was our first attempt, if not perhaps our first offense, and was ready to guy and laugh at our efforts."[6]

The troupe included Al Ringling (plate spinner, juggler), Alf T. Ringling (leader of the band), Charles Ringling (leader of the orchestra), E. M. Kimball (Old Man Dutch Big Von-Comedian), E. S. Weatherby (tuba and double bass), Fred Hart (song and dance), and Wm. Trinkhouse (song and dance, alto player, Indian club). M. A. Young was advance agent.[7]

Concert Company Program

RINGLING BROTHERS CLASSIC
AND COMIC CONCERT COMPANY

1.	Overture selected	Orchestra
2.	Vocal Trio (Brother soldiers, we've met here tonight.)	E. M. Kimball, Will Trinkaus, and C. E. Ringling.
3.	Cornet Duet. "The Enchanted."	Alf T. Ringling and E. M. Kimball.
4.	Japanese Specialties	Al Ringling
5.	Trinkaus and Hart in Songs and dances.	
6.	Euphonium Solo	Chas. E. Ringling
7.	Sketch, the Traveling Prestidigitator	By Company
8.	E. M. Kimball in character songs and sayings	
9.	Violin Duet (Der Barbier von Sevilla)	Charles and Alf Ringling
10.	Vocal Duet	Chas. And Alf Ringling
11.	Fred Hart in Unequalled Clog	
12.	Wm. Trinkhaus in Parlor Pastimes	
13.	E. M. Kimball in Dutch Character Songs.	
14.	Bass Solo, vocal	Chas. E. Ringling

The whole to conclude with Ringling Brothers original laughable farce entitled "A Cold Bath." Or as a failure a great success.

Admission, .25, .35 and .50.[8]

The aspiring performers survived their first show—just barely. "From the very beginning, the troupe in its entirety seemed to fly to pieces. . . . It seemed that as if every note from the cornet was a blue one, every tone from the violin a squeak, every blast of the clarinet a shriek, and as if all the different instruments were in a jangle."[9]

When they totaled their expenses ($25.90) and subtracted their income ($13.00), they could only hope for better times ahead. They continued on by train to the Wisconsin towns of Spring Green, Richland Center, and Boscobel, on their way to their former hometowns of McGregor, Iowa, and Prairie du Chien. John Ringling joined his brothers in Sanborn, Iowa, on December 18.

The Ringlings and their colleagues continued on, traipsing from small town to small town in Wisconsin, Iowa, Dakota Territory, and Minnesota. They were snowed in and snowed out; they arrived by train and from the trains by buggy, by horse and sleigh, and on foot. They played in cold, drafty halls in little towns—Emmetsburg, Spencer, Sanborn, Sheldon, and Peterson, Iowa; Fulda, Jackson, and Fairmont, Minnesota; Canton, Dell Rapids, and Egan, Dakota Territory; and West Salem, Bangor, Norwalk, Wilton, Kendall, Elroy, and Wonewoc, Wisconsin. The population of each town was but a few hundred people.

The Ringlings' advance agent, M. A. Young, secured the bookings and made local arrangements, put up advertising posters, and negotiated rental fees for halls. Hall rental for their first show in Mazomanie was $6.00, which they paid from ticket receipts. Other expenses for their first show included livery from Baraboo to Sauk City, $8.00; railroad fare from Sauk City to Mazomanie, $2.40; hotel bill, $7.50; and salaries for two amateurs, $2.00 (there is no record of which "amateurs" were paid).[10] The following year Otto Ringling joined his brothers and worked as advance agent.

To create excitement before each big show, the performers marched in a band parade down the town's main street each afternoon—a forerunner of the great circus parades the Ringlings later mounted.

They closed the first half of their 1882–1883 season in Oregon, Wisconsin, on February 3 and then rested for a few weeks before resuming shows on March 12 in Baraboo. They closed again on May 11 in Waunakee, Wisconsin. The Ringlings had performed 107 times in their first winter season; they took off Sundays but not holidays, performing on both Christmas Day and New Year's Day.[11]

Playing daily shows was an enormous accomplishment for a brand-new troupe, and meeting this grueling schedule taught the boys valuable lessons about scheduling and doing one-day stands. They gained invaluable experience in promotion and advertising, securing hotels and opera houses, and contracting for horses and wagons to travel from the depots to the show halls. They learned how to get along with people in the host cities, many of whom were more than a little skeptical of traveling actors. Above all they learned that pleasing the audience—and newspaper reviewers—had to be at the top of

Baraboo, 1880

By 1880 Baraboo's population had reached 3,266. The Chicago and Northwestern Railroad had come to town in 1871, and the telegraph had become the primary way for people to communicate. Baraboo included all the services one would expect in a small rural city: Carlos Bacon was the city undertaker and furniture dealer; the Baldwin Brothers manufactured monuments and headstones; John Barker was an attorney; Adolph Bender ran the Baraboo City Brewery ("Bottled beer for family use always on hand"); W. A. Boyd was a physician and surgeon; C. A. M. Burnham was a "lady physician and surgeon"; H. J. Case ran a stable; B. K. Cowles was proprietor of R.R. Eating House and Hotel; James Dickie, a competitor of August Ringling, made saddles and harnesses on Fourth Street; B. S. Doty sold flour, feed, and lime; August Ringling's brother-in-law G. G. Gollmar was a blacksmith, wagon maker, and horseshoer; W. Gust ran a meat market on Oak Street ("All kinds of meat, fresh and salt, of the best quality"); G. M. Reul manufactured sashes, doors, and blinds with a factory on the corner of East and Water Streets; F. Sneathen was a dentist ("New teeth at $12.00 to $20.00 a set. No extra charge for extracting; if desired, teeth taken out without causing pain. Gold filling reasonable."); and J. Van Orden was cashier of the First National Bank.[1]

___

NOTES

1. *Town and Country Business Directory, Sauk County, Wisconsin* (Baraboo, WI: Woodman and Powers, 1881).

their list of priorities. One review of the 1882 season read, "Ringling Bros.' Classic and Comic Concert Company made their appearance in our village on Tuesday and put up at the Park Hotel. . . . Their program was fitting to the occasion and well carried out. . . . The vocal and instrumental music by the company with a few exceptions was good."[12] Positive comments like these would nearly ensure an audience when the Brothers returned with their show.

With their first hall show season behind them, the Brothers spent the summer of 1883 gathering more experience, earning more funds, and planning the upcoming winter season. That summer Al Ringling performed with the Gregory Brothers Circus and worked as equestrian director for Parson's Great Grecian Circus of Darlington, Wisconsin.[13] Also in 1883 he found time to work with the Yankee Robinson's Double Show as manager of the equestrian department.[14] John also appeared briefly with the Great Grecian Show in 1883.[15]

According to Charles Ringling's recollections, Otto, Charles, and John spent much of the summer of 1883 in Baraboo.[16] The Ringlings had made little if any profit from their first concert season, but they would be ready to try it again when the cool days of fall returned to the Midwest, the crops were in, and rural people had time to attend a hall show in their town.

For their second season, the boys named their hall show simply "Ringling Bros. Grand Carnival of Fun." They tried to select towns that were growing and where local business was strong. The Brothers often picked lumber towns in the north, where lumberjacks had plenty of money and little in the way of entertainment.

That fall the traveling crew included several new faces: Otto Ringling, agent; Barry Stanwood, Geo Rowan and his brother, M. A. Young (agent for a short time), Jack Kernan, F. Taylor, Jas. Blainey, Harry Harmoyne, and Lottie Harmoyne. Continuing with the troupe were Alf T., John, Charles, E. M. Kimball, and, later that winter, Al Ringling.

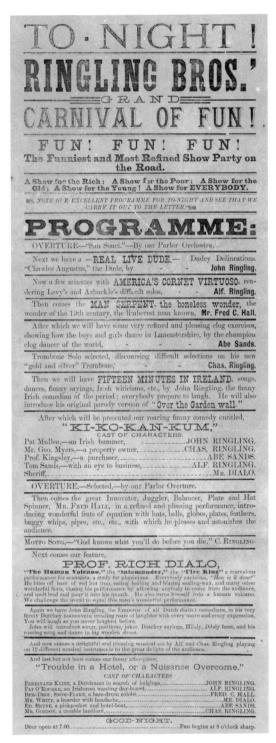

TO·NIGHT!

RINGLING BROS.'
═══GRAND═══
CARNIVAL OF FUN!

FUN! FUN! FUN!
The Funniest and Most Refined Show Party on the Road.

A Show for the Rich; A Show for the Poor; A Show for the
Old; A Show for the Young! A Show for EVERYBODY.

NOTE OUR EXCELLENT PROGRAMME FOR TO-NIGHT AND SEE THAT WE
CARRY IT OUT TO THE LETTER.

PROGRAMME:

OVERTURE—"San Souci."—By our Parlor Orchestra.

Next we have a —REAL LIVE DUDE.— Dudey Delineations.
"Chawles Augustus," the Dude, by - - **John Ringling.**

Now a few minutes with AMERICA'S CORNET VIRTUOSO, rendering Levy's and Arbuckle's difficult solos, - **Alf. Ringling.**

Then comes the MAN SERPENT, the boneless wonder, the wonder of the 19th century, the limberest man known, **Mr. Fred C. Hall.**

After which we will have some very refined and pleasing clog exercises, showing how the boys and girls dance in Lancastershire, by the champion clog dancer of the world, - - **Abe Sands.**

Trombone Solo selected, discoursing difficult selections on his new "gold and silver" Trombone, - - **Chas. Ringling.**

Then we will have FIFTEEN MINUTES IN IRELAND, songs, dances, funny sayings, Irish witicisms, etc., by John Ringling, the funny Irish comedian of the period; everybody prepare to laugh. He will also introduce his original parody version of "Over the Garden wall."

After which will be presented our roaring funny comedy entitled,

"KI-KO-KAN-KUM,"
CAST OF CHARACTERS

Pat Mullen,—an Irish bummer, - - - JOHN RINGLING.
Mr. Geo. Myers,—a property owner, - CHAS. RINGLING.
Prof. Kingsley,—a purchaser, - - - ABE SANDS.
Tom Sands,—with an eye to business, - ALF. RINGLING.
Sheriff, - - - - - - Mr. DIALO.

OVERTURE.—Selected,—by our Parlor Overture.

Then comes the first Innovator, Juggler, Balancer, Plate and Hat Spinner, Mr. FRED HALL, in a refined and pleasing performance, introducing wonderful feats of equation with hats, balls, globes, plates, feathers, buggy whips, pipes, etc., etc., with which he pleases and astonishes the audience.

MOTTO SONG,—"God knows what you'll do before you die," C. RINGLING.

Next comes our feature,

PROF. RICH DIALO,
"The Human Volcano," the "Salamander," the "Fire King" a marvelous performance for scientists, a study for physicians. Everybody exclaims, "How is it done?" He bites off bars of red hot iron, eating boiling and blazing sealing-wax, and many other wonderful feats, closing his performance by allowing anybody to come from the audience, and melt lead and pour it into his mouth. He also turns himself into a human volcano. We challenge the world to equal this man's wonderful performance.

Again we have John Ringling, the Emperor of all Dutch dialect comedians, in his very funny Dutchey maneuvers; creating roars of laughter with every move and every expression. You will laugh as you never laughed before. John will introduce songs, positions, jokes, Dutchey sayings, Hilsly, Didoy fazes, and his roaring song and dance in big wooden shoes.

And now comes a delightful and pleasing musical act by Alf. and Chas. Ringling playing on 12 different musical instruments to the great delight of the audience.

And last but not least comes our funny after-piece,

"Trouble in a Hotel, or a Nuisance Overcome."
CAST OF CHARACTERS

Ferdinand Kline, a Dutchman in search of lodgings, - JOHN RINGLING.
Pat O'Rourke, an Irishman wanting day-board, - ALF. RINGLING.
Dew-Drop, Snow-Flake, a base-drum soloist, - FRED. C. HALL.
Mr. White, a boarder with headache, - - Mr. DIALO.
Ed. Bryne, a pickpocket and hotel-beat, - - ABE SANDS.
Mr. Gordon, a trouble landlord, - - CHAS. RINGLING.

GOOD-NIGHT.

Door open at 7.00 - - Fun begins at 8 o'clock sharp.

They started out in Ironton, Wisconsin, on August 20 and played western Wisconsin towns until the end of September. Then they crossed the Mississippi River into Minnesota and put on shows there into November.

Unfortunately, as they moved from town to town, disagreements erupted among the Ringlings and several employees. One employee "began the habit of drinking," and two others "refused to attend to their duties."[17] On November 2 the disagreements reached an impasse, and the Brothers fired the entire collection. Charles Ringling later wrote:

> The Company did a good business but prosperity did not agree with the Rowan Bros. who were arrested in St. Cloud [Minnesota] and fined for disorderly conduct and discharged by us. As Kimball and Taylor thought they could do about us as they pleased and as Kimball thought we could not yet get along without him we concluded to run a smaller company and we left them at Campbell, Minnesota, November 2nd and ran the remainder of the season [with Otto], Alf T. John and Charles [Al joined January 6, 1884]. From this day, we commenced to make money fast and with less trouble.[18]

The company indeed was now smaller; the street band on November 3, 1883, consisted of Alf T., cornet; John, alto; Charles, baritone; and Otto, bass drum. As a marching band they were considerably short staffed, especially since Otto was no musician and was challenged to even pound on a bass drum. Even worse, the hall show performers now included only Alf T., Charles, and John (and later Al). But they marched on, determined to satisfy their audiences and relying more than ever on each brother's unique contributions to the success of their shows.

While the Brothers were busy on the road, back in Baraboo father August got the itch to move again. In November 1883 August, Salome, and children Henry and Ida packed

To raise money to start a circus, the Ringling Brothers put on hall shows starting in 1882. HANDBILL COLLECTION, CWM

Al Ringling married Eliza "Lou" Morris on December 19, 1883. She was a performer, seamstress, and snake charmer with the early Ringling circus. PRINT COLLECTION, CWM

their goods and moved to Rice Lake in northwestern Wisconsin. Rice Lake was a growing town in the midst of the lumbering region and had a strong demand for harness makers. What's more, they would now be closer to son Gus, who worked in the carriage-trimming business in Minneapolis.[19]

That winter the Brothers again played on Christmas Eve, Christmas Day, and New Year's Eve. They even played four Sundays, breaking their own rule. They performed every day from October 29 to November 15—eighteen shows without a break, although on December 19 Al married Eliza "Lou" Morris, who worked with the show as a performer, seamstress, and snake charmer. From mid-December to the first of the year they played small towns in Nebraska and then back in Iowa. Finally, in March they crossed the Mississippi and returned to Wisconsin.

For the 1883–1884 season the Brothers played 185 shows (starting on November 2, the staff consisted solely of five Ringling Brothers: Al, Alf T., Charles, Otto, and John). They closed on Friday, April 11, 1884, in Poynette, Wisconsin.[20]

The Brothers had one thing on their minds—starting a full-scale traveling circus—and they were focusing nearly all their efforts on accumulating enough money to do so. They were confident that they would have enough money to take a circus on the road in summer 1884, and they ran this notice in a national trade magazine in February: "Ringling Brothers close their specialty Company April 20 [1884; they actually closed April 11] and open their tenting season May 15. Wanted. Gymnasts, Acrobats, Leapers, Contortionists, Tumblers and people in all branches of the circus business. Sideshow and outside privilege to let. Address Al. Ringling, Baraboo, Wisconsin."[21]

For their first circus, in 1884, the Ringling Brothers enlisted the services of Fayette "Yankee" Robinson, a well-known circus man. Oversize Prints Collection, CWM

Al Ringling had worked for Fayette Lodawick "Yankee" Robinson during the summer of 1883, and he convinced the circus veteran (then sixty-six) to join the Brothers in forming their first circus.[22] One of the best-known circus showmen in the country, Robinson helped Al design a ninety-minute program and helped plan a wagon route for the circus that would start in Baraboo, stop in several Wisconsin towns, then move into Iowa and Minnesota, Illinois, and back to Wisconsin.[23] Recognizing Robinson's drawing power, the Boys named the show "Yankee Robinson and Ringling Bros. Great Double Shows, Circus and Caravan." It was the only time the Ringlings put someone else's name ahead of theirs in billing a show.

Despite having just completed their exhausting concert tour on April 11, the Ringling Brothers planned to open their circus on May 19—giving them scarcely seven weeks to prepare. But they had several things in their favor. Al and to a much lesser extent John had gained valuable experience working for other circuses. All five of the Brothers now in the circus business had learned how to perform day after day, each day in a different place. And they had accumulated $1,000 from hall show profits.[24]

Each of the five knew by this time that he did not want to spend the rest of his life in a harness shop, sewing leather, repairing harnesses and horse collars, and doing fancy leather work on a rich man's buggy.

And so the boys got busy bringing their circus to life. They bought lumber and made seats and supports. They purchased three second-hand farm wagons, one to be used by their advance agent and two to travel with the circus. For the advance agent's wagon they lettered the name of the show on the side and fashioned a canvas cover. They paid a farmer a few dollars and went into his tamarack swamp to cut tent poles. They cut stakes in a nearby oak grove. They removed the bark from the tent poles using a draw shave and left the stakes and poles outside to cure.[25]

The Brothers designed advertising sheets and ran ads in local newspapers. The *Baraboo Republic* reported:

> The Ringling Bros. arrived in this city Saturday night last for the purpose of organizing a circus with Yankee Robinson, one of the best and widely known showmen in the United States. . . . Their tent and circus property is being got together as fast as possible, and they will give their first show in this city May 19th. This circus will be known as "The Old Yankee Robinson and Ringling Bros. Double Shows." These young men have exhibited great enterprise and pluck, and we wish them financial success. Our circus going people should give the boys a good opening. We shall have more to say about the Baraboo Circus.[26]

A few weeks later, the *Sauk County Democrat* carried this story:

> This week a reporter of the *Democrat* visited the headquarters of the Yankee Robinson and Ringling Brothers double show in the Robert's building on Oak Street and found the boys working like beavers getting everything in readiness for their show which opens the season in this city on the 19th of the month. The tent has arrived and it is a mammoth affair. . . . Mr. Al Ringling, one of the head men in the concern, is an old show manager, having been in the business over fifteen years, and he thoroughly understands every branch of it. Yankee Robinson is a veteran in the show business having been in it over thirty years, and has been in nearly every town in the United States, his name is as familiar as Barnum, and old Dan Rice. He will be in Baraboo next week. The Ringling Bros. still claim this as their home, and our citizens will give the boys a big send off.[27]

The *Baraboo Republic* did a special two-column piece on Yankee Robinson prior to the first show. "Mr. Lafayette [sic] L. Robinson, who is one of the proprietors of the 'Yankee Robinson and Ringling Bros. Double Show,' is one of the oldest living showmen and actors, is familiar with all the events connected with the history of the drama and the show ring of this country. . . . Mr. Robinson has produced his comedy drama 'Days of '76' . . . over 5,000 times and has played in all the principal cities of the United States."[28]

There was great anticipation during the first warm days of May in Baraboo as the date for the opening of the circus grew closer. It was common for cities to charge circuses a license fee, anywhere from twenty-five dollars to more than a hundred dollars.

The city of Baraboo granted the Ringlings rights as "home artists" to put on their May 19 show without charge.[29]

The Brothers' main tent was forty-five feet by ninety feet and was designed to hold six hundred spectators. As the first show's eager audience crowded under the canvas, one seating section collapsed, sending several people to the ground. Yankee Robinson rushed to the site of the near-calamity, cracking jokes and assisting people to their feet while workers put the seats back in order.[30] After the chaos subsided, Robinson, who was small and frail but had a voice that echoed throughout the big tent, took center stage and gave a speech. He said the Ringling Brothers were "destined to become the greatest circus in the world."[31] And with that, the Ringling Brothers' Circus was launched. The show included "contortionists, jugglers, balancers and comedy acts interspersed with musical selections, but the Ringling boys were most of the show. They played various instruments in the band, danced, performed and led most of the acrobatic stunts and tricks."[32]

The Brothers had enlisted area farm boys and their wagons, and when the show was over, the hired workers took down the big tent, folded the canvas, pulled the stakes, took the seats apart, and loaded everything on wagons, including the long tent poles, which stuck out far behind one wagon. The motley procession of twelve horse-drawn wagons trailed out of Baraboo that cool spring night, across the Baraboo Bluffs to Sauk City, their next stop.

A newspaper review of the first show reported, "The afternoon's business was heavy, for Baraboo, as it does not usually patronize shows well in the afternoon. In the evening the tent was crowded so that it made it inconvenient for them to perform. The performances were very creditable considering the boys had never had any practice and we have not heard a single person find fault. They are proud of their home endorsement and desire us to return thanks to the citizens for their liberal patronage, and Mr. Al Ringling, one of the head men, says if business continues as good as it commenced he will come back to Baraboo with a big show."[33]

Each day they performed in a new town. The little time they had for sleeping they spent in local hotels or dozing off in the wagons as they made their way along the dusty or muddy roads. One performer noted, "Sleep was the dragon which pursued me with a relentless and irresistible power. It was like a vampire that took the zest and vitality out of my very life sources, and I went about almost as one walking in a dream."[34]

As the tour continued, newspaper reviews were mixed. After the show played in Argyle, Wisconsin, on Thursday, May 29, a local reporter wrote: "Yankee Robinson and Ringling Bros., double jointed, contracted, aggregation and exaggeration, has come, and gone, skipped, skedaddled, pulled out and perambulated toward the setting sun. Among the many curiosities were reserved seats, an Irishman, a Dutchman, an educated pig, and a full grown, live dude, plug hat and all. They also had a blind horse, which was mistaken by some as a 'living skeleton.'"[35]

They played in Dodgeville, Wisconsin, on Tuesday, June 3. A local editor wrote:

Yankee Robinson's show was in Dodgeville last Tuesday, and although by some mis-understanding with the king of Siam, the white elephant was not sent on, yet the Ringling Brothers did the best they could to supply the missing link caused by the absence of the elephant, by shoving a sandy hog and black horse into the void. The hog and horse constituted a double show exactly as was advertised in the Star last week. We are always very careful not to advertise anything except genuine articles, but in the case of this show we just made a hair-breadth escape; and had it not been of the timely appearance of the hog and horse, all our advertisement about a double show would have been false, and we would have incurred the displeasure of all the good people of the county. . . . As it is now, we have maintained our good standing with all the ministers, Sunday school superintendents and temperance commit-tees, at a great sacrifice.[36]

In the minds of many, for a circus to be a "real" circus, it must own at least one elephant. At this point the Ringlings did not yet own one.

The show moved into Iowa on June 21 and played twenty-seven towns there before pulling into Alden, Minnesota, on July 23. They played thirteen Minnesota towns and then forty more in Iowa.[37]

The circus caravan occasionally got lost, as country roads were poorly marked. Sometimes an outrider rode in advance, marking the road. "At a fork he would borrow a rail from a nearby fence and place it across the track that wasn't to be taken." When there were no fences, the outrider might use pieces of paper with rocks on them, or a handful of flour to mark the way.[38]

On rainy nights, the troupe packed up wet tents and lifted the heavy, dripping can-vas onto wagons as a team of cold, wet horses stood by. They drove all night through the mud and gloom, with no sounds but horses' hooves clopping through the mud and the slush of wagon wheels protesting the ooze.

Years later Al Ringling shared some of his wagon-show experiences with a friend. "[Al] recalled one rainy morning driving a team while sitting in a wet puddle high up on a wagon. An old razor back [circus employee] sitting beside him says to Al, as he had seen an old farmer coming out of his house and going to barn to do chores. 'Look at that rube.' Al turns to the man and says, 'You call him a rube. Well he is going into a nice dry barn and back to a dry house to eat and we are both soaking wet. We are the rubes.'"[39]

On such cold, wet nights, many disillusioned young farmers turned their teams and wagons toward home, remembering the warm, dry beds that they had left a few weeks earlier. The show constantly sought new recruits to replace those whose excitement for circus had turned to misery after one too many cold, rainy nights in the wilds of Wisconsin, Iowa, or Minnesota. As Alf T. Ringling wrote, "Every time it rained, or the wind blew, or the roads were bad, or the proprietor of one of the teams had seen enough of the country, the showmen had to skirmish for some other rural person with a pair of horses and an ambition to travel."[40]

Yankee Robinson appeared in every show. But he was ill and sometimes hardly able to walk out to center ring. His last appearance was August 16, 1884, in Correctionville, Iowa. In front of the crowd that day he said, "For 40 years I have followed a showman's life, during winter and summer. I have traveled through rain, hail, wind, frost and snow to please the public. For 40 years I have rested my head on a strange pillow and eaten at stranger's board. I have suffered all the reversals and hardships of an eventful career. And today I come from my sick-bed to attempt to please you and do my duty. For a number of years the public has said that I am dead but I am alive—as far as I have got—and when I die—I expect to die among strangers."[41]

Fayette L. "Yankee" Robinson died September 4, 1884, in Jefferson, Iowa. The Boys were left without their mentor and consultant. They were also now without their biggest drawing card. People came to see Yankee Robinson; they didn't know the Ringling boys.

Robinson's death was a turning point for the Ringling Brothers. If their circus was to succeed, they would have to do it on their own. On they drove, into September, playing the Iowa towns of Palo, Center Point, Center City, Hopkinton, and Cascade. They made three stops in Illinois before crossing back into Wisconsin with show dates at Shullsburg and Benton on September 26 and 27 and then back to Baraboo.

They had played 114 towns in four states and had been out nineteen weeks.[42] Upon arriving in Baraboo, the boys stored their equipment and began planning the 1885 season. But first they would mount another round of fall and winter concert shows.

As soon as November, the Brothers were on the road again as the "Ringling Bros. Carnival of Fun," playing the small town halls in Illinois, Iowa, Nebraska, and Wisconsin. They opened at Garden Prairie, Illinois, on November 12, 1884, and closed at Mount Horeb, Wisconsin, on March 14, 1885. They opened a second round of shows on April 6 in Warren Mills, Wisconsin, and closed May 5 in Barron, Wisconsin. Including their previous spring hall shows, their summer circus performances, and their fall Carnival of Fun shows, the boys put on 241 shows in 1884—an enormous accomplishment.[43] If nothing else, the Ringling Brothers had proved to themselves and to a largely accepting public that they could put on a show, move to another town, and do it all over again, day after day, week after week. They also proved that the five of them could work together as a team, sharing the duties of managing and performing and moving from town to town through all kinds of weather without destroying their relationship.

The Ringling Brothers

Albert Charles "Al" (1852–1916)

As the oldest, Al was the leader of the Brothers. He was equestrian director for the circus, in charge of the program and the hiring of performers. Al was nervous, always on the go, and a perfectionist, especially when it came to circus performance. For many years he was in front of the audience while the other Brothers worked in the background.

Al was a taskmaster, but he also had a soft side. His nieces and nephews found him warm, friendly, and always ready with a funny story. In one incident Al noticed a crying woman with a little girl hurrying away from the show grounds. Al caught up to her and asked her what was wrong, and she replied that she had lost her purse, which contained three dollars and her railroad tickets home. Al motioned for one of his men and instructed him to take the woman and her daughter to the show and sit with them, in the best seats. After the performance the man was to escort them to the best hotel for supper, buy the woman a new purse, reimburse her stolen money, purchase train tickets for their return trip, and make sure they got on the right train.[1]

William Henry Otto "Otto" (1858–1911)

Always fond of numbers, Otto was treasurer for the circus and became the financial genius of the Ringling operation. Quiet and methodical, he loved good books and built a substantial personal library. But he was always a frugal man. He never married and he never owned a home, living with his brother Alf T.

when he was not on the road. His brothers sometimes called him The King because he and he alone controlled the Ringling purse strings.

Alfred Theodore "Alf T." (1863–1919)

Alf T. was in charge of press relations. He established contacts with hundreds of newspaper people across the country, and as the Ringling Brothers Circus grew he oversaw a cadre of public relations writers who were constantly feeding news articles to the press about the circus at home and on the road.

Alf T. was somewhat of a free spirit. Although he was part of all major decision making, he left day-to-day operations to Al, Charles, and Otto. He had considerable musical abilities, playing the cornet during the circus's wagon-show days. For several years he penned the annual route books, chronicling the show's travels. He also wrote *Life Story of the Ringling Brothers* (1900), a history of the Ringling Brothers circus.

Carl Edward "Charles" (1864–1926)

Charles was in charge of advertising and promotion, including overseeing the vast army of bill posters, who plastered circus posters throughout the countryside prior to the show's visit. Charles also worked behind the scenes to keep the circus operating smoothly and efficiently. He was a favorite among the circus employees, laborers as well as performers, providing an even keel on the

(continued on page 24)

The Ringling Brothers

(continued from page 23)

circus lot where he spent a great deal of time. The staff affectionately referred to him as Mr. Charlie.

Charles was the most musically talented of the Brothers. Once a season up to the year before he died, he played a horn solo with the circus band. He also collected rare and expensive violins and was an avid fisherman.

John Nicholas (1866–1936)

John was in charge of scheduling and became an expert on where railroads ran and who ran them. He always dressed impeccably and never cared much for Baraboo; some found him a pompous show-off. He was tall, with curly hair and droopy eyes, and was considered a ladies' man. Even while his brothers were still living in Baraboo, he lived in a hotel in Chicago, and he later lived in New York.

In addition to his scheduling duties, John traveled widely in Europe on the lookout for outstanding circus acts. Along the way he became an amateur art collector and an entrepreneur. He built the Yellowstone Park and White Sulphur Springs Railroad between Ringling and White Sulphur Springs, Montana. He also purchased ranch land totaling more than one hundred thousand acres and founded the towns of Ringling, Montana, and Ringling, Oklahoma. He built a short-line railroad from Ardmore to Ringling, Oklahoma, and named this twenty-three-mile railroad the Oklahoma, New Mexico and Pacific.

August Albert "Gus" (1854–1907)

Gus signed on with the Ringling circus in 1890 and was content to work as an employee, not as a partner. He was in charge of Advertising Car No. 1, which was responsible for pasting circus advertising on the barns and sheds across the country. Gus was well read and, some said, the most gentle of the brothers.

Henry William George (1868–1918)

Though the youngest of the boys, Henry was six foot, three inches and weighed more than three hundred pounds—the largest of all the brothers. He joined the show in 1886 and later became superintendent of the main entrance to the Big Top.

When Otto died in 1911, he left his fifth of the circus to Henry, who then became a partner.

NOTES

1. "From Mud to the Field of the Cloth of Gold," *Show World*, September 17, 1910.

Photos on pages 23–24 from Print Collection, CWM

Establishing a Reputation: 1885–1889

"Waukon, Iowa. May 15, 1888. We have had the worst experience in business since we started."[1]

In the circus business—as in any business where public approval is essential—reputation means everything. As the Ringling Brothers struck out on their own, without Yankee Robinson's assistance and advice, they set out to establish an unblemished reputation and to create a show that would appeal to families and people of all ages.

They finished their spring 1885 Carnival of Fun hall tour just three weeks before returning to the road with their new show, "Ringling Bros. Great Double Shows, Circus, Caravan and Trained Animal Exposition." This year's shows would be bigger than ever, with larger tents—the main tent was an eighty-foot round top, and the sideshow tent was thirty by fifteen feet—and a street parade prior to each show.[2] They boasted "[t]he largest and best 25 cent show on earth, containing all the prominent features of the amusement world. . . . 50 new and startling features, great clowns, 3 hours of solid fun. . . . Amoor the largest Baboon living, and the largest snakes ever placed on exhibition."[3]

They opened in Baraboo on May 18. Some of the reviews were less than laudatory: "Ringling Bros. circus showed here last Friday to good crowds. The show contains several good features and is worth the price of admission. The band was the worst that ever appeared in this village, the performers knowing everything but music."[4]

A circus's success was measured in several ways. Most important, did the show make enough money to continue? Other gauges of success were the size of the main tent and the number of horses, wagons, and elephants. So far the Ringlings had no elephants (which were extremely expensive), but they were increasing the size of their main tent and adding horses and wagons each season. In 1885 the show had fifteen wagons and was making enough money to continue.

The Brothers closed the 1885 circus season in Randolph, Wisconsin, on Saturday,

Members of the Ringling Bros. Great Double Shows, Circus, Caravan, and Trained Animal Exposition, 1885. From left to right (standing): candy butcher (unknown), Al Ringling, Frank Sparks, G. P. Putnam, Rich Dialo, Alf T. Ringling, Sam Hardy, Frank Kissell. Middle row (sitting): George Hall, Vic Richardson, John Ringling. Front row: George W. LaRosa, Theodore Asmus, Charles Ringling, Dick Hunter (advance agent), Otto Ringling. Those not pictured include Lou Ringling, Al Ringling's wife. PRINT COLLECTION, CWM

October 3. They had presented 114 shows in Wisconsin, Iowa, and Illinois, the same number as in 1884. Six weeks after returning to Baraboo and winter quarters, they were on the road again with their 1885–1886 Carnival of Fun, opening November 12 in Ironton, Wisconsin. They added some of their summer circus regulars to their Carnival of Fun, including Rich Dialo, billed as "The Human Volcano. . . . He bites off bars of red hot iron, eating boiling and blazing sealing-wax. . . . [He closes his performance] by allowing anybody to come from the audience and melt lead and pour it into his mouth." John Ringling was promoted as "the Emperor of all Dutch dialect comedians, in his funny

Dutchey maneuvers; creating roars of laughter with every move and funny expression. You will laugh as you never laughed before." Alf T. and Charles Ringling were billed as playing twelve different musical instruments "to the great delight of the audience."[5] They closed January 30 in Fort Dodge, Iowa, and returned to Baraboo for a few weeks before starting a late spring run in Waunakee, Wisconsin, on March 2, ending in Rice Lake, Wisconsin, on April 23. They returned to Baraboo on April 24, with only a few weeks to prepare for another summer circus season.

The Ringling Brothers opened their 1886 circus in Baraboo on May 15. This year they had a ninety-foot round top tent (to which they added a thirty-foot middle section on July 3) and a seventy-five-foot by forty-five-foot sideshow tent. They now had eighteen wagons and had added a caged animal display consisting of a hyena, a bear, monkeys, and an eagle. According to a Ringling legend, they advertised the hyena as "Hideous Hyena *Striata Gigantium*. The mammoth midnight marauding man-eating monstrosity, the prowling grave-robbing demon of all created things."[6]

The Ringlings were developing a substantial menagerie, a big draw for rural people, who had little opportunity to view exotic animals. The previous January they had purchased a donkey and a Shetland pony—their first trick animal act. In November 1886 John Ringling purchased two lions, a kangaroo, a South American anteater, an elk, a ring-tailed monkey, and a cage of "rare and beautifully plumaged birds. . . . The boys will start out the spring with a well appointed circus and menagerie and will take the back seat for no show on the road. Success to the boys is the wish of the *Republic*."[7]

On September 6, 1886, young Henry, who had been in Rice Lake with the Ringling parents, joined his five brothers as an employee. He would turn eighteen on October 27. That fall and winter the boys were out twenty-two weeks, three more than in previous years. They played 127 stands: 65 in Iowa, 43 in Minnesota, and 19 in Wisconsin.[8]

Newspaper reviews of the 1886 show were generally good. One reviewer wrote: "Some of those who attended the Ringling Bros. Circus Tuesday evening were disappointed, for they expected a somewhat poor affair but the performance proved to be much better than most of the more pretentious shows that are traveling. It is not a big show but it is a very good one."[9]

Another writer proclaimed, "Ringling Bros.' circus was in this city [Darlington, Wisconsin] Wednesday, gave a creditable street parade in the afternoon and another in the evening and the attendance was fairly good. Now that Darlington has had its annual circus our people can saw up their wood piles, fill up their coal bins and wait for hoary winter, feeling that the town has been saved."[10]

That winter the Ringlings took over the former Bassett Factory on Water Street in Baraboo. There they stored their equipment and their growing menagerie. Working on next season's circus was top priority, but they were still short of money, so once again they took their hall show on the road beginning in November 1886 and closing in April

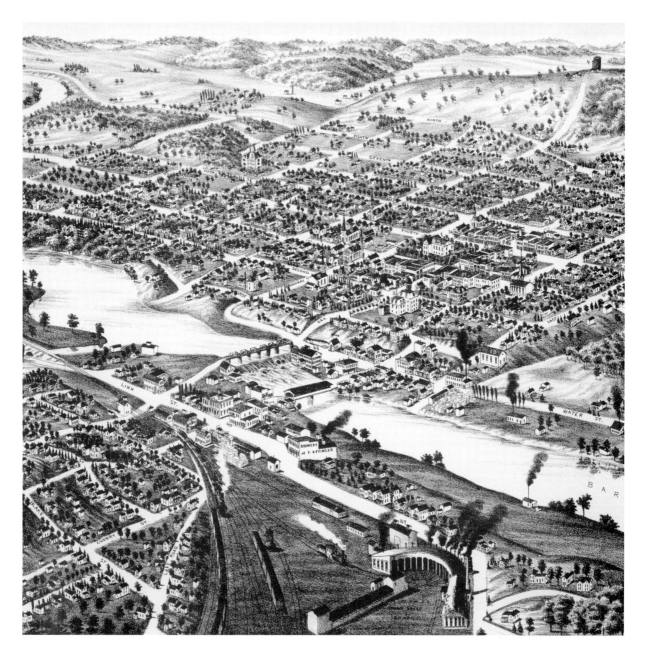

A bird's-eye view of Baraboo, Wisconsin, in 1886. The Ringlings located their winter quarters along the Baraboo River, on the north side of Water Street (toward the lower right of this image). In 1887 they purchased the Bassett property on Water Street, and in 1888 they built a ring barn and an animal house. Note the substantial railroad yards to the south of the river, including a railroad repair shop. The Ringlings rented the rail yards from the Chicago and Northwestern Railroad until they built their own railroad repair shops in 1893. SAUK COUNTY HISTORICAL SOCIETY

1887. They took time off in January and February, likely to rest and avoid the depths of winter. They put on only forty-eight hall performances that winter.[11]

The Brothers called their 1887 circus "Ringling Bros. United Monster Shows, Great Double Circus, Royal Menagerie, Museum, Caravan and Congress of Trained Animals." The main tent was a ninety-foot round top with a thirty-foot middle section. The sideshow tent was forty-five by fifty-five feet, and the menagerie was a seventy-foot round top. They had sixty horses and ponies. Five cages transported the wild animals that John had purchased the previous fall. They also added a camel while traveling, but it died before season's end. The show opened in Baraboo on May 7.

Why the Ringlings decided on such a verbose title for their circus is anyone's guess, but perhaps they wanted to make up for in words what they lacked in assets. Newspaper reviews of that season's shows were mixed. A Fond du Lac newspaper reported, "The show this afternoon was disappointing to those who attended and afforded less amusement than the average traveling dime museum." According to a Juneau, Wisconsin, paper, "The menagerie part of the business was not very extensive, the 'elephant' being conspicuous for his absence. The ring performance was up to the average 50 cent show, while the clown was far below the average buffoon." The Stoughton, Wisconsin, newspaper promoted the Ringlings with back-handed encouragement, "The home circus will be about all the shows the people will be apt to have a chance of seeing this season. The interstate commerce law makes the tariff of travel so high that the monster [railroad] shows from the east will be unable to make Wisconsin."[12]

In 1887 the Ringlings traveled the farthest yet from home, showing in Nebraska, Kansas, and Missouri. They traveled hundreds of miles by horse-drawn wagons over rough, rutted roads that were sometimes nearly impassable. They put up their tents

An 1887 advertising handbill for the Ringling Brothers show. Theirs was an overland circus, traveling by wagons until 1890, when they took to the rails. HANDBILL COLLECTION, CWM

For many people a circus was not a "real" circus until it had an elephant. The Ringlings purchased their first two elephants in 1888. PRINT COLLECTION, CWM

each morning, put on a parade and a show, took down the tents, and drove on to the next town—six days a week, resting only on Sunday. For everyone from the teamsters to the performers, it was hard, dirty work. Each night or early morning they faced another trip, usually along an unknown road, to an unknown place, often with little or no sleep and eating on the fly. No matter if the weather was bad, a wagon broke down or someone got sick or hurt, the show had to go on.

The Brothers closed the 1887 circus tour in Warrenton, Missouri, on October 22, and the group traveled back to Baraboo via a Mississippi steamboat to East Dubuque, Illinois, and from there by road.[13] They quickly sent out two groups of performers for the 1887–1888 winter hall show season. Company One included Alf T., Charles, John, and Henry Ringling plus five others and toured from mid-December to early February. Company Two had Al Ringling and his wife, Lou, plus five more employees and toured from early December to mid-March.

The winter hall shows had added to the Brothers' financial coffers, and they acquired two elephants in February. When John heard that the elephants had arrived in Baraboo, he quit the hall show five days early so he could see them.[14] Although the first of these exotic animals had arrived in the United States in 1796, few midwesterners had ever seen one.[15] Those along the circus route would now be treated not only to a long parade of wagons, horses, and cages of wild animals making strange sounds; they would

Albert "Butch" Parson was in charge of the Ringling show's candy and lemonade stand for many years. In this photo, from 1890, Butch is fourth from the left; his brother Frank is second from the left. PHOTO BY HUDSON & SHADLE, ALGONA, IOWA; PRINT COLLECTION, CWM

see two huge elephants shuffling along. The sight would stop anyone in their tracks, no matter what they were doing. With the purchase of these amazing beasts, the Ringlings' show became a "real" circus.

Along with two elephants, the Brothers now had two camels, three lions, a hyena, deer, kangaroo, zebu, emu, birds, monkeys, and eighty horses and ponies. The 1888 Big Top was 100 by 148 feet. The Brothers contracted out for refreshment services, and that year Al "Butch" Parson from Darlington, Wisconsin, had the privilege, selling pink lemonade and other treats. Al Ringling had worked for the Parson family as a performer and knew the Parsons well.

By early May 1888 the wagons were ready to roll. Since their first shows in fall 1882, every season had been more successful than the previous one; the Brothers could see no reason why this year wouldn't be the best yet. Otto kept his eye on the books, watching all expenses and keeping everyone on the budget straight and narrow. This included managing the Ringlings' contracts with various teamsters, who furnished horses and cared for and drove the teams—a major expense.

The circus had reached a size where the Brothers believed they could charge a higher admission without complaint, and they doubled admission to fifty cents for

The Ringling Brothers
had standard contracts
for everything, from
hotels to performers to
teamsters. In the 1888
teamster contract
shown here, they
agreed to pay fifty dol-
lars per month for two
teams, harnesses, and
services. RINGLING
BROTHERS COLLECTION,
CWM

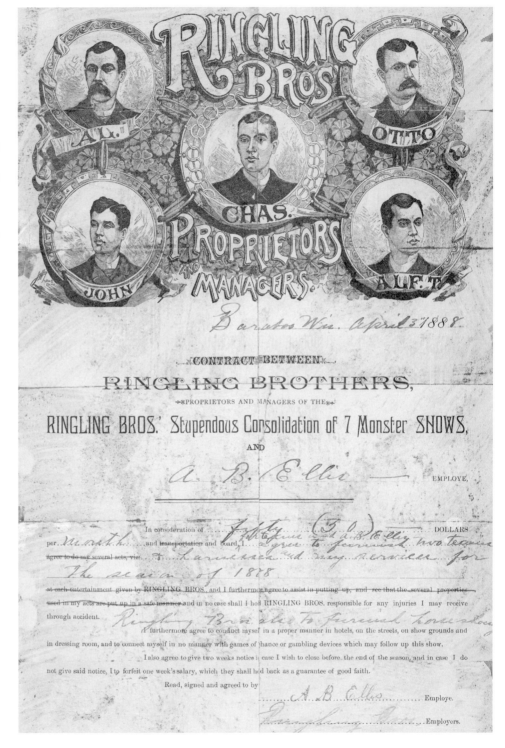

adults and twenty-five cents for children. The show opened in Baraboo on May 5 and drove on to Reedsburg, Cazenovia, and Hillsboro, Wisconsin. Then the rains began to fall—every day and every night, thunder and lightning and a steady downpour. Once dry, dusty roads turned to sticky quagmires. Everything was stuck in the mud. Everyone was wet and complaining. "[We] did not see the sun for four weeks. Missed many afternoon stands on account of mud and rain . . . were obliged to abandon advance wagons and bill by rail [advertising men traveled by train] for a short time."[16]

The Brothers soon found themselves in desperate straits, perhaps the worst financial situation since taking their circus on the road in 1884. Otto wrote to the Bank of Baraboo for help:

> It has been raining continually, and the roads have been in terrible condition. We were stuck in those clay hills at Ontario, Hillsboro & Cazenovia during the worst part of the storm. . . . During the past week commencing at Reedsburg we showed only one half of the time. The balance of the time was spent digging our wagons out of the mud—trying to meet our appointments. From Cazenovia to Hillsboro, 18 miles, it took us from 3 o'clock in the morning until 9 at night to get the show in town and then hired all the farmers we could find along the road to help draw our wagons to town. . . . The continual rain has put farmers behind with their work and it will necessarily make business dull for a short time. After considering everything carefully, we have decided that it will be better for us to cut down the show to 25 cents and reduce our expenses to a low notch and be entirely safe. In order to do this we must pay off the people we do not want next Saturday and ship what stuff we do not wish to carry [back] to Baraboo. If you could loan us enough to this effectually and before we meet with any more losses we will give you any security you may ask for (in our power).

Otto Ringling asked for a $1,000 loan. The postscript to the letter captured the depth of the Brothers' despair:

> You cannot form any idea of the terrible strain on us with everything at stake, in the rain and mud almost every day and night for over a week. . . . The wagons would sink down to the hubs and the poor horses could not budge them. We had to hire farmers at their own figures and we had to put all our men to work with shovels to get the clay away from the wheels. Our repair bills besides were enormous. Wagons continually pulled to pieces, springs broken, etc.[17]

The Ringlings had borrowed money from the Bank of Baraboo before and always promptly repaid it, so they had a good credit rating. This time the bank granted them a ninety-day loan of $1,000.[18]

Ringling Brothers Loans, Bank of Baraboo

May 1885: $100

May 1886: $300

May 1887: $500

November 1887: $1,000

May 1888: $1,000

May 1889: $1,000

All loans were at 8 percent interest.[19]

Otto sent a letter of thanks to the bank upon receiving the loan and indicated that they had not yet used any of the loan money and were "trying our utmost not to."[20]

In a follow-up letter Otto wrote:

Please find enclosed draft on Chicago for $1,000 payment for money sent us Caledonia, Minnesota. . . . The past ten days have been favorable and we have made about $1500 in that time. . . . [T]he past four days have been *excellent.* We can hardly realize that we have got through and overcome the difficulties that seemed to make it impossible to proceed any further. . . . We have now about $2,000 on hand, *cash,* besides returning your $1,000 and have paid for a new lot of paper [for advertising] have paid all expenses . . . and the prospects are brighter for the future. During the 4 weeks of Hell you could have seen a muddy, cold disheartened, dirty wet gang of *forlorn* people if you had been with the show, but the sun shines again. We are very thankful for the kind favor you have shown us and of course can not repay you by thanks alone. We believe it worried us more than yourselves and it is a great relief to be again on something like a paying basis. It was our first experience in a losing business and coupled with the terrible work and uncertainty of being able to get the show through the mud was disheartening. . . . We did not touch the $1,000 you sent us but got down to $1,220.00 that was cash on hand, besides your remittance. That was the low water mark.[21]

Once the skies cleared and the mud disappeared, the Ringlings were on their way with their usual confidence. After Minnesota and Iowa, they moved into Dakota Territory, Nebraska, and back to Iowa, finally returning to Wisconsin for eight stands in October.

Business was not especially good in Nebraska. In an August letter Otto wrote, "Business has been very bad during harvest (it always is) but is steadily improving and harvest is nearly over."[22]

Besides problems with the weather and harvest time, the Brothers faced other unforeseen events. For years circus people and local folks often got into tussles over one

A crowd of Ringling circus goers at Algona, Iowa, 1888. The person on the top of the tent at left (shown in highlighted area) is Joe Parson, doing a free ascension act. Photo by Saunders, Algona, Iowa; Print Collection, CWM

thing or another, leading to fist fights and worse. On June 23, when the circus was playing in Webster City, Iowa, James Richardson, a Ringling performer, was murdered, reason unknown. His killer, Thomas Baskett, was convicted and sentenced to fifteen years in prison.[23]

Accidents also plagued the circus. When the Ringlings played in Prairie du Chien the local paper noted: "During the grand entry act in Ringling's circus, Mrs. Al Ringling was thrown from her horse by stumbling of the animal. The knee of the horse struck her on the head, and the immense crowd thought she was killed as she was carried out of the ring to the dressing pavilion. Mr. Ringling soon came in and announced from the ring that she was not injured, and at the time she fell could not speak from fright. The news was received with loud shouts by the people."[24]

The 1888 season closed October 13 at Sauk City, Wisconsin. The local paper reported:

As anticipated, the appearance of Ringling Bros. colossal consolidation of seven shows at Sauk City on Saturday, attracted one of the largest crowds of people that has been seen here for some time. . . . The performance in the afternoon . . . about 1,500–2,000 people [were] present, and the features introduced in the ring were fully as entertaining as those of any first class show on the road. [The Ringlings] report this to have been the most profitable season since their organization, having

Al Ringling was always directly involved in circus activities. Here he is seen training show dogs in 1888. PRINT COLLECTION, CWM

more than doubled the net receipts of last year, and it is said to be over $50,000. Every resident of the county will be pleased to learn of the success which is crowning their efforts and hope for a continuance of the same.[25]

The 1888 circus season had been sufficiently successful that the Brothers offered no more winter hall shows. They returned to winter quarters in Baraboo in October and moved onto the Bassett property on Water Street that they had purchased in November 1887.[26] In fall 1888 they had built a new ring barn (sixty feet square) and a new animal house at the winter quarters.[27] The new ring barn included a standard-size circus ring (forty-two feet in diameter) where the horses and riders could practice throughout the winter.

The new animal house sheltered the exotic animals during the long, cold winter months. In Ringling circus parlance *barns* were unheated structures that primarily housed horses. Horses gave off sufficient heat to keep the buildings warm. *Houses* sheltered animals such as elephants and the other exotic animals that required additional heat from coal-fired furnaces.

Elephants

A circus wasn't really a circus until it owned an elephant. But elephants were expensive. The Ringlings didn't purchase their first ones (Babylon, or Babe, an Asiatic, and Fannie, an African) until February 1888, four years after they went on the road. By 1892 the Ringlings owned six elephants, and by 1908 they had forty huge beasts in their elephant herd. To many observers, the number of elephants a circus owned was a measure of its size and prestige.

In 1898 the Brothers purchased a "white elephant." The Ringlings heavily advertised the animal, named Keddah, as sacred, mythical, and "the most expensive of animals." It was not really white, but lighter colored than most elephants, with pink around the ears, white feet, light hair around its lips, and no tuft of hair at the end of its tail. Barnum & Bailey had a white elephant that had proved a disappointment in attracting crowds, so the Ringlings are likely to have purchased Keddah at a discounted price. Frugal as the Ringlings were, they converted a giraffe wagon into quarters for their prize "sacred" animal. Keddah traveled in this wagon on the train, to and from the lot, and in the street parade. He did not ride with the other elephants.[1] While traveling to Ft. Smith, Arkansas, on October 15, 1898, the wagon carrying the white ele-

Trimming an elephant's toenails was no small task. Notice the equipment: a hacksaw and a large file. This photo was taken behind the elephant house at Ringlingville winter quarters. PRINT COLLECTION, CWM

phant caught fire, and the animal suffered bad burns and smoke inhalation. As hard as his handlers worked to save the animal, it died five days later in Arkansas.[2]

The Ringlings were always on the lookout for additional elephants. In an exchange of letters with E. D. Colvin, an agent for Hagenbeck's, the German animal dealer, Otto inquired about the big beasts.

Colvin replied, "I quote you a list of all the elephants on hand at the present time: One male (Albert) 4 ft. 10 in. high—$1,400, One male (Tambus) 4 ft. 5 in. high—$1,375.00, one female (Clara) broken, 5 ft. high—$1,500." In March Otto learned from Colvin that the animals he had ordered from Germany could not get on the mail boat and had to come by way of Bulgaria on a ship that took fourteen days.[3]

On November 19, 1900, a spectacular event occurred at winter quarters: a baby Asian elephant was born, the first one in Baraboo.[4] A magazine reporter enthusiastically wrote:

> The Ringling Bros. are without question the proudest and happiest showmen in America today. The baby elephant is of course the cause of this

(continued on page 38)

Elephants

(continued from page 37)

joy. And such a dear little baby he is. A perfect miniature elephant, 34 inches long, weighing 300 pounds, carrying a trunk one foot in length. . . . Little Nick was born about 4:30 Monday morning, only a few hours after the show arrived in winter quarters. Alice, a monster elephant is the mother of the small wonder, and his father, Baldy, boasts of being the largest pachyderm in America today. When the calf was born the mother awakened the sleeping elephant men who were in the elephant building. . . . Like many animal mothers, Alice tried her very best to kill her offspring by trampling on him, and it was only by heroic measures little Nick was carried out of the mother's way into a place of safety. When picked up it was between life and death, but he lived, and today is as spry as a kitten. . . . [S]he was removed, together with little Nick, to the ring barn where the two are now kept. The mother is getting over her ferociousness toward the infant elephant, and it is firmly believed that after a few weeks she was become reconciled to him.[5]

The elephant was christened some days after its birth

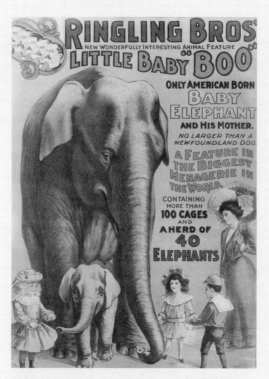

For the 1903 season the Ringlings advertised "Little Baby Boo" as an "American born baby elephant." The little elephant had in fact come from Ceylon with its mother. PRINT COLLECTION, CWM

by Wisconsin governor Edward Scofield and his wife, Agnes, who visited winter quarters.[6] The baby elephant would have been a great draw for the circus, but unfortunately it died before the Ringlings went on the road in 1901.[7]

Alice gave birth to an unnamed baby elephant on October 26, 1902, but she killed the calf. The Brothers ordered another elephant and calf from Hagenbeck's about November 22, 1902, and the animals arrived in Baraboo on December 18, 1902. The boys decided to advertise the new little elephant as having been born in Baraboo, and they named it "Baby Boo." This was an elaborate hoax—or advertising genius. An April 4, 1903, article in *Billboard* proclaimed: "Ringling Bros. possess quite an attraction this year in the shape of a baby elephant, which is about seven weeks old. It is named 'Baby Boo,' and she is about 30" high. She is the daughter of Baldy and Alice, two of Ringling Bros. largest elephants." In fact, the elephant and its mother had come from Ceylon (now Sri Lanka).[8]

Circus elephants sometimes caused problems. For the 1909 season, the Ringlings replaced Pearl Souder, elephant superintendent, with William Emery. Problems with the elephant herd began immediately. On July 30 five elephants ran away while the herd was unloading in Laramie, Wyoming. Two were captured immediately, but

Elephants

three others headed for the open prairie. One elephant was still on the loose when the train had to leave for Rawlins. Two elephants and three men were left behind to search for the runaway. They all returned to the show two weeks later, presumably with the recalcitrant elephant.

When the show played in Bakersfield, California, on September 19, 1909, five elephants ran away again, this time while the street parade was assembling. They knocked over the snake den and caused general havoc. The same five elephants bolted the next day in Santa Barbara. They were rounded up with great difficulty and were loaded back onto railcars, where they remained for the next seven weeks, with Al Ringling's approval.[9]

In 1910, while handlers were unloading the elephants from their railcars in Danville, Illinois, nine elephants ran away. They knocked down fences, destroyed outhouses, trampled gardens, and smashed sheds. The havoc went on for four hours before the escaped elephants were caught and brought under control. A reporter for the Rockford, Illinois, *Morning Star* wrote, "The attendance at both [Ringling] performances today were enormous, the thrilling events of yesterday having acted as a splendid advertisement for the show." Ringling lawyer John Kelley was busy settling claims.[10]

An elephant debarks the elephant car one early morning in 1902. The elephants were loaded side by side with their heads toward the car's center door.
RICHARD E. AND ALBERT CONOVER COLLECTION, CWM

NOTES

1. Richard J. Reynolds III, correspondence with the author, December 1, 2002.
2. *Red Wagon: Route Book of The Ringing Bros. World's Greatest Show, Season 1898* (Chicago: Central Printing and Engraving, 1898), pp. 78–79.
3. E. D. Colvin to Otto Ringling, March 3, 1900, Fred Pfening III, private collection, Columbus, Ohio.
4. To date this was the fourth baby elephant (all Asians) born in the United States. All were circus elephants: Howes Great London (1875)—the calf apparently did not survive—Cooper and Bailey (1880), and Barnum and London (1882). Richard J. Reynolds III, correspondence with the author, December 5, 2002.
5. "Shows in Winter Quarters," *Billboard*, December 12, 1900. Also see Richard J. Reynolds III, "Baraboo's Baby Elephants," *Bandwagon*, November/December, 1993, pp. 4–12.
6. *Baraboo (Wisconsin) Evening News*, December 6, 1900.
7. Mention of baby elephant's death in correspondence from the Standard Embossing Company of Chicago to Charles Ringling, March 11, 1901, Pfening collection.
8. Reynolds, "Baraboo's Baby Elephants."
9. William H. Woodcock Jr., unpublished lists of circus elephants and elephant history notes, CWM Library.
10. *Rockford (Illinois) Morning Star*, April 29, 1910; *Danville (Illinois) Commercial-News*, April 27, 28, 29, 1910; *Sauk County (Wisconsin) Democrat*, May 5, 1910, and May 10, 1910; *Baraboo (Wisconsin) News*, May 5, 1910, and June 23, 1910; *Baraboo Republic*, May 5, 1910; Richard J. Reynolds III, correspondence with the author, December 18, 2002.

The winter of 1888–1889 was a busy time for the Brothers as they made plans for their 1889 season. They called their 1889 show "Ringling Bros. and Van Amburgh's United Monster Circus, Museum, Menagerie, Roman Hippodrome and Universal World's Exposition." They had paid a small amount to include the name Van Amburgh, a once-famous trainer who had died in 1865. They opened on May 4 in Baraboo, with a larger, more elaborate circus parade preceding an all-new show. The parade was described as "The largest, longest, richest, rarest and most generously resplendent gratuitous display that human resources and effort can render possible. Arabian Nights and fairy tales made real. Wild Beasts, Bands, Gorgeous Chariots, Wide-open Dens and Glorious Art and Dress in ravishing array. Something that no one came afford to miss. It is worth going 100 miles to see."[28]

That year Gus Ringling, the second-oldest son, joined the show as advertising agent, although he remained an employee of the partners. Now all seven brothers were with the show. The Brothers also hired Spencer Alexander (nicknamed Delavan because of his connections to Delavan, Wisconsin) as boss hostler in charge of all the horses. That year the Ringlings had 110 horses and ponies. Butch Parson continued to manage the candy and lemonade stand.

By this time the Brothers had acquired another elephant, and this season's show traveled with those beasts plus two camels, nine cages of other animals, one cage of birds, and three advance wagons that traveled several weeks ahead of the others and were in charge of advertising, posting bills, and pasting signs on the sides of barns. During the muddy spring of 1888 the advance men briefly switched to rail travel, but they went back to driving wagons as soon as the roads allowed. The entire circus traveled by horse-drawn wagon in 1889.

The circus was out twenty-four weeks, closing in Lodi, Wisconsin, on October 15. The Ringlings made 147 stands, the most in their six years of operating an overland circus. And they made money. From May 10 to August 17 they deposited $22,731.00 ($437,000 in 2002 dollars) in the Bank of Baraboo.

Reviews for the 1889 show were generally positive:

> The Circus last Monday was far better than the majority of traveling shows, equal to any that ever visited Hartford. . . . There were probably as many as four thousand people from the outside in this city on Monday to see the street parade and circus, as by the ticket count 3,384 passed under the tent in the afternoon; besides these there was a large number of children in arms who gained admission free.[29]

Another writer said of the 1889 show:

> The glitter of tinsel, the gloss of varnish, the glare of vanity, and the glut of ambi-

tious men for the almighty dollar! What more was it than this? But then, comparatively speaking, the Ringling and Van Amburgh combination that squatted here on Wednesday was equal (magnitude aside) to the best of circuses, and probably not one that paid his or her ten cents to see the museum, or fifty cents to take in the "entire combined show," kicked, and there being no demands made for refunding of money, we conclude the public got all it paid for.[30]

Unlike many circuses, traveling medicine shows, and other rural attractions, the Ringling Brothers' show was an honest show—no shortchanging, pickpockets, or game-of-chance cheats. They even snagged pickpockets and turned them over to the local authorities. These immoral and illegal acts were known as "grift." A rural newspaper editor wrote, "The Ringling Brothers are personally known to many of our citizens and they are esteemed as upright young men. Their purpose to exclude every disreputable feature and 'snide' affair from connection with their show, is but characteristic of them."[31]

Once more in winter quarters, the Brothers immediately began planning for 1890. No one had forgotten the rains in the spring of '88, when they almost lost their show. One way to make sure muddy roads would no longer affect travel was to switch to rail. What's more, as an overland circus they could not grow much larger, and their routes would always be limited by how far horses and men could walk. By 1878 several circuses (Barnum starting in 1872, John Robinson in 1872, W.W. Cole in 1873, Cooper and Bailey in 1876, Forepaugh in 1876 or 1877, and Sells Bros. in 1878) traveled by rail.[32] The Brothers decided it was time to take to the rails as well. No more mud and dust. No more walking fifteen, twenty, or more miles a day, usually at night and often half asleep, through the dark and gloom on their way to the next town.

The Ringlings offered their road-show equipment for sale. An ad in a national trade magazine proclaimed: "From Road to Rail. The Ringling Brothers Great United Circus and Menagerie has closed the most successful season known in the history of wagon shows." The ad went on to list for sale tents, seats, lights, poles, ropes, cages, dens, baggage wagons, harnesses, costumes, banners, and more. "All property in first class condition, and can be seen at winter quarters in Baraboo, Wisconsin."[33]

Meanwhile, the Ringlings scoured the national trade journals searching for circus rail equipment. They discovered that the Adam Forepaugh Circus had surplus equipment for sale. Otto headed to Philadelphia, hoping to strike a deal. On November 8, 1889, he tentatively agreed to purchase several pieces of Forepaugh rail equipment, but his dealings with the Forepaugh Circus went on through December. When the negotiating dust cleared, the Brothers owned eleven railroad cars (three stockcars, one boxcar, one baggage car, three loaded flatcars, and three empty flatcars). The flatcars included one cage and six baggage wagons, and the boxcar included a zebra, kangaroo, and camel, "with enough feed and bedding for the trip." Total cost: $4,500. Otto Ringling also bought additional railcars and a bandwagon from the former Burr Robbins circus of Janesville, Wisconsin, bringing the total number of cars to sixteen.[34]

Now the Ringlings needed a place to store their train. In November 1889 the Ringlings were negotiating with a Mrs. Potter for land she owned across the Baraboo River from the Bassett property. They ending up leasing some of Mrs. Potter's land and began constructing a spur line for their newly purchased railcars. The Chicago and Northwestern Railroad had a major rail operation near the Potter property that included machine shops, a roundhouse, a water tank, wood yards, depots, and a switching yard.

The *Sauk County Democrat* reported: "The new buildings which are being erected at 'Ringlingville' for the accommodation of the Ringling Bros. Circus paraphernalia are getting along nicely under the personal supervision of Chas. Ringling."[35] This is the first evidence of the use of the term *Ringlingville,* and from this time forward, the Ringling buildings in Baraboo would be known as Ringlingville. A few years later, the cluster of Ringling tents on the road would also become known as Ringlingville.

Also during that busy winter of 1889–1890, the Brothers opened a new office over Horstman's Meat Market on Oak Street.[36] It was an extremely busy planning season: the Brothers established routes for the coming summer season, contracted the acts, developed advertising and promotional materials and budgets, organized and readied equipment, trained animals, and ordered supplies.

The city of Baraboo thought well of their efforts. "Ringling Brothers contribute no small amount to the volume of business of the city this winter. They have twenty-eight people on their payroll. Besides this the cost of keeping a large number of horses, animals, etc. to say nothing of the five Ringling Brothers' personal expenses, which help to reduce their bank account for the benefit of the community."[37]

In January 1890 August Ringling, now sixty-three, Salome Ringling, fifty-seven, and daughter Ida moved from Rice Lake back to Baraboo. The entire family was together again, for the first time in many years.

The Brothers were more optimistic than ever as they made the giant and expensive transition from an overland wagon circus to a railroad circus. If they managed well, routed carefully, and had a little luck, their opportunities would be unlimited. Their relationship to their hometown of Baraboo was strong. The community had been watching what they were doing down on Water Street, and it liked what it saw. The Ringlings had built a substantial reputation as an overland circus; now the challenge was to keep their reputation and enhance it as they moved to the rails.

Women and the Circus

The Ringlings' female performers were overseen by a circus mother, a combination chaperon, hospital nurse, friend, and counselor. Officially, she was matron of the women's dressing room.[1] Mother ruled with a heavy hand. There was no "hanky panky"; women were expected to do their work and adhere to a closely kept schedule.

The Ringling Brothers published a list of "Suggestions and Rules." It was said to be for all employees, but most of the rules applied only to women:

1. Do not dress in a flashy, loud style; be neat and modest in appearance.
2. You are required to be in the sleeping car and register your name not later than 11 p.m. and not to leave car after registering.
3. Girls must not stop at hotels at any time.
4. [Girls] are not permitted to visit with relatives, etc., in cities where show appears without permission.
5. [Girls] are not permitted to talk or visit with male members of the show company, excepting the management, and under no circumstance with residents of the cities visited.
6. The excuse of "accidental" meetings will not be accepted.

Note—if some of the rules seem harsh and exacting, please remember—experience has taught the management that they are necessary. It is intended to protect the girls in every possible way. Good order and good behavior are necessary, if you are to be comfortable and happy. The management urges each girl to live up to the spirit of the rules as well as to the letter.[2]

On the one hand, the circus strove to protect women, on the other hand it exploited them. Few places in late-nineteenth-century America would condone scantily clad young women as did communities embracing the circus. As historian Janet Davis has noted, "[I]t seems that pro-

A peek inside the women's dressing tent, 1902. Second from the right is the acclaimed strongwoman Katie Sandwina. DON S. HOWLAND CIRCUS COLLECTION SCRAPBOOK, CWM

prietors succeeded in selling the contradictions between titillation and respectability because sexual display at the circus escaped state regulations. Not only did state officials ignore the circus's spectacle of semi-nudity. They actually condoned it."[3]

In 1914 the Factory Department of the State Department of Illinois examined the wages and working conditions of Ringling Brothers' female employees. The department's report concluded that "the girls with the circus receive higher wages, perform easier duties and enjoy more wholesome physical and moral surroundings than girls working in Chicago department stores and factories."[4]

NOTES

1. W. C. Thompson, *On the Road with a Circus* (Self-published, 1903), p. 131.
2. Charles Ringling, Ringling Brothers, "Suggestions and Rules: Employees," ca. 1900, CWM.
3. Janet M. Davis, "Instruct the Minds of All Classes: The Circus and American Culture at the Turn of the Century" (Ph.D. diss., University of Wisconsin, 1998), p. 166.
4. Quoted in Davis, "Instruct the Minds of All Classes," p. 167.

Taking to the Rails and Growing: 1890–1894

"Give us fun and laughter,
And hand the smiles around.
We cannot laugh much after,
They put us in the ground."[1]

A railroad circus presented new opportunities and challenges for the Ringlings. Now the Brothers could travel anywhere in North America where there was a rail line. True, the Ringlings would now find themselves competing against the older and larger eastern circuses that had already been traveling by rail for several years. And they would now be at the mercy of the railroads' schedules and rules; although the Ringlings owned their own railcars, they hired locomotives to pull their trains. But entertainment opportunities remained limited, especially for rural people, and the Ringlings were confident they would succeed. At least they would never again be pulled down by muddy roads and unceasing rains now that they were on the rails.

The Ringlings called their 1890 show "Ringling Brothers' United Monster Railroad Shows, Menagerie and Museum." They wanted everyone to know that their overland days were behind them and that they were ready to compete with other rail circuses. They had about 225 employees, 18 railroad cars, and a Big Top that was a 125-foot-round top with two 50-foot middle sections. In the menagerie they featured three elephants, three camels, a "Bovalapus" (water buffalo), a zebra, a zebu, a hippopotamus named Pete (the Ringlings' first hippo), several monkeys, deer, two wolves, a couple of boa constrictors, and additional animals making up a total of fifteen cages. The show included 107 horses and ponies. Ringlingville was ready to roll.[2]

The last decade of the nineteenth century in the United States was a period of great expansion. In 1890 Congress passed the Sherman Anti-Trust Act, which sought to prevent companies from becoming monopolies and restraining trade. Initially, the act was

poorly enforced. On April 22, 1890, the first Oklahoma land rush took place. Within twenty-four hours, fifty thousand settlers claimed more than two million acres. The Oklahoma Territory was formed on May 2. North Dakota, South Dakota, Montana, and Washington had gained statehood in 1889, and Idaho and Wyoming were admitted as the forty-third and forty-fourth states in July 1890. In December 1890 two hundred Sioux Indians were massacred at the Battle of Wounded Knee in South Dakota.[3]

Many people were using Bell's telephone and Morse's telegraph to communicate. George Eastman invented a handheld camera in 1888; it became popularly known as a Kodak. Thomas Edison's lightbulbs and mercury vapor lamps were coming on the market in 1890, but his motion pictures didn't appear until 1893 (sound motion pictures were not perfected until the 1920s).[4]

In rural communities most farmers had shifted from hand-operated cradle scythes to McCormick's mechanical reaper to harvest their grain. J. I. Case's steam tractors began to power threshing machines and do limited farmwork. But horses continued to be the main power source and means of transportation in the country as well as in villages and cities.

This was the milieu in which the Ringlings mounted their new railroad circus. On April 12, 1890, Ringling Bros. Advertising Car No. 1 left Baraboo. A few days later Advertising Car No. 2 left. A Baraboo newspaperman noted: "A first class artist worked several months on these cars embellishing them with representations of the various features of the monster shows. They are each supplied with steam boilers for making paste, etc., and were loaded with tons and tons of bills [advertising posters]. A small army of bill posters accompanied them."[5] That small army consisted of sixteen men in Car No. 1, under Gus Ringling's direction, and fewer men in the other car.[6]

An 1890 handbill advertised the Ringlings' "Enormous Railroad Shows." It was the first year the Ringlings' circus traveled by rail instead of by wagon. HANDBILL COLLECTION, CWM

Ringling Brothers Circus performers, 1890. Lou Ringling is in the back row, first on the left. By this year the Ringling Brothers had about 225 employees. HERB JONES GIFT; PRINT COLLECTION, CWM

The Ringlings opened in Baraboo on Saturday, May 3. Their advertisement in the Baraboo paper featured a picture of a huge hippopotamus and the words: "The indescribable, tremendous monster of brute creation, the largest hippopotamus in captivity. The monster blood-sweating behemoth of holy writ. The new found monster mammoth amphibious Bovolapsus [an ordinary water buffalo], only real African Zebras in America, Royal Heathen Actors from Japan, Babylon, Largest Elephant on Earth . . . Jewel, the only umbrella-eared (i.e., African) elephant in the country."[7] The ad also pictured lion cubs, which had been born in Baraboo earlier in the spring.

The parade was described as "[t]he largest, longest, richest and most resplendent gratuitous display, representing with the most splendid effect and impressive truthfulness a grand triumphal march of nations. Never before in the history of American amusements has any show or combination of shows had the wealth, enterprise or pluck to attempt anything approaching in magnitude and magnificence this grand triumph of free street demonstrations."[8] With all that, who wouldn't want to plunk down twenty-five or fifty cents a see the circus?

The first show of the season went well. A *Baraboo Republic* reporter gushed:

The Ringling Bros. Circus and Menagerie, which exhibited in this city Saturday was a grand success. It was witnessed by thousands of people; their mammoth tents being crowded both afternoon and evening. . . . The wardrobe is entirely new and of rich material, the design and workmanship on the same being very beautiful, particularly creditable to Mrs. Al Ringling, under whose supervision the entire work was done. . . . The Ringling Brothers are all gentlemen and are bound to meet with success wherever they go. One thing very creditable to their show is the entire absence of gambling or anything of that nature, nothing of the kind being allowed on the grounds.[9]

The Brothers now included on their stationery, posters, and checks the slogan "Founders of the New School of American Showman." This is how the Brothers referred to those circuses that subscribed to their "no-grift" approach to the business. Some circus people began calling their show a Sunday school circus.[10]

After the Baraboo performance, the Ringling trains rolled on to Dodgeville, Wisconsin, where the show played May 5. On that cold spring Monday, it rained and snowed all day. No doubt more than one Ringling brother remembered the spring of 1888, when they had been stuck in the mud in similar weather conditions. But the trains rolled on, whistling into the night, foul weather or no.

But travel by rail did not eliminate all the dangers and delays of life in the circus. On May 20 three Ringling flatcars ran off the tracks, and on May 22 they arrived late because of a train wreck ahead of them. When they arrived in Whatcheer, Iowa, for a May 30 show, they discovered that the Grand Army of the Republic Civil War veterans did not think it right "for a circus to exhibit on Decoration Day"—but the Ringlings put on their show anyway.[11]

When the show was in Manson, Wisconsin, a railroad man was cut in two near one of the circus cars, killing him instantly. And after that night's show, a team ran away, throwing a gentleman and two ladies out of the buggy. The man broke his neck.[12]

On June 2 the Ringlings played in Tama, Iowa, where five hundred Indians from a nearby reservation attended. The Ringlings were developing a reputation for having something for everyone, no matter their age, their ethnic background, or where they lived.

With the grueling six-day-a-week schedule, circus employees enjoyed their Sundays, catching up on sleep, tending to laundry, writing letters, and resting. Fishing was a popular activity, although not always fruitful. The 1890 route book noted, "Sunday June 29. The Club went fishing, but it was on the bum."[13] (Luckily, the fishing seemed to improve as the season went on, as reported in the route book, "July 15. Best fishing of the season.")[14]

The crew also occasionally played baseball on Sundays, playing against local teams.

Afternoon shows in the rural towns drew larger crowds than the evening shows, as farmers wanted to drive home in daylight. This crowd, in Algona, Iowa, took in the spectacle of the circus on a hot, humid afternoon in July 1890. HERB JONES GIFT; PRINT COLLECTION, CWM

On Sunday, June 15, the circus team was edged out by the Monson, Iowa, ball team 14–13.[15] Through such activities, the Ringling Brothers were attempting to build strong community relationships as they traveled around the country. Sometimes such attempts were successful, but often they were not. While many local people came to the circus and enjoyed the show, there was often an element that despised circus people. Fights between circus employees and town ruffians were not uncommon. For instance, the 1891 route book reported, "At Bolivar, Missouri, on September 26th, a very fierce battle was fought between the show and the people of the town and vicinity. Many of the local bad men were badly injured."[16]

Business continued to improve, and full houses were reported in the route book as "down in front afternoon show," "afternoon house packed to the ring bank," "afternoon show big," and "had to close the ticket wagon." Crowds were so large on July 28 in Whitewater, Wisconsin, that the Brothers had to add another fifty-foot section to the Big Top. Two days later, in Hartford, Wisconsin, a huge windstorm blew down the Big Top, breaking a center pole. No one was injured, and the canvas was up and the show running in forty minutes.[17]

The Baraboo newspapers continued cheering on the Ringling boys. A short piece written in late August read, "We learn from responsible parties that Ringling Bros. are meeting with better success than ever this season. They are far overlapping last season's receipts. The boys are hustlers and no mistake. They are Baraboo boys."[18]

In September the show was on its way east, into new territory—Indiana, Ohio, Pennsylvania, Maryland, Virginia, and West Virginia. In Punxsutawney, Pennsylvania, they had record attendance: "Afternoon house ring bank [meaning that people were sitting near the ring], had to close the ticket wagon half an hour after the doors were opened, night house ring bank. This has been the banner day of the season."[19] The Ringlings' first year as a railroad circus was proving highly successful. The Brothers found that the "sophisticated" eastern audiences bought tickets as often as did the midwesterners.

Rumors began in 1890 that the Ringlings might leave Baraboo. "It is . . . rumored that the coming winter is the last one that the Ringlings will winter here; that they intend to go south where they can winter cheaper."[20] Such rumors swirled around the Ringlings nearly every year, their sources generally unknown.

Despite such speculations, the Ringlings were back in Baraboo for the winter of 1890–1891. There they learned that their cousins the Gollmars were starting a new circus. Now two circuses would winter in Baraboo.

That winter the Brothers rented the old Union Hotel near the winter quarters to house their winter employees.[21] Always trying to save money, the Brothers leased the Chicago and Northwestern Railroad buildings in Baraboo, including the roundhouse, where they painted and repaired railroad cars. They would rent these buildings until they built their own shops in 1893.[22]

Everything was abuzz in preparation for the 1891 season. The Brothers were expanding. They added several new railroad cars (they now had a total of twenty-six) and a third advertising car, and they laid more tracks in Mrs. Potter's field. They painted the railcars yellow with red lettering.[23]

In November 1890 John Ringling traveled to Great Bend, Kansas, to attend the sale of a "stranded circus" (one in financial trouble) owned by Charles Andress. (Andress later worked on the Ringlings' administrative staff, at one time supervising the sideshow performers; he is also credited with inventing a pneumatic stake-driver.)[24] John purchased a male African elephant named Zip, several camels, a llama, and an ibex (which, unfortunately, died on the way to Baraboo). The Ringlings also purchased a pair of tigers and a pair of hyenas.[25] The Ringling menagerie now included four elephants, five camels, four kangaroos, and assorted other exotic animals, including the "terrifying" hippopotamus.

In spring 1891 the Ringlings were still buying horses for the coming season. An April 8 newspaper ad read: "Ringling Bros. want to buy 25 head of horses. Must be good

In 1891 the Ringlings added the spectacle "Caesar's Triumphal Entry into Rome" to their show. It was the first year they used the phrase "World's Greatest Shows." HANDBILL COLLECTION, CWM

stock weighing from 1,000 pounds upward to 1,600 pounds."[26] By opening day in May, the show would have 130 horses and ponies, the largest number so far.

That winter the Ringlings developed an exciting new production number that would be the opening act for every performance and, they hoped, attract customers who wanted more than the usual circus fare. The new show reenacted "Caesar's Triumphal Entry into Rome." A description of the "Grand Spectacular Tournament" read, "Displaying all the pageantry and pomp of Rome's Victorious Legions, and introducing the unparalleled scenic and spectacular resources of the Ringling Bros. World's Greatest Shows." The 1891 promotions marked the first appearance of the name "World's Greatest Shows," a title the Ringlings would use for many years.

The Ringlings had come a long way from Al balancing a breaking plow on his chin, John telling stories, Alf T. and Charles playing their horns, and Otto struggling with a bass drum. For the first time, in 1891 they began advertising their show as a three-ring circus, with a "Millionaire Menagerie, Museum and Aquarium."[27]

The Brothers opened the 1891 season May 2 in Baraboo to a good afternoon house and an even larger evening audience. Then they traveled on, this year avoiding the eastern states, staying in the Midwest and South. They were out twenty-three weeks and showed in 143 towns. Some route book comments from the season included the following:

June 22, Grand Forks, N.D.: "Afternoon house packed to the hippodrome track; night house big. Temperance town, but thirty-five saloons across the river."

August 3rd, Streator, Illinois: "A great many of the company spent Sunday in the Windy City. Sam Cohn, merchant tailor of Chicago, visits and receives several thousand dollars worth of orders from the boys for winter clothes."

August 12, Trenton, Missouri: "The first band wagon got

stuck in a soft place, and it took eight horses and three elephants half an hour to get it out."

August 20, Monticello, Illinois: "We had the pleasure of witnessing the ascension of an air ship."[28]

Newspapers cheered the Ringling show. The Grand Forks, North Dakota, paper reported, "Ringling Bros. are now the leading showmen, and the five brothers who, in a few years have taken the front rank in popular favor, understand their business from the ground up, they know it pays best to be honest with the people and they aim to do more, rather than less that they advertise, and thus everyone sees their show becomes a free advertiser."[29]

The Galesburg, Illinois, paper mused, "Twenty-five years ago had anyone predicted that one day an enormous amusement enterprise of such vast dimensions as the Ringling Bros.' colossal railroad shows would wend its ponderous way to almost 200 principal cities of the Union each year, the statement would be listened to as veriest nonsense. Yet all of this has come to pass."[30]

Ringling Profits, 1891 (143 Stands)

Average daily receipts: $1,445 ($206,635 for the season; $3.9 million in 2002 dollars)

Estimated daily operating expenses: $538 ($76,934 for the season)

Estimated daily salary costs: $300 ($42,900 for the season)

Estimated total daily expenses: $838

Estimated daily profit: $607

Estimated season profit: $86,801 (about $1.7 million in 2002 dollars)[31]

Example of Ringling Daily Expenses, June 17, 1891 (Wahpeton, Minnesota)

Transportation: $200	Feed: $54.60
License fee: $25	Livery: $42
Lot expense: $5	Car department: $9.71
Hotel: $65.25	Animal department: $5.40
Billboards: $25	Chandelier department: $15.67
Cook house: $69.05	(gasoline for lights)

Total expenses: $516.69[32]

By 1891 the Ringlings' staff had grown to an astounding four hundred employees. The salary for working men (those who put up canvas, cared for animals, worked in the cook tent, erected Big Top seats, etc.) was about fifty cents a day ($9.60 in 2002 dollars)

Circus Horses

Until well into the twentieth century, horses were a major attraction for any circus. They had many roles, performing in the ring, competing in races around the Big Top tent, pulling the wagons from the train cars to the show lots, helping put up the heavy Big Top poles, and walking in the daily circus parade. Performing horses were known as "ring stock"; working horses were called "baggage stock."

In the 1870s there were more than 8.7 million horses in the United States. By 1900 the number had grown to 24.1 million. About 3 million horses were in urban areas in 1900.[1] Nearly all farmers and small-town people owned horses and depended on them. City folks knew horses, too, for they were everywhere. They pulled carriages that ferried passengers from railroad depots to downtown hotels. They moved heavy, high-wheeled wagons containing beer, coal, ice, lumber, bakery goods, and groceries. In many of the larger cities, before electricity arrived, horses pulled streetcars. Livery stables were available in most cities, where a person could rent a team and buggy much as we might rent a car today.

The most popular breed for circus baggage horses— those that did the hard work around the lot—was the Percheron. Percherons weighed up to 1,600 pounds, were sure of foot, and generally withstood crowds and

Mike Rooney, a bareback rider, was one of several Rooneys from Baraboo who performed with the Ringling Brothers over the years. Photo by Hudson & Shadle, Algona, Iowa; Print Collection, CWM

excitement with few problems. They were packed tightly in stockcars to avoid injuries when the car lurched forward or stopped quickly. They traveled wearing their harnesses, sometimes with the collars lifted slightly off their necks by overhead chains. The harnesses were removed on the circus lot while the animals rested in the horse tents during the afternoon.

In 1899 the Ringlings owned about three hundred horses, about one hundred of which appeared in acts of various kinds. Training of the horses and their riders took place during the winter months in the ring barn, which had at one end a forty-two-foot ring with a pole in the center. Attached to the pole was a pulley-and-rope device called a "mechanic." The mechanic consisted of a side arm with a pulley on the end. A rope was passed through the pulley and attached at one end to a leather harness that the rider wore. An assistant held the other end of the rope. If a rider fell from a horse, the mechanic helped to break the fall.

A reporter for the *Milwaukee Journal* described the horse-training sessions at winter quarters this way:

Male and female riders come in to practice their old tricks and essay new ones. They find it absolutely necessary to work in this way during the winter. Neglect means stiff limbs and ungraceful

Circus Horses

The mechanic, a device used to train horses and riders, protected fallen riders from injury. The mechanic was found at the end of the ring barn at Ringlingville winter quarters. Ralph Pierce Collection, CWM

carriage when the regular season opens. As much pain is taken with the practice as though the show was in full swing and thousands of spectators were present. Nothing is omitted so that the horses may become thoroughly familiar with their parts. Hoops are jumped through; hurdles leaped, fiery circles penetrated and the ringmasters whip cracks just as loud and at exactly the same moment as when the actual performance is on.[2]

Walter Gollmar, whose father was with the Gollmar Brothers Circus, recalled watching his father train horses.

Dad had a beautiful stallion Shetland pony that he wanted to train for the show. He used ropes to show the animal what he wanted it to do—and never harmed an animal. Never whipped an animal. He pulled the ropes to show the animal what he wanted it to do. He wanted this Shetland pony to put one foot up on a block of wood and hold the other foot out in a pose. The pony just wouldn't do it. Dad tried again and again. Day after day. But

the pony wouldn't do the trick. He was ready to sell it. While a potential buyer was there, the pony ran around the ring and, to Dad's surprise, stopped, lifted one foot onto the block of wood, and held the other foot in the pose Dad had been trying to teach it. The Shetland stallion turned out to be one of the best ponies Dad ever trained. Dad trained twenty-eight horses to ride one winter. Sometimes, though, the riders were more trouble to train than the horses.[3]

Ringling horses were trained both in winter quarters and on the road. This photo, labeled "training to cake-walk," was taken in Greenville, Texas, in 1902. Richard E. and Albert Conover Collection, CWM

NOTES

1. U.S. Census information quoted in Clay McShane and Joel A. Tarr, "The Centrality of the Horse in the Nineteenth-Century American City," in The Making of Urban America, 2nd ed., ed. Raymond A. Mohl (Wilmington, DE: Scholarly Resources, 1997), p. 107.
2. Milwaukee Journal, January 27, 1900.
3. Walter Gollmar, interview by the author, Evansville, Wisconsin, August 20, 2001.

The Ringling Circus Band, shown here in 1891, performed in concert before the show and played throughout the circus performance. William F. Weldon was director. PRINT COLLECTION, CWM

plus free room and board. Those in management positions received more, and some performers received handsome salaries. The Brothers divided up profits at the end of the season, drawing only expense money during the year.[33] Amazingly, the five partners had no written contract—they had only a verbal agreement to split the business five ways.

Profits varied among circuses; for the Ringlings it was about 40 percent for several of their most profitable years. Forty percent profit was certainly not the case for all businesses; circus profits, especially for the Ringlings, were outstanding, and some circuses turned in even higher profit margins. According to circus historian Stuart Thayer, profits for some pre–Civil War circuses reached 60 percent.[34] Profits represented all cash money—no accounts receivable, no credit. And they were earned by selling twenty-five-cent and fifty-cent tickets to mostly ordinary country folk who thirsted for some good, clean entertainment.

The Ringlings had to earn almost all their money from April to October. The rest of the year they had essentially no income, only expenses. The animals kept on eating, and the winter quarters crew had to be housed and fed—and paid. Supplies had to be purchased and equipment repaired for the coming year. And if the Ringlings wanted to keep expanding, they had to add more of almost everything.

It is unlikely the residents of Baraboo had any idea of the vast amounts of money the Brothers were taking in, other than knowing that the boys were buying things in town and employed a number of locals at winter quarters. While the name "Ringling Bros." was becoming well known throughout the land, back in Baraboo they were just a bunch of local boys with a crazy idea that seemed to have paid off. It had to be difficult for local businessmen and farmers, who could barely scratch out a living, to understand the Ringlings' success.

In 1891 rumors persisted that the Ringlings might move from Baraboo. A local paper carried a brief notice: "The report that the Ringlings were about to change their place of rendezvous from Baraboo to Milwaukee is denied, on authority of the Brothers."[35]

The Ringlings had no intention of moving. They were focusing on their recent accomplishments and trying to figure out how to expand and compete with much larger circuses, such as Barnum & Bailey, which had a tremendous reputation in the eastern United States and was known throughout the country. The five young Ringling partners had a taste of success, and with some luck, hard work, and careful attention to thousands of details, they were on their way to becoming a show that other circuses needed to worry about.

While in winter quarters in 1891–1892, the Brothers planned an even larger circus for the coming season. In October they bought two more elephants, three camels, a Russian elk, a mountain lion, a leopard, and a Sumatra tapir.[36] The animals had been a part of Sam MacFlinn's Great Eastern Circus.[37] In February the Ringlings acquired a large polar bear to add to their menagerie.[38]

That winter the Ringlings turned the former Peck and Cramer Building, at the corner of Water and Ash Streets in Baraboo, into a carpenter shop where workmen built new seats for the Big Top. In a three-story building on the "corner near Hoyt's mills," leather crafters under the experienced eye of the Brothers' father, August, made harnesses. The second floor was the lithograph room, "filled with tons of attractive advertising paper," and the third floor was used for making mattresses for the "Ringling hotel," a private facility where many Ringling winter employees lived. A brick former feed store near Noyes corner at Ash and First Streets was used as a paint shop, and tent canvas was stored in the back. And in a building at the corner of Oak and Fourth Avenue, in the Wright Block, seamstresses under the careful direction of Mrs. Al Ringling were reported to be "manipulating the needle and thread in the manufacture of their sparkling and costly new wardrobe."[39]

The *Sauk County Democrat* reported that the Ringling hotel (at the southwest corner of East and Water Streets) "was crowded with employees of the show, and the room

In 1892 the Ringling Brothers commissioned a new bell wagon, shown here in a parade that August in Black River Falls, Wisconsin. PHOTO BY C. J. VAN SCHAICK; BLACK RIVER FALLS HISTORICAL SOCIETY

of other hotels is also being infringed upon as the newcomers arrive." The *Democrat* also declared that in the Ringlings' business office, "typewriters, pens and pencils are almost constantly in motion," and it described the car repairing department as "keeping a force of men at work in making improvements in rolling stock. The wagon manufactories of Moeller and Sons [located on Third near Broadway] and Gollmar Bros. are also compelled to run extra forces in order to build all the necessary new vehicles. Space will not permit further mention of one of Baraboo's greatest industries."[40]

The Brothers began the 1892 season with a larger Big Top, a bigger menagerie, and twenty-eight railcars (increased to thirty-two before season's end). They added several other new features, including an impressive bell wagon—the nine bells weighed more than five tons and were cast especially for the Ringlings—and a huge J. I. Case steam tractor, referred to as a traction engine.[41] The tractor had a steam whistle and a cab similar to one on a railroad locomotive. With their massive size and unusual characteristics, the new wagon and tractor became important attractions in the Ringlings' parade.[42]

By April everything was in order for the season's grand opening in Baraboo. Charles was sufficiently relaxed two days before the opening that he went fishing, catching "thirteen speckled trout that together weighed 15 pounds."[43]

For many years Gus Ringling managed the activities of Advertising Car No. 1 and its bill posters, shown here in 1892.
PRINT COLLECTION, CWM

The city of Baraboo designated opening day, Saturday, April 30, "Ringling Day." A long list of businessmen advertised that they would close their doors at 7:30 p.m., "in order to give all proprietors and employees an opportunity to attend Ringling Bros. Circus."[44]

Rain began falling after the parade and continued all afternoon and into the evening, making it an uncomfortable "Ringling Day." Nonetheless, thousands of people sloshed through the mud and water into the relatively dry tents to see what new thrills the Ringlings had in store this year. After Baraboo, it continued raining, day after day, town after town. A month of rain—and muddy show grounds, and missed appearances.

While the circus was traveling from Madison, South Dakota, on June 9, an animal cage blew off the train and a kangaroo escaped, "wildly hop-step jumping over the seas of plains." The following day the kangaroo was captured. The brief bit of freedom must have been too much for the animal, however, and it died three days later.

Glowing newspaper reviews for the Ringlings' show continued. A writer for the Duluth, Minnesota, paper reported, "Ringling Brothers' Show, [June] 27th had fully 10,000 people at afternoon and over 10,000 at evening performance. It was pronounced by all to be the best exhibit ever given in Duluth of the kind."[45]

The Ringlings were working hard to maintain their reputation as an honest, family-friendly circus, and they even employed Pinkerton detectives to assist. When the show played in Waupaca, Wisconsin, on July 14, 1892, the local newspaper carried this story:

> Thursday morning last the Ringling Brothers notified the mayor that there were five pickpockets in town who had followed the show. Chief of Police Larson spotted them and made them leave town on the noon train, before they got in any fine work. It is seldom that showmen take such pains to preserve the reputation of their shows as did the Ringling Brothers.[46]

In August, while in the show was in Garrett, Indiana, the assistant master of properties, a Mr. Kelly, was killed. The route book account relates the incident:

> The night was very dark, recalling what the Bible says about those who "love darkness rather than light because their deeds are evil." Mr. Kelly was lured from the door of the dressing-room tent, no doubt with the intention to rob and waylay. He probably made resistance, and then came a struggle, a blow on the head with a coupling pine, and finally the sudden shot which startled all in the dressing room, laying the victim low. Mr. Kelly was borne to a neighboring house where he lived an hour and a half in great apparent agony. . . . In the excitement and darkness the murderer escaped.[47]

During the 1892 season, the Ringlings showed in thirteen states, mostly in the Midwest but as far away as Oklahoma Territory. That year they played a third of their stands in Iowa and Wisconsin, old and well-known territory for them. The biggest day of the year was June 27 in Duluth, where they took in $5,183. They closed in Cape Girardeau, Missouri, on October 26, having played 153 stands (10 more than in 1891).

The Ringlings' receipts for 1892 exceeded those of 1891 by about $122,000 (in 1891 they took in $206,635; in 1892, $328,878).[48] Assuming a conservative 40 percent profit, the Ringlings banked about $131,551 in 1892 (about $2.5 million in 2002 dollars).

The Ringlings arrived in Baraboo on Saturday night, October 29, 1892, and immediately proceeded to tuck animals and equipment away for the long, cold Wisconsin winter. There was no denying that they had become a major force in the circus world. For those not privy to account books, a circus's success was judged by the number of railroad cars, horses, and elephants, the size of the menagerie, the number and size of tents, especially the Big Top, and the quality of the Big Top show. All of these were on the increase for the Ringling Brothers—with the possible exception of the quality of the Big Top show. Some historians argue that the quality of the Ringling show hadn't reached that of the Barnum & Bailey Circus, which often competed with the Ringling Brothers. "The Ringlings were a Chevrolet show, the Barnum & Bailey show was a Cadillac."[49]

If the Brothers were aware of an unfavorable comparison, they didn't let it bother them. With their assets and confidence on the rise, they immediately began preparing

Train Wreck

The circus train rolled through the dark and rainy early morning of May 17, 1892, on its way to Concordia, Kansas. Suddenly, everyone was jarred awake by a terrific crash and then the screams of injured and dying animals and the cries of workers caught in the rubble. A railroad bridge had washed out, and the train had hurtled off the tracks.

Pouring out into the night, our men perceived by the flickering light of lanterns a chaos of wrecked [rail] cars, some crushed to utter kindling wood, and others hurled headlong or sidelong into a lake of mad waters that held both sides of the track, and whose undermining power had wrecked a trestle and train. This lake was full of dead and drowning horses. . . . With humane bravery, our men plunged into the waters and cut harness right and left, or pulled the necks of drowning horses out of the water with halters. As the gray of morning came on the situation grew worse. Robert O'Donnell, of Gratiot, Wisconsin was found in a mass of blood-stained wreckage, with a splintered piece of two-by-three scantling driven clear through his head. . . . Nearby, mid twisted rails and rack and ruin, was the body of Albert Dietzler, aged sixteen, from Freeport, Illinois. The poor boy's head was crushed as if by a sledge hammer. Twenty-six magnificent draught horses, heavy Clyde stallions, Normans and Percherons, floated dead in the lake on the other side of the track. Other poor brutes had broken legs or ripped bellies and had to be killed.[1]

Four other men were severely injured and were taken to a Kansas City hospital. Immediately after the wreck, a handbill began circulating, "Wanted, Draft Horses, weighing from 1,200 to 1,600 pounds. Will pay what they are worth. Ringling Brothers' Circus."[2]

No time was taken off. The circus performed as scheduled on May 18 in Concordia.

NOTES

1. O. H. Kurtz, *Official Route Book of Ringling Brothers: Season of 1892* (Buffalo, NY: Courier, 1892) pp. 53–54.
2. Ibid.

Sideshow performers (shown here circa 1893), including the tattooed man, fat man, bagpiper, and snake charmer, had similar contracts and salaries to other performers' and were treated no differently than other show people. PRINT COLLECTION, CWM

The Ringlings bought this giraffe from the John Robinson circus during the winter of 1892–1893. WALTER SCHOLL COLLECTION, ILLINOIS STATE UNIVERSITY, NORMAL, ILLINOIS

for the 1893 season. They were considering new acts, John Ringling was scouting new towns to play, and they were adding to their menagerie. They purchased more elephants, increasing the herd to eight: Babe, Jule, Fannie, Lou, Fanchon, Prince, Duke, and Sultan. (Zip, the huge African elephant, died during that winter.) They bought a gnu (often referred to as a horned horse) and a giraffe. "During the winter of 1892–93, we purchased of John Robinson one female giraffe [named Mamie] and shipped it to Baraboo on a flat car in a cage over which was built a shanty—unloaded when the thermometer registered zero."[50]

Exaggeration had always been a part of circus promotion, and the giraffe offered a new opportunity. In 1893 Ringling posters proclaimed, "Largest living giraffe." She was a big one—but as a female, hardly the largest living one. She remained a major feature of the Ringlings' menagerie until her death in July 1896 while the circus was in Iowa.[51]

By the end of January 1893, the Ringlings had a new car shop adjacent to the

Baraboo contractor Carl Isenberg and his brother, George, constructed most of the Ringling winter quarter buildings as well as several homes for the Brothers. SAUK COUNTY HISTORICAL SOCIETY

Chicago and Northwestern yards on the south side of the Baraboo River.[52] Local contractor Carl Isenberg did the work and would build several other buildings for the Ringlings in ensuing years. The Ringlings also built a paint shop near their railroad tracks in Mrs. Potter's field.[53]

By late 1892 plans were well under way for the World's Columbian Exposition, to be held the following summer in Chicago. The international exhibition would commemorate the four hundredth anniversary of Christopher Columbus's discovery of America and was purported to cost $31 million. The show would display wonders of technology, including the first movable sidewalk and the forerunner of the movie projector, and showcase unheard-of products that are now familiar: Cream of Wheat, Shredded Wheat, Aunt Jemima syrup, Juicy Fruit gum, and Pabst Blue Ribbon beer. Visitors would stand in awe of the huge Ferris wheel, invented for the World's Fair; this one was 250 feet across and held more than two thousand passengers. Admission would be only fifty cents for adults, twenty-five cents for children age six to twelve, and free for those under six. It was predicted to be the event of the year.[54] The word was that people would forgo a visit to the "ordinary" circus and would travel to Chicago to see this extraordinary World's Fair.

While Americans eagerly awaited the World's Fair, they were also about to enter one of the most severe economic depressions in the country's history. Early in 1893 banks around the country began to fail. Panic spread, farm prices fell, and soon thousands of businesses had closed and individuals had gone bankrupt. Within a year three million workers—20 percent of the workforce—would be unemployed, and thousands of homeless and starving men would aimlessly walk city streets, searching for their next meal.[55]

With both the World's Fair and the country's economic woes to consider, it seemed clear that businesses, especially those in entertainment, should hunker down and ride out the economic storm. Many of them did.[56] But the Ringlings decided to go on with their show no matter what. They opened in Baraboo on Saturday, April 29, World's Fair and depression be damned. With 35 railcars, 3 advertising cars, 207 horses, 20 cages of wild animals and birds, 7 elephants, 3 camels, and about 700 employees, the 1893 Ringling circus was the largest ever.

On May 1, opening day of the World's Fair in Chicago, the Ringlings played a little more than a

Many thought the spectacular 1893 Columbian Exposition would steal customers from the Ringling Brothers Circus. It did not. WHi(X3)40415

hundred miles away in Sterling, Illinois. The show included three rings and two stages, sometimes with five events going on at the same time. There were clowns and acrobats, trained horses, and tight-rope walkers. Charles W. Fish, well known for his horsemanship, was one of the featured performers. He was billed as "The world's champion summersault rider."[57] And of course, the "Largest Living Giraffe" was boldly promoted.

The show also featured an eight-piece sideshow band under the direction of John Marshall, a Grand Concert Band of twenty-one members directed by William F. Weldon, Minstrel Orchestra of eight (an entire minstrel show was part of the performance), three parade bands ranging from nine to thirteen members, and a four-member Parade Field Band with fife and drums.[58]

The Brothers quickly discovered that even though times were tough, farm prices were low, and many people were out of work, families still went to the circus. The color and splendor, the animals, and the music took people's minds off their problems, at least for a short time. The boys reported an "enormous crowd" in Mankato, Kansas; "business was big" in Phillipsburg, Kansas. In Wayne, Nebraska, "the number of tickets sold exceeded by several thousands the entire population of this county." In Minneapolis a newspaper reported it as "the largest [business] ever done by a circus in Minneapolis, and the show as the most satisfactory ever seen here."[59] One day's receipts in Minneapolis were $3,510.[60]

The Ringlings' business was flourishing, and yet the country's economic situation grew more dire. On May 12 there was a run on the Plankinton Bank of Milwaukee, precipitated by the failure of a big furniture company to which the bank had lent money. The bank closed on June 1.[61]

While in Milwaukee in late July, the Brothers saw firsthand the effects of the depression. Many local firms were closed or operating with limited hours. Unemployment was high and money was short, but still, people came to the circus. Milwaukee's *Evening Journal*

An 1893 handbill advertised "The Giant Giraffe, Tallest Animal on Earth" and "Mr. Charles W. Fish, the Acknowledged Champion Bareback Somersault Rider in the World," among other features. HANDBILL COLLECTION, CWM

reported an afternoon attendance of fourteen thousand people, with every seat taken and people sitting on the hippodrome track. The paper reported, "The show was superior to any circus performance ever seen in Milwaukee."[62] Afternoon and evening receipts for the Milwaukee performance totaled $3,234.45.[63]

It became a Ringling tradition that at the end of the season, chef E. C. Hailey would serve up a special meal for all the employees. In 1893 the keeper of the route book described the bittersweet event: "The band plays, 'Home, Sweet Home,' and the hundreds who have lived together for six long months as one great family scatter to the four winds of the heavens."[64]

Farewell Dinner Menu

Soups: Cream of chicken with rice. Tomato.

Fish: Baked white fish. Egg sauce. Boiled trout. Cream sauce.

Boiled Meats: Boiled leg of mutton. Caper sauce. Beef. Horse Radish Sauce.

Roast Meats: Roast beef. Brown gravy. Pork roast. Apple sauce. Roast Lamb. Green peas. Roast veal dressing.

Poultry: Boiled fowl. Oyster sauce. Roast duck dressing. Roast chicken dressing.

Entre: Kidney stew. Mutton stew. Maccaroni [sic] and cheese.

Vegetables: Green corn. Mashed potatoes. Baked sweet potatoes. Stewed tomatoes. Stewed onions with cream.

Dessert: Chocolate cake. Cream cake. Coconut Cake. Green apple pie. Lemon pie. Peaches. Oranges. Grapes. Nuts.

Refreshments: Coffee. Tea. Ice tea. Milk.[65]

The Ringling circus ended its season in Havana, Illinois. Despite the depression and competition from the World's Fair, the Ringlings' gross income for the 1893 season was $318,451 (138 stands) compared with $328,878 in 1892 (153 stands). The average income per stand in 1893 ($2,308) was higher than in 1892 ($2,149).[66]

Back in Baraboo the Brothers once again rented the old City Hotel on Water Street for the winter, put away their animals and equipment, and immediately began planning for the coming year. Could they top their 1893 season?

In 1894 the World's Fair was over, but the depression continued. The Ringling Bros. World's Greatest Shows, now with thirty-nine cars and three advance cars, opened in Baraboo on April 28 and then went on to the Midwest, East, Northeast, and South.

Crowds were good, the weather tolerable. They competed with Sells Brothers Show in Iowa and won hands down. Alf T. later described the May 28 show in Des Moines: "In spite of the fact that the big top had been enlarged for the occasion by the addition of an extra center-pole and many extra seats, it was utterly impossible, both at the afternoon and night performances, to furnish seats for all of the thousands, and many occupied standing room."[67]

While the circus was traveling in Iowa, one of the property wagons caught fire when the train was moving, most likely caused by sparks from the steam locomotive. "It was a novel sight to see our train speeding along at the rate of twenty miles an hour while the large wagon was in flames." The fire was put out before it spread.[68]

Crowds continued to be good to excellent. It was the Ringlings' first time in several eastern states and their first time in the South. Alf T. wrote: "Our first stand in Texas is a corker. People here are overcome with the merit of the World's Greatest Shows, and welcome the change from the inferior concerns that have been playing this region so long."[69] Nothing like a little self-congratulation. But the boasting was well earned. It had been a stroke of genius to take the circus to Texas, where they played twenty-two dates and did extremely well. In Dallas in mid-October, even with extra seats, the Ringlings had to close the doors at 1:30 and give evening show tickets or refund money to nineteen hundred people. That evening's show sold out as well.

They also did outstanding business in Louisiana and Mississippi. They expanded their 1894 season to 175 stands, the most yet, and were on the road for 205 days. They closed in Water Valley, Mississippi, on Saturday, November 17, and were back in Baraboo the following Tuesday.

Not only did the Ringlings have more stands in 1894, but the average gross receipts for each stand were higher than in the previous two years. They took in $5,858 in Dallas, their biggest day so far. They brought in $4,829 in Fort Worth on October 17, $5,143 in Waco on October 24, and $5,019 in San Antonio on October 30. Earlier in the year, their biggest day had been May 2 in Davenport, Iowa, where daily receipts were $4,596.[70]

Ringling Average Daily Gross Receipts

1891: $1,445

1892: $2,149

1893: $2,308

1894: $2,484[71]

Gross income for the 1894 season was $419,768—the largest amount ever for the Brothers. Of course, expenses were up, too, although the salary for most circus workers remained at fifty cents a day, with board and a bunk on the train included.

One Day's Expenses: Fort Dodge, Iowa, June 5, 1894

Transferring cars: $75

Billboards: $100

License: $100

Oil: $3.75

Sledge hammer handles: $8.25

Hay: $7.00

Hotel: $178.25

Shears: $.85

Gasoline [for lights]: $14.34

Animal feed: $55.25

Lot permit: $25.00

Meat: $5.25

Cook house: $116.65

Livery: $44.50

Police fines [details unknown]: $25.00

Newspaper ads: $80.00

Total Expenses for Fort Dodge, Iowa: $839.09 [excluding salaries]

Receipts for Fort Dodge, Iowa: $2,677.95

Profit for Fort Dodge, Iowa, excluding salaries: $1,838[72]

Using the conservative 40 percent profit figure, the Ringlings netted approximately $168,000 (about $3.2 million in 2002 dollars) for the 1894 season.

Five years on the rails had placed the Ringling Brothers among the top circuses in the nation. Even during a severe depression they attracted thousands of people to their shows. They had demonstrated that they could compete in the eastern and northeastern states, as well in the South and as far west as Texas. And their solid midwestern support never wavered.

They had suffered blowdowns, a devastating train wreck, and a lightning storm that killed several people, yet they persevered, always with an eye toward becoming larger, entertaining more people, and making more money.

Now, as they faced the last five years of the century, it seemed nothing stood in their way. They had both reputation and monetary resources, and all seven brothers were involved, contributing their unique skills and honing their expertise. When the city of Baraboo welcomed the Brothers home in the fall of 1894, a local newspaper man wrote:

> "The Ringlings are home again!" was the good news heralded about town Tuesday afternoon. The four large trains bringing their paraphernalia and many of the people connected with the show rolled into Baraboo between one and two o'clock Tues-

day afternoon [November 20], and as usual many eager spectators were on hand to take a look at the outfit and to greet the proprietors and resident employees of whose faces Baraboo people never tire. Upon the arrival of the show one could not avoid thinking that the Ringlings were certainly born lucky, and we're glad of it. All went well again during the entire season, which will go on the records of these successful show managers as the best of all.[73]

The circus was contributing considerably to the economy of the community, and the Ringling boys were local heroes. But big changes were about to take place that would affect Baraboo and would have a great impact on the future successes of the Ringling Brothers.

Noncompete Agreements

One way the Ringlings sought to lessen competition with other circuses was to sign noncompete agreements with other shows—a fairly common practice among circuses at the time. For instance, on June 8, 1893, the Ringlings signed a noncompete agreement with the Adam Forepaugh Show, which agreed to cancel appearances in all Wisconsin towns, the Red River Valley, and all towns north of Minneapolis except St. Cloud, Willmar, and Litchfield. The Forepaugh show also agreed not to advertise in Mankato, Minneapolis, or St. Cloud, Minnesota, until after the Ringlings had played the towns. The Ringlings agreed to not play in any towns west of the Mississippi River except Mankato, Minneapolis, and St. Cloud. The document also specified that it "be treated strictly confidential between the parties hereto." The fine for violating the agreement was set at $20,000.[1]

In 1894 the Ringlings struck a similar agreement with Barnum & Bailey. The Ringlings agreed not to show in a specified list of towns in Ohio, Wisconsin, Indiana, Iowa, Illinois, Michigan, Minnesota, and Missouri. Barnum & Bailey agreed not to show in specified towns in Iowa, Minnesota, Illinois, Missouri, Wisconsin, Nebraska, and Kansas. The Ringlings also agreed not to "circulate or cause to be circulated any advertisements of any kind or description" in New York, New Jersey, Pennsylvania, Connecticut, Massachusetts, and Rhode Island during the 1894 season.[2]

NOTES

1. Noncompete Agreement, June 8, 1893, Adam Forepaugh Show and Ringling Brothers, CWM.
2. Noncompete Agreement, March 7, 1894, Barnum and Bailey and Ringling Brothers Shows, CWM.

A Giant Emerges: 1895–1899

"The unrivaled success of the World's Greatest Shows in Chicago and on the road had aroused the expectations of the amusement-loving people of St. Louis to a fever heat."[1]

The economic depression dragged on into 1895 and wouldn't be over until 1897. But the Ringlings, fortified by their successful 1894 season, were already looking past the depression. How could they surpass what they had accomplished the previous year? How could they become an even greater presence in the circus world and take the undisputed lead?

As the Brothers looked ahead to the coming years, they saw the Barnum & Bailey circus as their major competitor. For several years Barnum & Bailey had opened their season indoors at their open-air building in New York City, the "Monster Hippodrome," later renamed Madison Square Garden. The Ringlings considered opening indoors in the Midwest. They could start their season a month earlier and thus earn more money. Showing indoors for an extended time would also help performers perfect their acts before going on the road. Indoor shows wouldn't require putting up and taking down tents each day; there would be no railroad expenses moving from town to town; and the show would require fewer employees than when on the road.

Early in February 1895 the Brothers announced that they had leased the Tattersall's building, an exhibition hall for horse shows, in downtown Chicago. The show would play there April 6–28. It was the first time that a circus show, menagerie, and hippodrome track would be under one roof in Chicago. The Ringlings had never exhibited in Chicago and had never shown in one place for more than a few days, so the Brothers were taking a risk. Would city people attend a circus? For three weeks?

The Tattersall people quickly began remodeling the building for the Ringlings, adding opera chairs, reconstructing entrances, setting aside a section under the seating

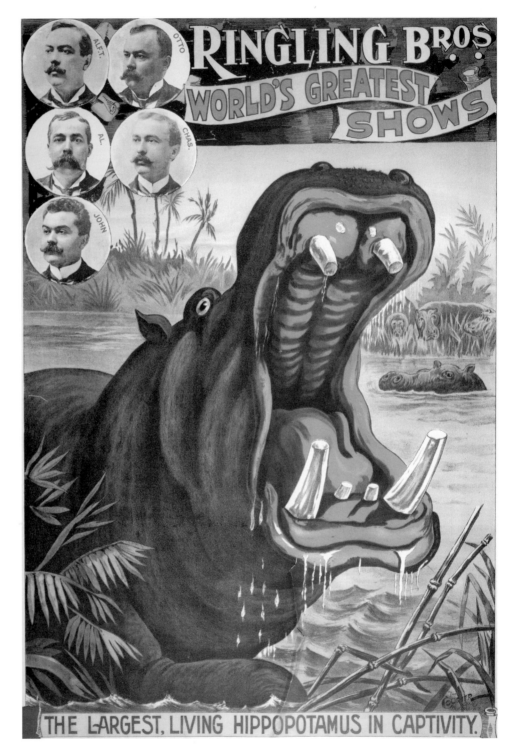

An 1895 Ringling Brothers' poster announced the "Largest Living Hippopotamus in Captivity." Poster Collection, CWM

In 1895 the Ringlings opened their show season indoors for the first time, appearing at the Tattersall's building in Chicago. By opening indoors in April they could extend their season by several weeks. They would open at Tattersall's for several years. COURIER COLLECTION, CWM

platforms for the menagerie, and hanging five thousand flags of many nations under the building's dome.[2] The show would include two rings (a third would be added in succeeding years) plus an elevated stage.

The Ringlings added several new features to their 1895 show. They formed a forty-eight-member band and hired world-famous musical director Signor Alessandra Liberati to present an hour-long band concert at 1:00 and 7:00 each day. They offered several new European circus acts in addition to their already-popular acts, such as Mike Rooney's somersault riding act and their famous clowns. They also hired Speedy, a human high diver, for the last week in Chicago to keep attendance high. Speedy dove about eighty feet from the dome of the roof into a tank of water about three-and-a-half

Five Brothers in a Row

The Ringlings began using an image of the five partner brothers as their signature logo in 1888 on their employee contracts, when only Al and Otto wore mustaches, and John, Charles, and Alf T. were clean shaven.[1] An 1890 ad displayed the five brothers in pinwheel fashion, with one brother in the center and one at each corner. Now each had a mustache.[2] In 1891 the five mustachioed brothers were presented in a horizontal row.[3]

　　Their signature image, with Alf T. in the upper-left corner and Charles in the lower right, was developed about 1898. In this photo each had the same expression, each had a similar moustache, and each was wearing a standup white collar. There was a striking similarity among the five, which was surely the intent. When someone saw an ad, a poster, correspondence, or anything associated with the Ringling show, there were the likenesses of the five partners, all in a formidable row. The picture became their trademark.

The "five brothers in a row" image was developed around 1898. It became one of the most recognizable icons in show business. COURIER COLLECTION, CWM

NOTES

1. Ringling Brothers contract, April 3, 1888, Pfening collection and CWM.
2. Reproduction in *Bandwagon*, March–April 1984.
3. *New York Clipper*, August 1, 1891, p. 362.

feet deep and miraculously survived each time.[3] The Ringlings now had fifteen elephants, eight camels, their famous "gigantic giraffe," a hippopotamus, and a yak—in all, twenty-four cages of wild animals. They had forty-four railcars and three advance cars.

　　The first two sections of the huge show left Baraboo the evening of March 23, 1895, and arrived in Chicago the next day. The last two sections, which largely included the baggage horses and the menagerie, arrived in Chicago on March 27.[4] On Thursday evening, April 4, the Ringlings mounted their first-ever night parade. It was reported that four hundred thousand people saw the extravaganza of horses, wagons, wild animals, elephants, and circus performers.[5]

　　The show opened at Tattersall's Saturday evening, April 6. The usual posters, newspaper ads, and news stories announced the gala event throughout the city. A local writer had this to say about the show:

> The present experiment for the Ringling Brothers might have been a most costly one had the circus been less meritorious. The preliminary expenses were large, more than the lay reader would perhaps believe if the figures were given. The opening night proved a happy (predicator) of all the nights and days which followed. The

Ringlings doubtless figured on the possibility of dropping some money here. As a matter of fact they will leave here several thousand dollars to the good, with an enhanced reputation, and the knowledge that the success of the Chicago engagement is already heralded through the territory they make in the immediate future.[6]

As the Ringling Brothers Circus grew, so did their concert band. The 1895 Military Concert Band comprised forty-eight musicians and was led by Alessandra Liberati. Circus goers could take in the exotic menagerie, the spectacular circus show, and a preshow concert of classical music, all for one fifty-cent ticket. F. Beverly Kelley Collection, CWM

The Ringlings spent twenty-three days in Chicago and put on forty-five performances. Their gross receipts were $52,157; the average daily take was $2,267.[7]

The Ringlings now had confirmation that not just farm and small-town people were attracted to their show. No matter where they lived, people loved the Ringling Brothers Circus. After Chicago the Ringlings loaded their trains and went under canvas April 30 in Ottawa, Illinois. They showed in St. Louis May 6–11. Alf T. Ringling later wrote, "The unrivaled success of the World's Greatest Shows in Chicago and on the road had aroused the expectations of the amusement-loving people of St. Louis to a fever heat, and the six

Ringling Organization, 1895

By 1895 the Ringlings employed 775 people. The various functions of the circus business were headed by managers, who each supervised up to several hundred employees. About seven hundred people traveled with the show; approximately one hundred of them were performers, and the rest were in labor and support roles. Another seventy-five worked in the advance and advertising department.

Departments

- Music, William F. Weldon (eighty-three performers, including a ten-person sideshow band, forty-nine-piece military concert band, and twenty-four-piece Grand Circus Band).
- Transportation, Robert Taylor (thirty-one men responsible for railroad operations).
- Canvas Department, John "Happy Jack" Snellen (205 men responsible for putting up and taking down sixteen tents, including erecting seats and constructing rings).
- Horse Department, Spencer "Delavan" Alexander, Boss Hostler (114 men including teamsters, grooms, pony boys, stable men, blacksmiths, a harness maker, and a wagon repairer; Mr. Rhoda Royal was in charge of ring stock, the performing horses).
- Menagerie, James Rafferty (twenty men who cared for twenty-four cages of exotic animals and birds, plus camels, sacred cattle, and elephants; Mr. Pearl Souder had specific responsibility for the fifteen elephants).
- Properties, Charles Miller (twenty-two men responsible for show performance equipment).
- Wardrobe, W. W. Rees (seven employees responsible for keeping all costumes in good repair).
- Chandelier Department (lights), Charles W. Roy (seven men).
- Dining Department, E. C. Haley (fifty-three men prepared and served three meals a day for all the employees).
- Refreshment Department, A. E. Parsons (twelve men). Privately operated by Parsons, who paid a percentage to the Ringlings to sell pink lemonade, peanuts, cigars, and the like to the circus audiences.
- Ticket Department, Otto Ringling (twenty-seven men); Henry Ringling was Big Show door tender.
- Sleeping Car Department, Paul Cunningham (nine men).
- Sideshow, Charles Andress (sixteen employees and performers).
- Performers, Al Ringling, Equestrian Director (one hundred performers).
- Financial Department, Otto Ringling (two employees).
- Advance and Advertising Departments, John Ringling, router and railroad contractor; Charles Ringling, general advertising agent; Alf T. Ringling, general press agent, Gus Ringling, manager of Advertising Car No. 1. Three advertising cars: Car 1, approximately thirty-five men; Car 2, approximately twenty men; and Car 3, approximately twenty men.[1]

NOTES

1. Alf T. Ringling, *With the Circus: A Route Book of Ringling Bros. World's Greatest Shows, Seasons of 1895 and 1896* (St. Louis: Great Western Printing, 1896).

days' visit to the metropolis of Missouri was one continuous ovation."[8] The show took in $22,803 for the six-day run, with average daily receipts of $3,800.[9]

The show moved east and played Boston from June 24 to June 29. "Rain or shine, they [the crowds] thronged into the great amphitheatre [Big Top], and when the engagement was brought to a close the record of Boston amusements, like that of St. Louis had been broken; for those who were competent to speak declared that never before in the history of Boston entertainments had so many people passed through the entrance of a circus tent in a single week."[10]

Newspapers praised the show. The *Boston Journal* announced: "The Ringling Brothers not only have the greatest show on earth, but also the greatest show that ever was on earth." And the *Boston Globe* declared: "The Ringlings' is the best circus, by all odds, that ever visited Boston."[11]

They played 201 stands during the 1895 season, with average daily receipts of $2,685. The season's gross income was $539,753. Ringling profits for the year, assuming a 40 percent profit margin, were about $216,000 (about $4.3 million in 2002 dollars).[12]

Having found great success in 1895 with their indoor opening at Tattersall's, the Ringlings returned there for the 1896 opening. On April 2, 1896, they loaded their railcars in Baraboo and headed for Chicago. (The trip, in near-zero temperatures, resulted in the death of three boa constrictors.) Once again the Ringlings held a nighttime parade in downtown Chicago prior to the April 11 opening. The *Chicago Times-Herald* said of the parade, "It had the right of way over everything except the United States mail . . . the street cars waited to allow the long procession to pass. The line of waiting [street] cars was many blocks long, yet the passengers did not complain for they saw a good show from an excellent vantage point."[13]

Ringlingville Baraboo

During the winter of 1895–1896, Ringlingville Baraboo consisted of thirty-seven Ringling employees, three listed as part time. They included Spencer Alexander, superintendent of livestock; James Rafferty, superintendent of animals; Rhoda Royal, superintendent of ring stock; John Snellen, boss canvasman; Wilson Reese, superintendent of wardrobe; and Pearl Souder, superintendent of elephants. In addition there were four animal keepers, nine teamsters, two grooms, two cooks, one dishwasher, one canvas maker, two harness-makers, two advance agents, and eight "general" employees.[1]

It is unlikely that nine teamsters were required during the winter months. Like other employees, teamsters did various tasks as needed during the winter off-season. One way the Ringlings were able to keep experienced team drivers—it took considerable skill to drive multi-horse teams—was to provide them winter employment.

NOTES

1. *1895–1896 Angell's Baraboo City Directory.*

Newspaper reviews were strong:

Ringling Bros.' World's Greatest Show closed the season at Tattersall's this evening.
The business during the past few weeks has been phenomenal, and the standing-
room-only signs are liable to be displayed at the performance for the remaining day.
The great show has added wonderfully to its reputation during the present stay, and
all lovers of this style of entertainment pronounce it the best and biggest ever seen
in Chicago. . . . Chicago emphatically likes the Ringling show, and prefers it to any
other.[14]

Rain and wind were the Ringlings' constant companions in the spring of 1896. It
rained so much in Peoria, Illinois, that the entire lot was under four inches to two feet of
water. "It was impossible to give any further performance as the trunks in the dressing
rooms were floating, so the audience waded out to terra firma and the show people
turned their attention to saving their wardrobe and other properties from floating
away."[15]

On August 12 the Ringling Brothers bought the failing W. B. Reynolds Circus.
William B. Reynolds had started his overland circus during the winter of 1891–1892. The
show became a railroad circus in 1893 but did not fare well because of the depression.
Reynolds managed to go out for two more years, but by 1895 they had only eight cars. In
1896 they went out with only five cars and admission at twenty and ten cents; they spent
much of the season showing in the Chicago suburbs before selling to the Ringlings. The
show's properties included four advance wagons, twenty baggage wagons, a ticket
wagon, two bandwagons, seven passenger wagons, and twelve cages of animals. They
also included two elephants, Baldy and Queen, who remained with the Ringling show
for many years.[16]

On August 22, in Kankakee, Illinois, five hundred patients at a nearby "insane asylum" attended the show. A fierce windstorm came up and blew down three horse tents,
the Big Top, the dressing room tent, and the menagerie. Ten thousand people, including
the asylum patients, were soaked. "During the excitement 29 lunatics escaped from
their keepers and at dusk were not yet found."[17]

The Ringlings moved on to the South with great success and closed on November
26 in Luka, Mississippi. As usual, rumors circulated about whether they would winter in
Baraboo, and now it seemed there might be some truth behind the speculation that they
would leave their hometown. The season's route book closed with these words, "Had
arranged to winter at Philadelphia but changed and returned to Baraboo."[18]

Other circuses, including Barnum & Bailey, Forepaugh-Sells, and the Buffalo Bill
show, had been watching the Ringlings' growth with alarm, and several circus owners
devised a plan to drive the boys out of business. The idea was for one competing circus to
show just ahead of the Ringlings, and one just after, "to make a sandwich" of the Ring-

ling Brothers' show. When the press learned of the scheme, the idea collapsed. The "press began to resent the idea and called it a conspiracy against America's only real live show."[19]

During the 1896 season the Ringling circus made two hundred stands, including twenty-two days in Chicago, where they took in $46,668 at an average of $2,121 per day. For the entire season they took in $501,968, with average gross daily receipts of $2,510, down somewhat from average daily receipts in 1895 ($2,685). Their largest daily income to date, $6,388.30, occurred in Atlanta, Georgia, on November 2.[20]

The continuing economic depression was affecting attendance and receipts. A Berlin, Wisconsin, newspaper included this in a review of the circus: "The hotels we are informed did not do quite as large a business as that of two years ago, the last visit of the big show. The threatening weather of the night before is probably responsible for this. Then again, there is not so much money in circulation as there was two years ago."[21] The attempts of several circuses to crowd the Ringlings likely also had some effect on income.

Back in Baraboo for the winter of 1896–1897, the winter quarters were crowded with the growing number of horses and other circus animals the boys were acquiring. By the time the show returned to the road in 1897, the elephant herd alone had grown to twenty-five animals.[22]

The Ringlings opened the 1897 season in Chicago, where the average daily gross receipts were only $1,417, compared with $2,121 in 1896 and $2,267 in 1895.[23] Perhaps this was a sign of the continuing recession. Or perhaps the newness of the circus had worn off for Chicago people.

After Chicago and a few stands elsewhere in the Midwest, including a week in St. Louis, the boys moved west, with stops in Colorado, Wyoming, Utah, Idaho, and Montana. They played St. Louis with huge crowds and daily receipts averaging $2,157.[24]

During the 1897 season, under "the largest tents ever constructed," the Ringlings had their highest average daily receipts to date. HANDBILL COLLECTION, CWM

They showed six days in Colorado, averaging $3,148 each day, and then moved into Wyoming with a stand at Rock Springs, where they took in only $841.90. The keeper of the route book had this to say about Rock Springs:

Hot and dusty. Business light. A cosmopolitan crowd of Huns, Fins, Norwegians, Poles, Dagoes and other foreigners who work in the coal mines here. A desolate, barren mining camp, with a cosmopolitan bunch of weather in keeping with its people. It was clear, cloudy, sunshiny, dusty and rainy, by fits and starts. One show was given, and no one was sorry to leave the place.[25]

In Utah and Montana, daily receipts averaged about $3,000 per day. The Ringlings were back doing what they had done several years before—going to small towns in out-of-the-way places, for the most part drawing huge crowds of people thirsting for entertainment.

They swung back east, with several dates in Michigan, Minnesota, and Wisconsin, and on July 15 played in Baraboo for the first time in two years. The route book noted, "Hot and clear. Business good. The home of the big show. Mr. and Mrs. Ringling, senior, and a number of relatives of the firm, visited the afternoon show, and later had dinner in the dining car."[26]

They were in Janesville, Wisconsin, the next day, where a reporter wrote, "Ringling Brothers' big show—Wisconsin's own circus—is in town, and so are ten or twelve thousand people who want to see the show is carrying the fame of the Badger state to every nook and corner of Uncle Sam's domain."[27]

As had been true the previous season, competition from other shows was fierce, especially in the Midwest. Two or even several circuses might play in the same town, sometimes just weeks apart. The Ringlings showed in Detroit on July 26 and faced Barnum & Bailey, who were already advertising their upcoming show in that city. The route book writer noted:

This has been the hottest opposition fight of the season so far. Every effort has been made by the opposition to get the people to "wait," and even the weather is with them. In spite of pouring rain, the street parade went out on time, and the streets were thronged with a dripping crowd to witness it. The afternoon house filled the big top, and at night it was all but a turn-away.[28]

One feature of the 1897 show was the black tent, or projectoscope tent. Inside a tent with a painted or dyed black ceiling was a moving picture machine.[29] Circus goers interested in seeing a silent movie bought separate tickets to enter the tent. Little did the Brothers know that moving pictures would eventually become the circus's major competitor.

The 1897 season included only 177 stands, but average daily receipts were the highest ever, and their total income approached that of 1895, when they had 201 show dates.[30] For three years in a row, the Ringlings' gross revenue had exceeded $500,000 ($9.9 million in 2002 dollars).

Seven-Year Summary of Ringling Finances				
Year	Gross Revenue	Average Daily Receipts	Stands	Railcars
1891	$206,635	$1,445	143	29
1892	$328,878	$2,149	153	32
1893	$318,451	$2,308	138	38
1894	$419,768	$2,484	169	42
1895	$539,753	$2,685	201	47
1896	$501,968	$2,510	200	50
1897	$524,153	$3,081	177	56

Since the Ringling Brothers put their circus on the rails in 1890, it had grown each year (going from twenty-nine railcars to fifty-six). They had survived the competition, although at times it lowered their income. And they had faced the national economic depression head on. Although there were dips in receipts, the depression years were good ones for the Brothers.

By the end of the 1897 season, the United States had become involved in the Spanish-American War, fighting in Cuba and in the Philippines. The depression of 1893 was ending. The economy was humming again, and people had a little more money in their pockets.

The Ringlings looked forward to 1898 with more enthusiasm than ever. The economy was promising, and their nemesis for the past several seasons, the Barnum & Bailey show, had packed up and moved to Europe for an extended stay. The Ringlings' main competition would now be Forepaugh-Sells, Buffalo Bill, Great Wallace, and the smaller shows.

"When the news was published that Bailey was to go to Europe, . . . Otto Ringling, who is the real business man of the outfit, thought it was the opportunity of their lives. That fall there was plenty of money in the country, as we were enjoying a wave of McKinley prosperity. . . . During the winter of 1898, they purchased a new line of railroad equipment, new cages, . . . and extensively added to their menagerie."[31] It was an exhilarating time for the Ringlings, but their excitement was dampened by the death of their father, August Frederich Ringling, on February 16, 1898.

Then, shortly before the start of the 1898 season, in April, a fire at the winter quarters put a scare in everyone. The *Baraboo Republic* reported:

Wednesday afternoon before three o'clock a fire alarm was sent by telephone to the electric light plant and the fire whistle was sounded. The fire was located at Ringlingville, but by the time the department arrived it was out. The fire is said to have originated in the paint shop from oil that was being heated on the stove. At Ringlingville the employees got out the fire hose that is always kept for the purpose and had a stream of water on the roof of the building in less time than it takes to tell it. In this building were several wagons, one the new hippopotamus cage and the other a lighter but expensive animal cage. Had the fire gotten under good headway it would have been difficult to have saved the big four and a half ton cage. The damage is but slight.[32]

The Ringlings had enough confidence and money that they decided to put two shows on the road in 1898—their own and the John Robinson Greatest of All American Shows, which they leased. The Robinson show had twenty-two railcars plus two advance cars and consisted of Robinson property combined with Ringling animals and equipment. Animals for the show included six elephants and one Ringling-owned hippo, plus fourteen cages. The Robinson circus opened in Baraboo on April 27 and toured the Midwest with numerous stops in Wisconsin and Iowa. It closed on November 7 in Rogers, Arkansas.[33]

Charles Ringling traveled with the Robinson show for its first twelve weeks, while it was getting established. Henry Ringling served as manager of the show for the entire season, and John G. Robinson traveled with the show as an employee.

Meanwhile, the Big Show, as the Ringlings referred to the Ringling Bros. World's Greatest Shows, opened in the Coliseum Building in St. Louis, Missouri, on April 11, 1898. It is possible the Ringlings didn't return to Chicago for the season opening because of declining revenues there and the clear possibility that Chicago residents were losing interest in circus performance. A circus had never before played indoors in St. Louis, and the community looked forward to the event. City leaders knew the Ringling shows had opened indoors in Chicago in previous years and were flattered that the Brothers picked their city for their 1898 opening.

The show traveled with fifty-seven cars (twenty-eight flatcars, twelve stockcars, ten coaches, four elephant cars, and the usual three advance cars). The show had nineteen elephants and thirty-two cages of exotic animals.[34]

On April 11, opening day, festivities begin with a parade that tied up traffic, disrupted streetcar schedules, and was enjoyed by thousands of people lining the parade route. The parade included four hundred horses and a herd of elephants, all of which had known peace and quiet since the previous October. Suddenly, an eight-horse team pulling the yellow bandwagon bolted and ran away. The writer of the Ringling route book described the event:

> [W]ith rare presence of mind and consummate skill George "Buggy" Stump, the driver, seeing that he was powerless to check them, kept them in the middle of the street until he met an electric car, against which he dashed. The sudden shock of it had a quieting effect on the team, one of the "wheelers" being thrown under the car wheel, resulting in a broken leg, thus averting what might have been a terrible catastrophe, with great loss of life. The side show band, who participated in this mad flight, were not slow at this point to escape from their perilous position on the wagon, and with blanched faces thank their lucky stars they were still numbered with the living.[35]

Gross receipts for the ten-day stand in St. Louis were $21,479.75. The Ringlings paid the exposition center one-eighth of the gross—$2,684.90.[36]

While they were in St. Louis, the Ringlings heard news of the United States' involvement in the Spanish-American War. They sent a telegram to Washington.

Telegram to War Department

Russell A. Alger, Secretary of War

    In the event of war can we place at the disposal of the War Department twenty-five elephants for special artillery service in Cuba. Some of them have served in the Punjaub, and neither the climate, food, swamps nor underbrush of Cuba could interfere with their utility. In the heavy underbrush they would be particularly useful, where horses cannot travel freely. They could be armored so heavily as to be utilized as moving forts. We have men competent to handle the animals, who are anxious to enlist, and the value of the elephants in the light artillery has been fully demonstrated in India. Ringling Brothers.[37]

Alf T. made sure the newspapers knew about the telegram. The *St. Louis Post Dispatch* printed a long article with the headline, "Elephants for Cuba. Ringling Brothers make a tender of their herd to the War Department."[38]

There is no record that the Ringlings' offer was seriously considered. But what would the Brothers have done if the government had accepted the elephants? It had been long established that a circus wasn't a circus without elephants.

The Ringlings did not wait around for an answer from the War Department. From St. Louis they moved east, through Illinois and into Kentucky and West Virginia. The show quickly ridded itself of early season problems. The route book entry for April 27 reads:

Mt. Sterling, Kentucky. Fine day. Arrived early. Parade out on time. Everything is working as smoothly as if the show had been out for months. Everyone has learned his place and the clock-like regularity so much wondered at by the thousands who view the working forces handle the trains, horses, tents and other departments, has assumed its mid-summer aspect. The show grounds were lined with snack stands from which colored folks dispensed hot coffee, barbecued shoat, 'possum cake, fried fish and Washington cherry pie. Weather fine. Business good.[39]

Reception in the East was positive. When they played in Troy, New York, on a Monday at the end of May, all the businesses and factories closed, "and the city was veritably given over to the circus."[40]

The 1898 season had its usual assortment of accidents and unusual happenings. While playing in Fitchburg, Massachusetts, on June 7, everyone heard a terrific explosion about 8:00 p.m. War fever was high, and someone said it must surely be a Spanish bomb. In fact, a tank of gas used to feed one of the lights had exploded, blowing two workers over a tent wall for a distance of twenty feet. No one was reported killed.[41]

When the show played in Jackson, Michigan, on August 13, the Brothers suggested to the warden of the nearby prison that they do a show at the prison. The warden accepted the offer, and several performers made their way to the huge building inside a walled compound. Alf T. Ringling described the event this way:

After passing through numerous corridors and passageways, they were ushered into the open court, or prison common. It was a grotesque procession—the musicians with their instruments, the clowns, bedecked in grease paints and attired in their mirth-provoking costumes . . . a motley assemblage of "troopers" indeed, and one that recalled the days of wandering troubadours who strolled from place to

Alf T.'s Farm

In 1898 Alf T. Ringling traveled in Europe and spent some time in a chalet in Switzerland. He fell in love with the setting, and upon returning to the United States he went looking for a place that was similar. He learned from a friend that only six miles east of Baraboo, in Greenfield Township, was such a place. On December 3, 1901, Alf T. bought 120 acres for $5,800; the following March he purchased an additional 20 acres for $1,000.[1] In 1903, 1905, and 1907 Alf T. bought additional nearby land, making his total holdings 280 acres. There he built a chalet and a guest/carriage house, where over the years he entertained such well-known celebrities as Buffalo Bill Cody, Tom Mix, and Babe Ruth. (The Aldo Leopold Foundation of Baraboo currently owns the property.)

NOTES
1. Greenfield Township, T.11, R.7 E., Section 2. Land ownership records. Aldo Leopold Foundation, Baraboo, Wisconsin.

Circus Families

Many Ringling clowns joined the Puff Club, shown here in 1910. Print Collection, CWM

Circus people traveled, worked, and ate together for up to seven months of the year. Many formed close friendships and even makeshift families.

Some of these "families" devised names for themselves. The "Pot Gang" consisted of animal caretakers who gathered in the evenings around a campfire after the closing of the menagerie to eat, tell stories, and pass the time before loading the trains for the next stand. And the "Puff Club" consisted of the show's principal clowns; one of the club's rules was that each member must use a powder puff as part of their making up. The initiation fee was twenty-five cents.[1]

The residents of Ringlingville shared joys and suffering like any family. When there was an accident or a death, it touched everyone in Ringlingville. While the show was in Athol, Massachusetts, on June 4, 1898, an employee's son died. "The sad news of the death of little Georgie Conners, who passed away at 4 o'clock this morning, in the Springfield hospital, from appendicitis, fell like a pall over the entire show. . . . He was the only child of Mr. and Mr. George Connors, an unusually bright and lovable boy, who had grown into the affections of many of the members of the show. Many hearts ached with loving sympathy for the sorrowing parents in this, the dark hour of bereavement. . . . The following day the body was tenderly laid to rest in the cemetery at Springfield. Mrs. Al Ringling and Miss Ida Ringling attended the funeral obsequies."[2]

NOTES

1. Alf T. Ringling, *The Circus Annual: A Route Book of Ringling Brothers, Season 1901* (Chicago: Central Printing and Engraving, 1901), p. 37.

2. *Red Wagon: Route Book of The Ringing Bros. World's Greatest Show, Season 1898* (Chicago: Central Printing and Engraving, 1898), p. 47.

place giving exhibitions. On reaching the courtyard a sight never to be forgotten greeted our eyes. The prisoners were massed on the green sward. . . . [T]he ringing of bells caused a hush to fall upon the assemblage as the "troopers" walked in. All was quiet for a moment and then, out of the afternoon air burst a glad shout of welcome which echoed and re-echoed down through the long corridors of the prison.[42]

After a series of acts, the 854 prisoners had a chance to see several elephants put through their paces. Alf T. wrote:

> At its conclusion, the prisoners marched into the prison, the band leading and playing "Auld Lang Syne." The air was taken up by the convicts and they sang with feeling almost indescribable. As they filed by the expression depicted on the long line of faces showed joy, excitement, pleasure and pain. Here and there a tear stained face betokened the mission of the players had not been in vain. On entering the corridors the men marched silently and took their places in front of their respective cells. The great gong sent out a deep detonation, the cell doors opened and each prisoner entered there to resume the dreary monotonous life of a convict.[43]

As the circus crisscrossed the country, the quality of the show lots varied considerably. In Huntington, West Virginia, the lot was covered with big sewer pipe, and the lot in Syracuse, New York, was a dumping ground filled with ashes, tin cans, "hoop skirts and a worn out washing machine." As Alf T. reported, "The aroma rising from this odoriferous combination was unlike anything we have ever met before. The English tongue, comprehensive as it is, fails to find anything in its vast vocabulary that can begin to express what was wafted o'er the 'dump.'"[44]

The weather remained an unpredictable factor in circus life as well. In 1898 the rains began in late summer and continued into November. Many of the show lots were in miserable condition, making everything about showing difficult and at times nearly impossible. The only bright spot was a five-day stand in New Orleans, where good crowds turned out. But even the New Orleans lot was far from ideal. On Thursday, November 17, upon returning from their parade in a heavy rain, the circus workers found the lot under water. They hauled in cinders, hay, and straw, placed planks in the menagerie tent, and built walks from the streetcar lines to the show lot. And people flocked to their performances. As Alf T. wrote, "It is said that our business surpassed that of any circus that has ever visited the city and this fact alone is a source of much satisfaction to the management."[45]

For 1898 the Ringlings had planned their longest season yet—opening in St. Louis on April 11 and scheduled to close on December 8 in Kosciusko, Mississippi. But the weather caught up with them. They closed on November 28, canceling nine stands in

The Ringlings opened the 1899 season at Tattersall's in Chicago and then went under canvas at Rockford, Illinois. Here the circus prepares for the parade before the Rockford shows. CHARLES S. KITTO CIRCUS COLLECTION, CWM

Mississippi and Alabama. "Show closed and shipped to Baraboo, canceling . . . stands on account of mud, cold, rain, and conditions of lots and roads."[46] Even with the cancellations, the Brothers played two hundred stands for the season, including ten days in St. Louis. The John Robinson Show played 167 stands. Thus, with two shows, the Ringling Brothers offered 367 circus stands in 1898.

After the two shows closed in November, the staff sorted the equipment and shipped that belonging to Robinson back to Cincinnati. However, the Ringlings had been so impressed with some of the Robinson wagons that they bought four of them. These "cottage cages," resembling fancy dwellings with pitched roofs, dormers, bay windows, domes, and corner towers, were some of the most unusual circus cages ever built. The quaint wagons appeared in many of the Ringlings' subsequent parades.[47]

The boys continued to expand winter quarters in Baraboo. On October 24, 1898, they paid $275 for another plot of land on the river immediately to the east of the land they acquired in 1897.[48] They also bought the former Lavoo Hotel, which had been across from Stewart's Lumber Yard, and began remodeling it for winter housing for workers.[49]

For the 1899 season, with the Barnum & Bailey show in Europe, the Ringlings had clear sailing. They seemed content to go on the road with their main show only, and the Robinson show went out of Cincinnati on its own that year.

The Ringlings returned to Tattersall's in Chicago for their April 15 opening and then headed to St. Louis for a week's stand under canvas. Special features for 1899 included three herds of elephants performing at the same time, in three rings, and John O'Brien's horse act, which included sixty-one horses performing at once.

Even with occasional weather problems, crowds were huge as the show traveled through the West as far as Washington State, with stops along the way. Then it was back through Montana, North Dakota, South Dakota, Minnesota, and Wisconsin (there was no show date in Baraboo). Always dependable Iowa was next with several dates, followed by Nebraska, Kansas, Oklahoma Territory, and the South, with three dates in New Orleans, including the closing on November 22. The Ringlings made 186 stands in 1899.

The year 1899 had been an old-fashioned, conservative year for the Ringling circus. Other than traveling to the Northwest, the Brothers tried few new things. Their good reputation and credit rating continued. The Martindale Mercantile Agency in New York (a kind of credit-rating agency of its day) received a request from the Strobridge Litho Company of Cincinnati concerning the Brothers' ability to pay bills. The agency replied:

> Referring to your request of August 12 that we obtain for you a report as to the responsibility of Ringling Bros. of Baraboo, Wisconsin, we beg to submit the following information which we have obtained from F. R. Bentley, the Attorney for this Agency in Baraboo:
>
> The firm of Ringling Bros. is composed of five brothers, (Charles, Al, John, Alfred and Otto), . . . are known to be prompt in meeting their obligations. They have never failed, nor been sued, nor asked an extension. They have valuable real estate in their own name, unencumbered. They all own their own homes and have about $15,000 worth of other real estate. Their supposed total net worth real and personal, is $500,000. So far as known, they have no indebtedness, nor no judgments, or chattel mortgages.

The attorney concluded by stating that "these people are perfectly good in every respect."[50]

At the end of 1899, Alf T. wrote, "It is scarcely necessary to dwell upon the great success of the Ringling Brothers' show during the past season. Financially it has been three seasons, and as to its artistic and exhibitional achievements the comments of the press and public give the most forcible and convincing expression."[51]

Ringlingville on the Road

By 1895 Ringlingville on the road functioned like a sophisticated small city. It included sleeping and eating facilities, a huge livery, a blacksmith shop, a barbershop, a candy store, and even a post office. Ringlingville's postmaster for many years was Jules Turnour, a clown in the circus. Because the circus's routes were planned well ahead of time, circus employees' families knew where to send mail. Upon arriving in a city each morning, Turnour hitched up a team and drove to the local post office, where he picked up the mail for the circus people.

As Turnour wrote:

I know every performer by name, and I am the agent that brings joy or ache. Many eager hopes hang on those post-office trips of mine. The dashing bareback ladies and the daring trapeze performers look for letters that never come. Human nature is the same the world over, whether it is in the gilded palace or under the canvas of the big tent. I send away money orders for all the performers, and in this way I find out some of their secrets. The gruff strong man, whose giant muscles are the admiration of the crowd, sends part of his wages each week to his old mother in Germany; the bewildering little rider, who moves in a gay world of motion and color, has a sick husband,

(continued on page 86)

Ringling employees picked up their mail at the Ringlingville post office—a circus wagon (shown here in 1915). Print Collection, CWM

Jules Turnour was both circus clown and Ringlingville postmaster for many years. Print Collection, CWM

Ringlingville on the Road

(continued from page 85)

whom she supports. I become the friend and confidant of all of them, and it makes life richer and deeper and more worthwhile for me.[1]

By 1908 Ringlingville included a doctor, a chaplain, a veterinary surgeon, detectives, barbers, blacksmiths, and a storekeeper—everything one would expect to find in a small city. And as in many cities, the circus population was, as one writer noted, "a congress of nations." In that year Ringling employees, both performers and workers, included 16 Japanese, 40 French, 10 Swiss, 30 Italians, 5 Portuguese, 4 Bohemians, 10 Austrians, 50 Russians, 65 Germans, 8 Belgians, 10 Scots, 8 Spaniards, 10 Poles, 4 Egyptians, 2 Singalese, 6 Cossacks, 12 Hungarians, 4 Burmese, 6 Welsh, 390 Americans, 460 Englishmen, and a hundred or so others of unknown origins. The writer concluded that Ringlingville on the road was "a Tower of Babel for tongues, a congress of religions, a gathering of clans and families."[2]

Ringlingville on the road was a traveling city that boasted most of the services found in any rural village, including a barbershop, shown here circa 1890–1891. The Ringlings wanted all employees to be well groomed for the public. Note the razor strap and straight-edge razor in the barber's hands. PRINT COLLECTION, CWM

NOTES

1. Jules Turnour (as told to Isaac. F. Marcosson), *The Autobiography of a Clown* (New York: Moffat, Yard, 1910), pp. 78–79.
2. *Duluth (Minnesota) Herald*, June 24, 1908.

The blacksmith shop was an essential service in Ringlingville on the road. PRINT COLLECTION, CWM

The Brothers had been in the circus business a scant fifteen years and had achieved success beyond anyone's imagination. Now they were about to enter a new century. Although they had seemed content to run a rather conservative circus in 1899, could they afford to do this indefinitely? The bigger question they faced was, What would be circus's place in a rapidly changing society?

The introduction to the 1899 route book includes these words:

> The circus of today is decidedly an institution of our own country and of our own time. It has grown up with us. Early in the nineteenth century it was small, like our country, and its marvelous growth has been measured only by the equally marvelous development of America.
>
> Society needs amusement. Human nature craves entertainment. The nerves and subtle brain forces of man were not made to stand the physical and mental strain incidental to life's struggle, without relaxation.
>
> To be good, mankind must be happy. The sunshine of this world inspires hopes for a brighter day.
>
> Amusement unfetters the mind from its environs and changes the dreary monotony of the factory's spindles to the joyous song of the meadow lark; it removes the ball and chain with which man feels himself bound to his duties and lifts him above the cares of life. . . .
>
> This is the mission of amusement, and the circus, with its innocent sights of joy for the children and its power to make all men and women children again for at least one day, comes the nearest of any form of amusement to fulfilling this mission.[52]

By the end of the century, the Ringling circus had clearly become a giant. Would it maintain its lead among competing circuses? And perhaps more important, could it compete with the many new entertainment opportunities, especially the moving picture?

Facing a New Century: 1900–1901

"The only circus in the world covering the entire continent in one season."[1]

The new century opened with prosperity and optimism. William McKinley, who had taken office in 1897, continued as president of the United States. The first automobiles appeared; baseball was growing in prominence; barbershop quartets harmonized in village bandstands, often preceding a performance by the local band. Moving pictures were becoming the rage.[2]

In 1900 the average worker earned about $13 for a sixty-hour workweek; schoolteachers received $325 per year. The Montgomery Ward and Sears, Roebuck catalogs were read more than any other books, including the Bible.[3] In a Baraboo newspaper an ad offered for rent a modern house with furnace, bathroom, cistern, well, and barn for $12 per month. A six-room home could be purchased for $1,500. W. M. Little, a Baraboo tailor, advertised: "For that cold feeling, wear an overcoat, one of the warm kind." Another ad encouraged storekeepers to put in telephones. One could purchase a Blickensderfer typewriter at the Baraboo News office for $40. The Bank of Baraboo, where the Ringlings did much of their business, boasted that its capital was $50,000, and the South Side Cash Shoe Store bragged that it had "The Best shoes that tread the earth."[4]

That year Alfred T. Ringling published *Life Story of the Ringling Brothers,* a colorful report of the beginnings of the Ringling circus. He was sometimes prone to exaggerate for the sake of a good story—but a great story it was. During the winter of 1899–1900 the Brothers took stock of their menagerie, and Otto ordered several animals. A January 1900 letter from the German animal dealer Hagenbeck's read:

Enclosed I am sending you 2 photos of an alive walrus, which I have now since 2 years 5 months in my possession. It is a wonderful beast, now about 3 years old. It did weigh in June last year over 400 pounds, and I think, by the description my man

By the turn of the twentieth century, people were attending circuses by the thousands. In this photograph the crowd has gathered, decked out in Sunday finery, to hear a "talker" describe the incredible sights awaiting inside the sideshow tent.
<small>PRINT COLLECTION, CWM</small>

gives me, that he has now at least 600 pounds. His tusks are about 2 inches long. It is a splendid trained animal, and I am sure it would be a wonderful success, if you had this animal in your show. The very lowest price for the animal is $5,000.00, delivered free to Hoboken, duty paid by me.[5]

There is no record that Otto bought the walrus, but he must have ordered a tiger from Hagenbeck's in January, along with an eland and a "big monkey."[6] Otto complained about the price of the monkey and received a $100 reduction.[7]

Although they were well aware of the rapid changes taking place in society and technology, including increasing competition for audience members' attention, the Ringling Brothers made few changes to their circus for the 1900 season. They did open in an eastern state for the first time, debuting in Wheeling, West Virginia, on April 10. "All Wheeling fell in love with the show almost from the day of its arrival because of the splendid conduct of the people and their courtesy to visitors."[8]

The Brothers advertised the 1900 show as "Ringling Bros. World's Greatest Shows: The Invincible Monarch of Amusements, and beyond all dispute or doubt The Greatest Show on Earth."[9] The Barnum & Bailey Circus was known as "The Greatest Show on

Al Ringling was an avid fisherman, and he often took off from circus duties for a few days of angling. In this 1902 photograph Al is at right and Mike Rooney, a performer from Baraboo, is at left. RICHARD E. AND ALBERT CONOVER COLLECTION, CWM

While Barnum & Bailey toured Europe, the Ringling Brothers conveniently "borrowed" their famous "Greatest Show on Earth" slogan. HANDBILL COLLECTION, CWM

Earth," but with Barnum & Bailey still safely away in Europe, the Ringlings apparently saw little wrong with "borrowing" a catchy slogan from one of their biggest competitors.

After West Virginia the Ringling trains rumbled on to Pennsylvania, New Jersey, and Connecticut, where they did a stand in Bridgeport, home of Barnum & Bailey. By June they were back in the Midwest. The tour was going so well that Al took time off for two fishing trips in July, the second one with his wife, Lou, and brother Henry.

On August 6 and 7 the Ringlings played in Denver and claimed to turn away as many as seven thousand people. They traveled on to Leadville, Colorado, a city with one of the highest elevations in the country and then moved on to the Northwest. In Montana, Indians came from miles around, pitched their tents, and attended the show. The Ringlings turned away people in Seattle and then showed in California for the first time. The 1900 route book noted, "[D]uring its five weeks' stay there it averaged nearly three turn-aways a week. In San Francisco and Los Angeles people were turned away by the Thousands."[10]

The boys closed in Monticello, Arkansas, on November 14 and headed home for the winter. "The tour of the circus this year was one long run of prosperity. Never before in the history of tented amusements has such an enormous business been done by any show. We have traveled from the Atlantic to the Pacific; have touched one point in Canada and gone to the South as far as the Mexican line, exhibited in twenty-eight states, two territories and British Columbia. . . . [W]e have not had a single accident of any consequence, and little or no sickness." Even noting the obvious exaggeration in the route book summary, it was probably the Ringlings' best season ever.[11]

Despite all its success, not everyone was happy with the Ringling Brothers' show. In Richland Center, Wisconsin, the *Richland Rustic* noted: "The show itself was as good as ever, but to those who have seen it once or twice it was a disappointment. . . . It was in fact much the same show it was four years ago."[12]

But most reviews of the season were laudatory. The *Appleton (Wisconsin) Crescent* proclaimed:

> By all odds the biggest, cleanest and best circus and menagerie that ever visited Appleton was the Ringling show which exhibited here Monday. Every feature was perfect, and every promise of the program made good to the letter. No crooks or tramps were in the wake of the show, and not an arrest was made during the day as a result of the presence of the circus and its attendant throng in the city. . . . In the afternoon over twelve thousand people paid admission to the circus and the evening crowd was half as large. Everybody pronounced it the most novel and satisfactory arenic exhibition ever seen here.[13]

The *Columbus (Ohio) Dispatch* reported, "The people of this city evidently liked the Ringling Brothers show, for a big audience of Columbus people saw the afternoon performance, went out, talked about it and then came back in the evening bringing their sisters, their cousins and their aunts."[14]

The Ringlings returned to Chicago for the opening of their 1901 season. They held a two-hour parade before huge crowds on the crisp night of April 8 and then opened the show at the Coliseum on April 10. They played mostly two shows a day in Chicago through April 27. (One exception was Sunday, April 14, when a nearby church complained: "The Reverend Ernest M. Stires and his flock, fearing that the commingling of the strains of Handel and Mendelssohn from the church pipe organ with the 'Rag Time Life' of the circus brass band would be conducive neither to musical harmony nor to religious devotion, refused to give permission to the granting of a Sunday night license to the circus people.")[15]

From Chicago the circus played several shows in Ohio and then went east for a two-day stand in Washington, D.C. Many of the show people visited the Capitol, the White House, and other government buildings and, according to the route book, "pronounced

Winter Activities

Ringlingville on Water Street, Baraboo, circa 1905. PRINT COLLECTION, CWM

Winter at Ringlingville was planning and training time. Alf T. Ringling wrote:

A big show is a show all year round. It does not go into a comatose state in the winter, like the frog, and sleep until the warm breath of spring thaws it out . . . it goes into plain work-a-day winter quarters, which means, in the case of the Ringling Brothers, seven large barns capable of housing 350 horses, great, commodious and heated animal-houses with massive dens for the menagerie animals, car shops, 4,800 feet of railroad tracks, machinery building and planing mill, practicing-ring building, heated elephant house, giraffe

building, paint shops, wagon shops, training barn, blacksmith shops, wardrobe rooms, large hotel, harness shop, carpenter shop, and storage building for canvas, paraphernalia, etc., hay shed, chariot and wagon sheds, office rooms, and what not in the way of buildings, in all covering over twelve acres of ground.

After the season is over it usually takes from two to three weeks to get everything back in the different buildings.[1]

Baraboo residents have passed down many stories—some have become legends—about Ringlingville winter quarters, particularly about the exotic animals housed

Winter Activities

Training animals was an important part of winter quarter activities. Here zebras practice a tandem act in the ring barn, circa 1908. PRINT COLLECTION, CWM

there. Locals often commented on the trumpeting of the elephants, the roar of the lions, and the other strange sounds coming from Ringlingville down by the river.

One winter a black panther escaped its cage and ran across the street from Ringlingville, taking refuge in an old woman's outhouse. When the woman went for a visit, there was the panther, sprawled across the toilet seat. The resourceful woman went back to her house, grabbed a broom, and shooed the big cat out. Workers later captured the dangerous animal and returned it to its cage.

Residents also tell of the time a python that stiffened up from the cold was left for dead on the manure pile just outside the animal house. Local farmers often used the circus's manure as fertilizer. Later, when a farmer pitched the manure onto his wagon, he uncovered the huge snake, very much alive and now agitated at having its warm nest disturbed. The farmer shrieked and took off running; workers returned the snake to its den. The farmer had the scare of his life.[2]

NOTES

1. Alf T. Ringling, *Beneath White Tents: Route Book of Ringling Brothers, Season 1894*, p. 144.
2. C. P. "Chappie" Fox, interview by the author, Baraboo, Wisconsin, August 20, 2001.

This photo, circa 1904, was taken behind the Baraboo animal house to emphasize the height of a Ringling giraffe. Giraffes were quite capable of eating feed placed on the ground. PRINT COLLECTION, CWM

FIRST TIME IN CANADA

RINGLING BROS. WORLD'S GREATEST SHOWS.

The Absolute Monarch of All Tented Amusements
The Acknowledged and Unquestioned Biggest Shows on Earth

THE ONLY GIRAFFE

KNOWN TO EXIST TODAY IN THE WORLD.

Sole and Lonely Survivor of a Once Numerous Family.

ONLY GIRAFFE KNOWN TO EXIST IN THE ENTIRE WORLD

Secured at the Cost of a FORTUNE SHOWN AT EACH EXHIBITION OF THE LARGEST MENAGERIE ON EARTH

LAST OF HIS KIND HUMAN EYES WILL NEVER BEHOLD ANOTHER

ONE 50-CENT TICKET ADMITS TO EVERYTHING.
CHILDREN UNDER 12 YEARS, HALF PRICE.

OTTAWA, MON. June 10

them fully waterproof."[16] (One appreciates a comment about waterproof buildings from circus people, who lived under leaky tents!)

After an extended tour in the Northeast, including five days before huge crowds in Boston, the Ringlings moved into Canada for the first time. They played there from June 6 to June 26 and then moved back across the border into Michigan. While showing near St. Thomas, Ontario, Al and Henry had time for a two-day fishing trip. They brought back six hundred pounds of black bass—"Enough to feed the show."[17]

The troupe was back in Pennsylvania by early July. On July 4, in Pittsburgh, the Ringling employees took a break from their rigorous schedule to celebrate the holiday with a special dinner prepared by A. L. Webb, steward of the cook tent.

Ringling Employee Fourth of July Dinner, 1901

Mock turtle, radishes, olives, sliced onions, baked lake trout, parsley sauce, shoestring potatoes.
Boiled ox tongue, lemon sauce.
Braised pork tenderloins, tomato sauce.
Veal loaf, with mushrooms.
Orange fritters, wine sauce.
Prime ribs of beef, dish gravy.
Spring lamb, mint sauce.
Chicken, with dressing.
Lemon ice. Chow-chow. Sliced cucumbers. Mixed pickles. New potatoes in cream. Mashed potatoes. Green peas. Beets. Braised cabbage. Cabbage salad. Chicken salad.
Fruit pudding, brandy sauce. Lemon pie. Strawberry pie. Assorted cake. Ice cream. Fruit. Crackers. Cream cheese. Coffee. Tea. Milk.[18]

The Ringlings took their show to Canada for the first time in 1901. Ads that year boasted that the show included "the only giraffe known to exist today in the world"— a huge exaggeration. HANDBILL COLLECTION, CWM

The circus staff usually celebrated holidays with a special meal in the Ringling dining tent. PRINT COLLECTION, CWM

By mid-July the show was in the Midwest. A freak accident occurred in Muncie, Indiana, on July 11. In midafternoon two young men drove up with a team of horses just as the elephants were let out for water. The horses bolted and threw the young men from their buggy. The runaway team tipped over the ticket box and smashed into the sideshow banners, bringing down the entire front of the sideshow promotional banner before galloping toward town. No one was seriously hurt, although a woman "was stunned by a falling banner pole."[19]

The show reached Wisconsin by the end of July. Several people from Baraboo, including Mrs. Al Ringling, Mrs. Alf T. Ringling, Richard Ringling (Alf T.'s son), the Ringling brothers' sister, Ida, and their mother, Salome Ringling, traveled to Janesville to see the show.

In Topeka, Kansas, on August 6, the audience continually interrupted announcer

Moeller & Sons

Local craftsmen in Baraboo, such as H. Moeller & Sons (the Moellers were cousins of the Ringlings), depended on the Ringlings for a large portion of their income. In the winter of 1899–1900, the Moellers collected $2,139.45 for repair work they did for the Ringlings, including the following:

Cage No. 71: $9.10

Cage No. 70: $8.25

Blacksmith bellows, extra long: $13.70

Elephant hooks: $.75

Bell wagon: $7.75

Menagerie pole wagon: $33.10

Cook wagon: $28.30

Ticket wagon: $89.71

Elephant whip: $.50

Two new plank wagons: $450.00

Chandelier wagon: $53.10

107 stake bands at $.05: $5.35

26 seat brackets at .20: $5.20

50 layout pins at .05: $.2.50

Balancing pole: $.50[1]

NOTES

1. H. Moeller & Sons account book, April 1899–April 1900, Fred Pfening III, private collection, Columbus, Ohio.

Lew Graham as he tried to promote the after-show concert. Then, performer Joe Le Fleur did his usual backward flip from a pyramid of chairs and came down hard. Several men, including Graham, rushed to his side. As they lifted his limp body, the audience was at last completely silent. In a loud voice, Graham called, "Is there a doctor in the house?" He paused, gazing at the apparently severely injured performer. He called again, "Is there a doctor in the house?" There was no response from the deathly quiet audience. Graham paused, then said loudly, "If there is, then I would like him and all of you to remain and see our grand concert." Le Fleur jumped to his feet, and a huge cheer came from the crowd.[20] Audience members had been taken in by the ruse, and they loved it. Graham had clearly found a way to get their attention.

The show played in San Francisco from August 26 to August 31 to huge crowds. It was a critical time for the show to be in San Francisco as the local teamsters had been on strike for several weeks. Circus workers were offered as much as eight to ten dollars a day to be strike breakers. But no one from the circus responded, deeming the proposition too dangerous. The circus appeared to be neutral ground between labor and management—everyone seemed to enjoy the circus no matter which side he was on.[21]

On September 14 the Ringlings were in Pomona, California, when they received the horrifying news: President William McKinley had died of gunshot wounds. He had been shot by anarchist Leon Czolgosz on September 6, 1901.

The Brothers held only a night performance on September 19. That afternoon they organized a special memorial service for President McKinley in the Big Top, for Ringling employees only. It was an elaborate affair featuring speakers, a specially decorated stage with an immense American flag serving as the backdrop, and an oil painting of the president, draped in black. The Reverend J. F. Leland of the Universalist Church conducted the memorial service. The circus band played a dirge. In attendance were all the Ringling Brothers, their wives, members of the executive staff, performers, clowns, and workers of every stripe—about five hundred of them. The service closed with the singing of the hymn "Nearer My God to Thee." "When the last note died away and Dr. Leland stood up to pronounce the benediction, suppressed sobs were heard and scarcely a dry eye could be observed under the spread of canvas."[22] The Ringlings made sure the press was present at their memorial. The *Los Angeles Times* carried a lengthy story about the event, with the headline "Unique Memorial by Circus Folk: Ringling Bros.' Employees join in Mourning."[23] The Brothers held their service five days after McKinley's death; it no doubt took a while for everyone to assemble in San Francisco, but one could also argue that they wanted to hold the event in a large city, and not down in San Diego or Santa Ana, which had less-prestigious newspapers.

The Ringlings had done extremely well during the years McKinley had been president (1897–1901). Their love for McKinley was genuine. Theodore Roosevelt, known to be a reformer, was the new president, and the Brothers had to wonder: Would major political change create problems for their circus?

From California the Ringlings took their show to the Southwest and South, closing in Mississippi on November 16. The show had had yet another successful season.

Back at winter quarters, the Ringlings were once more running out of room. In the fall of 1901 they built a new 36-by-110-foot brick animal house and a 56-by-120-foot horse barn.[24] It is unclear when the Ringling Brothers' new office building was constructed on Water Street, and whether the old office, constructed in 1897, had been moved to the new site and additions made. A reasonable estimation is that the new office was constructed in 1901, certainly before 1904. Sometime between 1904 and 1913 a records vault was added to the office building. The office was of balloon-frame construction in the Queen Anne style. It was rectangular with an added front porch, and it looked like an ordinary farmhouse, similar to thousands built in this period.

As 1901 came to a close, the future seemed much less certain than it had at the start of the century. Not only were new entertainment opportunities challenging the circus, but a new president might not treat big business—and the Ringling Brothers circus was surely a big business—as well as his predecessor had. The Ringlings looked to 1902 with some unease.

Weather Challenges

Weather was a constant challenge for the circus. High winds and lightning storms, which could lead to what was known as a "blow down," were especially dangerous—even deadly.

windward side and the Big Top crashed to the ground. There was "a heaving mass of broken seats, splintered poles and torn canvas. The dressing room tent quickly followed, but the menagerie top to which the audience

When storms, high winds, or accident damaged a circus top to the point that it could not be used until it was repaired, workers would erect only the sidewall of the tent so that the animals were still hidden from those who had not paid the price of admission. Here the Ringling menagerie is set up with sidewalls. Print Collection, CWM

A terrific storm came up during the evening show in Sedalia, Missouri, on May 25, 1893. Al Ringling quickly warned the two thousand people under the Big Top. It was hardly a moment after the last person exited that a gigantic gust of wind snapped all the tent ropes on the

had fled remained standing." Several people were injured, but everyone survived.[1]

The Brothers missed their next appearance, but by May 27 they had had the canvas, poles, and seats repaired and were back in business. A few weeks later, in

Weather Challenges

York, Nebraska, high winds struck again. The menagerie tent blew down, soaking the wild animals, and the cook tents fell, but the Big Top remained standing.

The weather turned lethal when the show played in River Falls, Wisconsin, on June 21, 1893. An Associated Press writer reported:

A terrific thunder storm raged in this vicinity this afternoon. Rain fell in sheets, and great floods of water formed almost in an instant in the streets. . . . The circus proper had just finished its perform-ance, and as the concert was about to begin a number of people who did not care to attend the latter were making their way through the menagerie tent when a terrific bolt of lightning struck one of the center poles of the menagerie tent, and more than fifty people were prostrated. Seven were killed instantly, and the balance is now regaining the normal use of their limbs. . . . [I]t was only by the exercise of rare presence of mind on the part of Messrs. Ringling and their employ-ees that a more serious and probably fatal stam-pede was averted. . . . . The bodies of the dead were taken to the village engine house, where some dis-tressingly sad scenes were enacted. . . . This com-munity is a gloomy one this evening, and the calamity is universally deplored. None of the show people were injured. . . . The circus will, of course, give no performance tonight.[2]

On the morning of June 10, 1897, in Wahpeton, North Dakota, a severe thunderstorm blew out of the west while the canvas crew was setting up the tents. Lightning struck a center pole where twenty-two men were working. C. E. Walters and Charles Smith were killed instantly, and twenty others were knocked unconscious. The hat was passed and money was collected for the

men's funerals; a monument, a replica of a shattered center pole, was placed over their graves.[3]

Even when severe weather left people unscathed, it could take a serious toll on both circus equipment and ticket receipts. When a huge prairie storm blew into Ellsworth, Kansas, on September 15, 1897, the route book scribe reported:

Threatening clouds began to gather a little after 4 o'clock and by six the storm had assumed alarming proportions. The first blow struck at about 6:00 o'clock but, although severe, the canvas withstood the force of it and nothing gave way. The storm then veered around and came back, whirling with terrific speed. It struck the big top and the black tents and in a second there was nothing by a mass of wreckage and debris where they had stood. The attendance at the afternoon show had been tremendous and another crowd was expected at the night show, but in consequence of the storm, the night show was abandoned. All hands were set to work all night in a pouring rain to untangle the mass of ropes, canvas, seats, stringers and shat-tered center and quarter poles, and it was daylight when the last section pulled out of the town. A great deal of valuable wardrobe and paraphernalia were damaged or destroyed, but there were no casualties.[4]

The Ringling circus even confronted a sandstorm in Butte, Montana, on September 4, 1902:

Small particles of dirt and stone were dashed into the eyes and faces of the workingmen and many of them were almost blinded, but like true soldiers they stayed at their posts and soon had the tents

(continued on page 100)

Weather Challenges

(continued from page 99)

erected. . . . One could scarcely see ten feet from the front doors at one o'clock, yet an enormous crowd was in waiting long before the chains were taken away. Great difficulty was experienced by Henry Ringling's little army of ticket takers, as their eyes were filled with dirt and dust and at times it was impossible for them to see the people. All the available men assisted at the door and the crowd was soon handled. When the circus commenced, swirling dust was so thick in the big top that all the chandeliers were lighted and even the persons on the seats could scarcely discern the actors. The storm continued all day and late into the night, and everybody, from the Ringlings to the smallest pony boy, was glad when Butte was in the distance.[5]

NOTES

1. *Route Book of Ringling Brothers, Season of 1893* (Buffalo, NY: Courier, 1893), pp. 46–47.
2. Quoted in the *Route Book of Ringling Brothers, Season of 1893*, pp. 55–56.
3. *The Circus Annual: A Route Book of Ringling Brothers World's Greatest Shows, Season of 1897* (Buffalo, NY: Courier, 1897), p. 103.
4. Ibid., p. 112.
5. *The Circus: A Route Book of Ringling Bros.' World's Greatest Shows, Season 1902* (Chicago: Central Printing and Engraving, 1902), p. 24.

Making Money and Pleasing People: 1902–1903

"The Biggest Circus on Earth."[1]

The Ringlings had learned early on that pleasing their customers and treating them honestly took high priority. When their customers were pleased, they made money. The challenge, of course, was continually figuring out what pleased people.

The Barnum & Bailey Circus would not return to the United States until fall 1902, so that summer the Ringlings' major competition were the Forepaugh-Sells Circus, Buffalo Bill's Wild West, and the Great Wallace Show. But circus historian Fred Dahlinger notes that "by 1900–1902 the Ringlings could go where they pleased, at will, such was their drawing strength."[2]

The Ringlings added a few new acts for 1902, including a pageant "representing the inaugural ceremonies of the grand fetes of ancient Rome," using all three rings and both stages. But mostly the Brothers relied on what worked—elephant and horse acts, acrobats, aerialists, jugglers, and horse races of several stripes: monkeys riding Shetland ponies, a ladies' jockey race, a four-horse Roman chariot race, and more.

They opened indoors in Chicago, but this time without a parade. It was becoming increasingly difficult to offer a circus parade in large cities crowded with streetcar traffic, horse-drawn carriages, and even a sprinkling of horseless carriages. They gave two performances a day from April 9 to 26, and then on the evening of April 26, the Ringlings' sixty-five railcars rumbled on to Champaign, Illinois, for the April 28 opening under canvas.[3]

The 1902 season began with a string of accidents and mishaps. On April 23, just before the season opening, the big pole wagon, which carried the giant Big Top poles, broke through the Ash Street Bridge in Baraboo. Although just one wheel broke through, the workmen had great difficulty getting the wheel back on the bridge. One of the jacks they were using in their efforts fell in the river and was lost. When the wheel broke the bridge plank, four of the horses bolted and ran away; they were eventually corralled in front of the Effinger Brewery. The rest of the circus wagons were rerouted over the Oak Street Bridge, where one of them collided with Webber's dray wagon, which was loaded with flour. Now traffic was stopped on both bridges. As a reporter wrote, "For a time it looked like a blockade on the streets of Chicago."[4]

Accidents and injuries were common in the circus. Putting up and taking down tents was dangerous business. Working with horses, elephants, and a host of other animals often placed workmen in danger. And of course, the constant exposure to windstorms, lightning, and floods added to the possibility of injury. Performers were also prone to injury; on May 19 in Ohio, aerialist Frank Smith fell thirty feet and broke his left arm in two places, dislocated his right shoulder, and was severely bruised. He was treated by circus doctor Arthur H. Gollmar and moved to a nearby hospital for treatment and recovery.

While the Ringling trains were moving from West Virginia to Ohio on May 22, one section had a minor derailment. While waiting for some repairs, a group of circus performers walked to a nearby farmhouse. There were introductions all around, and soon the farmer's daughters were offering bowls of milk and bread for the babies and children who were with the troupe. The farmer's family and the performers had a party on the lawn. The route book included the following note: "The afternoon spent at this house in good old West Virginia will long remain fresh in the memories of the troopers as one of the bright events of the season."[5]

The show played in Canton, Ohio, on May 28. Many of the performers and workmen visited President McKinley's grave "to pay silent respect to the memory of that great and good man who was shot down by a cowardly assassin on that long to be remembered day at the Buffalo Exposition."[6]

By mid-June the Ringlings were back in Wisconsin with shows in Watertown, Chippewa Falls, Stevens Point, Fond du Lac, Milwaukee, and Madison. From there they headed west. While in Denver, one of the performers and a ticket seller were married in a downtown church. "It was the first circus wedding of the present season and presents and congratulations were poured upon the happy couple until they were swamped."[7]

As the circus traveled from Tacoma, Washington, to Portland, Oregon, the mishaps continued. The third train section was moving slowly when two elephant cars and a flatcar left the track and plunged into a ditch filled with several feet of water. One man suffered a broken ankle, another had a dislocated shoulder, and another received severe bruises. Pearl Souder, superintendent of elephants, suffered a scalp wound but refused treatment until the elephants were cared for. All the elephants but one were little more than shook up. Fanny, the oldest of the Ringling elephants, had landed under a small bridge and couldn't get up. "Souder dosed her with whiskey, and after placing chains

The Ringling parade entertained thousands in Madison in 1902. Al Ringling (in buggy), representing the owners, was usually first in the parade. Next came the lead bandwagon. PRINT COLLECTION, CWM

around her neck, used two other elephants to pull her to terra firma."[8] There is no record of Fanny's injuries.

Another car derailment near Lexington, Missouri, sent the cook tent and the black-smith van into a ditch, with extensive damages. Breakfast was late the next morning as the crew helped the cooks put things back together.[9]

And then the rains came. In Kansas City the lot was so muddy that the stake and chain wagon and other big wagons sank to the hubs. According to the route book, "On several of the wagons, 24 horses were used and by nightfall the baggage stock was completely tired out. Monday's [September 22] parade was held in the rain and the lot at noon was a veritable sea of mud. Hundreds of bales of straw were scattered about in order to make the interior of the menagerie and big tops presentable. Big business, rains and oceans of mud were features of the day."[10]

The Ringlings left the rains behind and traveled on to Texas, where they played from October 8 to November 7. They played Lake Charles, Louisiana, on November 8, and finally closed in Monticello, Arkansas, on November 15. Despite troubles on the road, it had been another prosperous year. The Ringlings' prestige continued to increase as newspaper reviews lauded their efforts, and thousands upon thousands flocked to their shows.

The Ringling Brothers Circus had become arguably the most successful circus ever. As an institution, the circus—the Ringlings' included—was in fact quite conservative. There were tents, rings, aerialists, clowns, horses, elephants, usually a menagerie, a band, and a parade. What could the Ringlings do that was new and yet didn't stray too far from what people had long expected of the circus?

Every Christmas the Ringling Brothers gathered in Baraboo for a family celebration and an annual meeting. It was at these meetings that they made their plans for the

The Ringlings appeared in Texas in October 1902.
RICHARD E. AND ALBERT CONOVER COLLECTION, CWM

coming season. At the 1902 meeting the Brothers surely discussed how to compete with the Barnum & Bailey show, which had returned from Europe in October and was currently at winter quarters in Bridgeport, Connecticut, preparing for the 1903 season.[11] They had already met with James Bailey in May 1902, to work out route arrangements for 1903 to avoid overlap.[12] The Ringlings also knew that Barnum & Bailey had ordered new parade wagons from the Sebastian Wagon Company of New York, and that winter the Ringlings ordered six new parade wagons from the Bode Wagon Company of Cincinnati and the Moeller Brothers in Baraboo. The Ringlings' order comprised a pipe organ

Come One, Come All

The circus had nearly universal appeal. Because it did not depend on language the way the theatre did, for instance, circus audiences usually included English as well as non–English speakers. Understanding English was not necessary to enjoy the music, the clowns, the elephants and horses, the aerialists, and the menagerie animals. When they were in heavily populated ethnic areas—Germans and Norwegians in Wisconsin, Swedes in Minnesota—these groups came. When the circus played in Indian country, Indians came. In San Francisco Chinatown residents turned out in large numbers.[1] In Utah wagonloads of Mormons came "from one end of the valley to the other and patronized everything under the acres of canvas."[2] And being illiterate didn't matter either—even those who

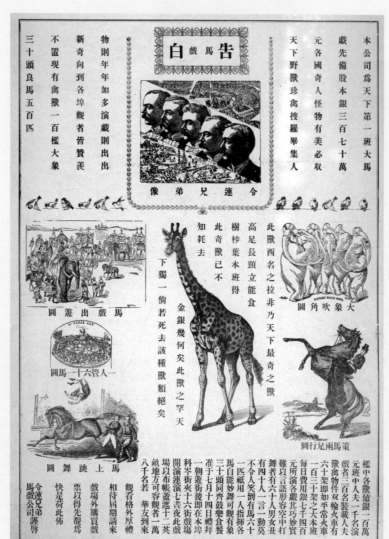

couldn't read a word could soak up the sights, sounds, and flavor of the circus. From the very beginning the Ringling Brothers worked hard to ensure that everyone was welcome under their canvas.

NOTES

1. Alf T. Ringling, *The Circus Annual: A Route Book of Ringling Brothers, Season 1901* (Chicago: Central Printing and Engraving, 1901), pp. 69–73.
2. *The Circus Annual: A Route Book of Ringling Brothers' World's Greatest Shows,* Season 1903, p. 66.

The Ringling Brothers worked hard to provide a show for all ethnic groups, often advertising in several languages. This handbill, printed in Chinese, was prepared for their September 1903 appearances in Chinatown, San Francisco. HANDBILL COLLECTION, CWM

In winter 1902–1903 the Ringlings ordered six intricately decorated wagons from the Bode Wagon Company, including the Great Britain Tableau (left, top), the Russia Tableau (left, middle), and the Germany Tableau (left, bottom). The Great Britain Tableau survives today in a modified form at Circus World Museum in Baraboo. ALBERT BODE GIFT; CWM

wagon ($1,425) to be used in the cathedral scene in "Joan of Arc," United States and Great Britain Tableau wagons ($1,500 each), Russia and Germany Tableau wagons ($1,900 each), and a snake den wagon ($850). (The Ringlings paid about $1,700 on average for their big tableau wagons, while Barnum & Bailey forked out about $3,333 for each of their tableau wagons.) Additionally, the Ringlings ordered five flatbed wagons that would represent Egypt, France, India, Persia, and Spain and four cages (hippo den, paradise cage, rhino den, and lion cage) from the Moellers in Baraboo. The carvings on these wagons were created by the Milwaukee Ornamental Carving Company.[13]

The Brothers received a letter from Hagenbeck's, the German animal dealer, telling them which animals Barnum & Bailey had ordered for the 1903 season and what new animals the Ringlings should consider purchasing in order to compete.[14]

For the 1903 season the Ringlings promoted their show as "Ringling Brothers World's Greatest Shows and the Libretto of the Sublime Spectacle Jerusalem and the

Crusades." The new "Jerusalem and the Crusades" act would, they hoped, compete not only with Barnum & Bailey and other circuses but also with vaudeville, which had become extremely popular and successful.[15] The new pageant would include a ballet troupe of ninety-five young women, making this the Ringlings' largest circus yet. Now the Brothers could squelch the critics who said they were in a rut and repeating what they had always done.

The show opened with a three-week stand in Chicago. The spectacle paid off. The boys turned away audiences for fourteen of the sixteen days.[16] The 1903 route book includes this comment: "[T]he Jerusalem spectacular was the crowning feature . . . [T]he notices and criticisms in the papers were of the kind that make a circus man forget his troubles and feel at peace with the world."[17]

The first stop after Chicago was South Bend, Indiana, and then they traveled east and up into Ontario, Canada. A reporter for the Canton, Ohio, paper wrote:

> That old saying, "There's nothing new under the sun" is utterly disproved in Ringling Brothers' colossal circus, menagerie and hippodrome which exhibits in Canton, Thursday, May 21st. The Ringling Brothers have millions of dollars invested in their stupendous enterprise, and in addition to the most complete and startling arenic performance in the world, which introduces all the marvels of the present age, the five famous brothers present this year, on a scale of grandeur and magnificence never before attempted, a gorgeous spectacular production of Jerusalem and the Crusades.[18]

It was a laudatory piece to be sure, and one wonders how many of these words were written by Alf T. Ringling or one of his press agents and presented to the paper in a tidy package, a common practice. Nonetheless, the papers printed the statements.

After Canada, it was back to the Midwest. The worst storm of the season occurred in Springfield, Illinois. The sky was darkening as evening customers filed into the Big Top by the thousands. Shortly after the Jerusalem spectacle concluded, the storm struck. Wind pummeled the tent, lightning flashed, and thunder shook the ground. The thousands inside the tent began to panic and surge toward the door. Charles Ringling took charge, telling people, "It's more dangerous outside, please take your seats." Some did, but many did not. The band continued to play, as the nervous customers awaited the worst.

Meanwhile, the canvas crew outside was working frantically. They took down the menagerie, cook tent, and horse tents, but not before the wind snapped one of the menagerie tent poles. Then workers quickly attached extra guy ropes to the Big Top, and it remained standing. To keep the audience's mind off the storm, one performer volunteered to do her bareback act. The storm passed without further incident. It was a night that everyone would long remember.[19]

For the 1903 season the Ringlings debuted the spectacle "Jerusalem and the Crusades," in part an attempt to compete with vaudeville. The new spectacle was hugely popular. COURIER COLLECTION, CWM

Elephant Training

New elephant acts were perfected during the winter months in Baraboo. PRINT COLLECTION, CWM

At the turn of the century, the training of elephants began with physical conditioning. Pearl Souder, the Ringlings' superintendent of elephants, explained:

> Elephants when we first get them are just like men who do not exercise. . . . Their muscles are soft and flabby. . . . We want them to stand on their heads, balance on their fore-legs and do various other stunts that are wonderful for elephants, but before educating them we [condition them]. We take a green elephant and give it a thorough physical culture course. First we walk it for miles a day, and then we induce it to run. Exercise of this kind takes the kinks out of the legs and hardens the flesh.

Souder related how trainers used well-trained elephants to assist in the training of novices. Using ropes, trainers helped the new elephant rest its front legs on the back of the trained elephant; from there, again with help from ropes, the new elephant would stand on its head. After a few tries, the elephant's muscles became hardened, and the tricks became easier. "Week after week and month after month the training continues until we have a herd of real athletic animals."[1]

Animal trainer Jorge Barreda, who has worked for Circus World Museum, described modern elephant training:

> The first thing you do is to teach them to pick their feet up. Touch the back of the foot, pick

(continued on page 110)

Elephant Training

(continued from page 109)

the foot up, and say "foot." You start talking to the elephant. Elephants are naturally capable of everything they do in a performance. Elephants are very intelligent and have a huge memory bank. The old saying "An elephant never forgets" is true.

You have shy elephants and some that are tougher and more challenging. It's a matter of repeating over and over again. Once the elephant understands you want it to pick up its foot, then it does it automatically by command. So you keep repeating the task you want done. You work on all the feet, constantly repeating. When they have learned a trick, you give them a carrot treat. Elephants love carrots.

The next thing is to walk the elephant by your side. We put collars on ours at first. We would hold on to the collar and walk alongside the animal. You want the elephant to walk forward when you say "move out." You say "back up," and the elephant backs up. It is important to have the elephant stay with you when you are walking and not run away.

When walking, you teach the elephants to stay behind each other. Some trainers teach them to hold the tail of the elephant in front [of them] with their trunk. You teach them that by using a stick at first, having them put their trunk around the stick. When they do it, you say, "good" and give them a treat. There are films of wild African elephants doing this, so it is a natural thing.

The next level of trick is getting them to stand on a tub—first two feet, and then all four feet. Some elephants with treats do it quickly; one of my elephants took almost two months [to learn this trick]. For her we first buried the tub so it was only six inches off the ground. Slowly we raised the tub. Now she is fine [with the trick]. She is very timid and shy.

After they are comfortable standing on a tub, we teach them to back up to the tub and sit on it. Then we teach the elephant to pick up its front feet while it's sitting on the tub. These are not unnatural positions. Watch them playing in the mud—they will often sit on their behinds. They will also stand on their hind legs to reach high branches in trees. About everything we teach them, they do in the wild. It's a matter of communication [getting them to understand what we want them to do]. . . .

Most people in circuses have used Asian elephants. There were often one or two African elephants with a show, but most were Asian. Asian elephants are easier to work with. They are a little less nervous, a little more tolerant, but not as smart as the African elephant. The African elephant is taller; the Asian elephant is stockier and heavier.[2]

NOTES

1. *Columbus (Ohio) Dispatch*, May 10, 1903.
2. Jorge Barreda, interview by the author, Baraboo, Wisconsin, September 12, 2001.

Even though the circus showed in a new town almost every day, there was a considerable tedium associated with doing the same tasks day after day, with only a Sunday respite. The Brothers were well aware of this, and they sometimes provided interesting opportunities for employees during their days off. For instance, when the show played in Burlington, Iowa, on July 13, the circus cars were spotted on a levee adjacent to the Mississippi River. A route book entry states:

> Seeing a tug and barge at anchor, Mr. Charles Ringling engaged it and invited the weary troopers to take a trip down the river. Following an early dinner, the show folks clambered aboard the river craft and floated down with the current, singing and dancing just like a group of merry children. The impromptu affair was very enjoyable and served to pass away several hours that otherwise would have been tiresome ones.[20]

While in Colorado Springs, many of Ringling employees climbed Pike's Peak and the Garden of the Gods.

The Brothers were confident enough in their department superintendents that they often took extended trips away from the circus. The 1903 route book notes that "Mr. and Mrs. Al Ringling returned to the show here [Denver] and will make the western tour. They have been up north angling and tell some interesting stories of the game fish they hooked."[21]

Business continued to boom for the show as it moved west. "To write big business at every stand and in every story becomes monotonous, but it's the truth just the same. Phenomenal business has been the Ringlings' since the opening day in Chicago, and as the west is very prosperous, it bids fair to continue to make the present season the best financially the Ringlings have ever had."[22]

Of course, the 1903 show also had its share of problems. While the circus was unloading in Youngstown, Ohio, on May 20, a horse kicked one of the zebras and broke its neck, killing the animal. The zebra's carcass was sold to the local butcher, who had the skin tanned and prepared as a rug.[23]

In Ogden, Utah, a "tramp" carrying a .44-caliber pistol shot one of the train's watchmen in the arm. (The watchman survived.) Then in Boise, Idaho, the roof of an elephant car caught fire; elephant superintendent Pearl Souder sounded the alarm, and the elephant men leaped from their bunks, formed a bucket line from the locomotive tender (a railroad car attached to the locomotive that contained coal and water for the engine), and soon had the fire out.[24]

In Port Huron, Michigan, in June, there was a runaway during the circus parade. According to the *Detroit Free Press*:

As the procession was turning onto Military Street off Union some of the horses attached to the band coach . . . drawn by a team of sixteen, became unmanageable
and started a stampede. The horses and coach went down the street at a mad gallop,
defying the efforts of the driver to bring the frightened steeds under control, and
they were not stopped until one of the wheelhorses and two out of the middle had
fallen and were being dragged along on the pavement. They were finally halted just
north of Pine Street, having gone four blocks along a crowded thoroughfare. E. B.
Henderson, one of the bandsmen jumped from the coach and suffered a broken
limb.[25]

The 1903 show played Washington State to huge audiences and then headed south
to California and an eight-day stand in San Francisco with turn-away audiences. The
show lot was in such tight quarters that when workers put up the Big Top, they had to
drive stakes in the backyards of nearby homes and pass the ropes though holes cut in the
fences.[26]

The Ringlings moved on to the Southwest and then closed in Malden, Missouri, on
November 6. The *Baraboo News Republic* reported that "the five Ringling brothers each
pocketed $50,000 from the profits of the past season. The season just closed is said to be
the best they ever had."[27]

Despite the Ringlings' concerns, the Barnum & Bailey Circus did not prove to be a
great problem in 1903. Barnum & Bailey was clearly not the show it had been before
leaving for Europe five years earlier. It had added several expensive parade wagons to its
inventory, presented an exceptional street parade, and offered an outstanding Big Top
show, but its infrastructure was worn and tired. According to historian Fred Dahlinger,
"It was a bust. The show was too heavy to move quickly; they missed parades and, worst
of all, performances; and the train and baggage wagons were in tough shape."[28]

Despite its tremendous growth and huge staff, the Ringlings' circus continued to
maintain its reputation as a clean, family-oriented show. As a reporter for the *Baraboo
Evening News* proclaimed:

Absolutely no profanity is permitted on the grounds and the use of an oath is considered sufficient grounds for discharge. Many of the men are active Christian
workers, and next year a minister of the gospel will be a part of the circus organization who will hold service twice on Sunday in the great tented city. The leading
clown is a religious crank. He is a wealthy farmer and his home is in South Dakota.
He goes with the show in summer and lives at home in the winter. Many of the others performers and some of the clowns are members of leading churches and
among the employees are a number of college graduates and men wealthy enough
to retire who do this work merely as a diversion. It is the cleanest show that travels
and no hangers on will be permitted for a moment.[29]

(Of course, no circus, not even the Ringlings', was that lily white; this piece was most likely penned by a Ringling press agent.)

The Barnum & Bailey Circus was also an upright show, but according to circus historian Richard J. Reynolds III, "Bailey just didn't trumpet it like the Ringlings did. . . . New Yorkers and other sophisticated easterners were probably blasé about the matter whereas it would have been a big deal to the God-fearing and righteous folks of mid-America where the Ringlings focused."[30]

By the end of the 1903 season, the Ringlings had clearly and undeniably reached the pinnacle of the circus world. Their main rival, Barnum & Bailey, had lost its competitive edge. If the Ringlings kept their customers' wishes always in mind and updated their show, they would continue to prosper.

Keeping the Lead: 1904–1905

"The announcement that the Ringling Brothers had bought a one-half interest in the Forepaugh-Sells Bros. Circus came as a surprise to a number of circus men."[1]

The Ringlings would take their enormously successful Jerusalem spectacle on the road for the second year in 1904, and they hoped for another overwhelming response. A 1904 display ad proclaimed: "Ringling Bros. World's Greatest Shows. Now added without any addition in price to the biggest show on earth, depicting with historical accuracy and truth the trials and triumphs of the delivery of Jerusalem from the Saracens by the Crusaders."[2] Another ad stated that, because of all the equipment and performers needed for the Jerusalem show, "[a]bsolutely an additional train of cars [an earlier report said fifteen cars] is required to carry the scenery, wardrobes, armors, war implements, accessories and people of the newly added and enormously grand spectacle of Jerusalem and the Crusades."[3] In another ad they claimed to have twelve hundred cast members for the spectacle, including three hundred dancing girls, two hundred chorus singers, fifty musicians, and a sixty-eight-stop pipe organ.[4]

The show opened March 30 in Chicago and played there until April 20. Then the show moved west, with dates in Illinois and St. Louis, and then east and into Canada before heading to the West Coast.

News reports continued to applaud the Jerusalem show. A Newark, Ohio, newspaper declared:

This circus is the standard of the world, more than twice as big as any other, and must be copied by all that see [sic] success. Last year it was thought to have reached the climax of size and inventive genius, but this season's display proves the idea to have been fallacious. Not only are there a greater number of imported ring features, and startling home creations, including the spectacular production of Jerusalem and the Crusades, but all the other departments of the show life—the menagerie, aquarium and horse fair—have enlarged nearly double.[5]

New ring acts also attracted attention. One act that left people gasping was called "Looping the Gap." With the circus band playing slow music, performer Walter Lowe entered the ring and carefully examined his special bicycle. Al Ringling shouted, "Are you ready?" Lowe nodded his head. A great hush came over the audience. Lowe and his bike rolled down a steep incline, rapidly gaining speed, and then flew across the gap of several yards to alight on another ramp. The crowd cheered and clapped. Surviving the leap, Lowe stood next to his bicycle bowing and smiling.[6]

A new horse act was another crowd pleaser. "The three Hobsons have developed the bare-back riding act, and three of them ride one horse, ending the performance with a concerted leap from the ground to the back of the galloping animal."[7]

Crowds across the country continued to flock to the Ringling Brothers show. A reporter for the *Columbus (Ohio) Dispatch* wrote, "Truly, there were 'masses' and 'classes' and classes in masses present when the circus arrived early in the morning over the Big Four from Springfield. The train consisted of four sections, in all numbering 80 cars."[8]

The Ringlings caused some controversy when they played in Duluth, Minnesota, on July 4. The city had planned a big Fourth of July celebration, and when officials learned the Ringlings would be in town that day, they knew their own gathering would fizzle and have little participation. Headlines in the local paper proclaimed, "Too Much Circus, Fourth of July Celebration is Likely to Be Dropped. Many of those on the committee are of the opinion that it would be foolhardy to go to great trouble and expense in arranging for a big celebration when it is known that the circus will be here for the national celebration."[9]

The show closed in Grenada, Mississippi, on November 18 and headed back to winter quarters in Baraboo. Space in Baraboo for the ever-growing circus was an ongoing concern, and that fall the boys had hired contractor Carl Isenberg to construct a new horse barn on Water Street. It was 56 feet wide and 120 feet long and would house about one hundred horses. The building cost $4,500.[10]

Then in January 1905, big news shook the circus world: the Forepaugh-Sells Circus, headquartered in Sellsville (Columbus, Ohio), would be sold at auction.

James A. Bailey, of Barnum & Bailey, who already owned one-fourth of Forepaugh-Sells, bought the rest of the show for $150,000 at auction. After the sale, Bailey sold half of the Forepaugh-Sells show to the Ringlings. The two owners agreed that the circus would continue under its present name, Forepaugh-Sells. When asked if there would be changes, Otto Ringling replied, "Oh, yes. There will be a great many. In the first place we expect to improve the circus and put in an increased menagerie. . . . We will not retain all of the present employees."[11]

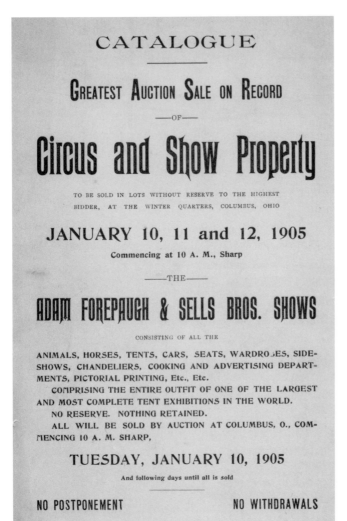

Much to the surprise of many in the circus world, the famous Forepaugh-Sells Circus was put up for auction in January 1905. James Bailey, who already owned one-fourth of the show, bought the remaining three-quarters at the auction. He then sold half of Forepaugh-Sells to the Ringling Brothers. RICHARD E. AND ALBERT CONOVER COLLECTION, CWM

While the owners of the big circuses were in fierce competition, they were also businessmen who knew when to cooperate. The Ringlings were reaching the pinnacle of their success, while Barnum & Bailey was in decline. Becoming partners in the Forepaugh-Sells Circus would allow the Ringlings to keep growing. And the aging James Bailey was assured that the Ringlings would take an active role in managing the Forepaugh-Sells show. It looked like a winning move for both big circuses. Together, the Ringlings and Barnum & Bailey decided to keep the Forepaugh-Sells show intact, including its name, since it had considerable name recognition and a good reputation. Most of the public would have no idea that Forepaugh-Sells was really owned by Barnum & Bailey and the Ringling Brothers.

Henry Ringling (along with a representative of the ailing James Bailey) would manage the Forepaugh-Sells show. He and Otto spent considerable time during winter 1905 in Columbus, Ohio, preparing the Forepaugh-Sells show for the summer season.

James Bailey and Otto Ringling discussed the 1905 dates and locations for the three shows. The *Duluth Herald* reported:

> Territory is now being mapped out for the three circuses, and from present arrangements the Barnum & Bailey circus will open in Madison Square Garden the last week of March; the Forepaugh-Sells Brothers circus [will open] in Columbus, and the Ringling Brothers [will open] in the Chicago Coliseum April 1. The Barnum circus will work west, the Ringling circus east, and the Forepaugh-Sells Bros' circus North and South.[12]

Before the Forepaugh-Sells purchase, James Bailey and the Ringlings had signed an agreement "for the purpose of promoting the mutual interests of these respective shows" on November 1, 1904, for the 1905 season. Some of the provisions of the agreement included the following:

> That the route of said shows shall be determined by a division of territory east, west, north and south, alternating each year during the life of this agreement as follows: That the city of Greater New York is to be considered the exclusive territory of the Barnum and Bailey Shows and that Messrs Ringling Brothers are to have the City of Chicago as their exclusive right of exhibition.[13]

Upon acquiring Forepaugh-Sells, they expanded this 1904 agreement.

The new year brought a flurry of activity for the Ringlings as they hustled to organize two major circuses for the 1905 season. Letters went from Baraboo to Columbus, Ohio, on a variety of topics. As always, Al and Otto were sticklers for detail, and they continued their hands-on approach to management. The following letters, all directed to Henry, are good examples of their attention to the minutest considerations.

Al Ringling wrote detailed suggestions about riding gear for two of the Forepaugh-Sells performers:

> We suggest one to ride in side saddle with English hunting dress or riding habit; that would be Miss Ida Miaco. The other to ride astride with divided skirt, who is Miss Mamie Kline. Regarding dresses for them, we have none here neither have we ordered same. Perhaps you have dresses there for them but hardly think so. You can see Mr. Gorman or Fred Schafer. They will know. If they have none would suggest you order dress or riding habit for Ida Miaco, black skirt, red waist and black velvet jockey or hunting cap. You could have this made at Lilly and Company. Regarding Miss Kline's dress—she is in Columbus. You could have Gorman see her regarding same. Think it would look nice to have one lady in side saddle and the other astride. Ida Miaco has never ridden astride but I think Miss Kline has. Will mail you Ida Miaco's measurements. Yours, Al.[14]

Otto bought twenty-three horses in March from Abe Klee and Son in Chicago for $275 each, including shipment to Columbus. He paid $50 less than he would have paid on the Columbus market. He wrote to Henry:

> They are fine ones. The difference $50.00 in price is very much in favor of buying them here in preference to the Columbus horses. . . . I enclose you herewith bill for the horses. I have signed a draft for the amount of $6,325 which you will pay when presented. I have told them to draw on you through your bank in Columbus. Otto.[15]

Music in the Ringlings' Show

Historian and circus music authority Fred Dahlinger has written that "[t]he most emotionally stirring component of the circus experience is the music. Nothing evokes the elegance, spectacle and grandeur of the big top better

For many people, especially those from farms and small towns, the circus concert was their first opportunity to hear first-class music played by top-notch musicians. Music was also important when things went wrong—when a windstorm threatened to blow down the tent, a performer was injured, or some other calamity occurred. When adversity struck, the band immediately began playing, and the clowns rushed in. It was a way to calm and distract an agitated audience.

The Ringlings recognized music's importance to their show and spent time and money expanding their musical offerings. In 1902 the Ringling Brothers concert band, under the direction of George Ganweiler, had twenty-seven members. In 1903

The Ringlings employed a huge number of musicians, and many of the circus acts and shows, such as the sideshow, had their own bands. Print Collection, CWM

than the galops, waltzes, marches and other specialized compositions which descriptively augment the live action in the ring."[1]

Along with its integral part in the circus performance, music played several other roles. Every circus parade featured strikingly dressed musicians riding on gaily decorated bandwagons pulled by high-stepping horses. The Ringlings also offered an hour-long concert for the public before the big show began, including selections from Schubert, Bach, Verdi, Sousa, Wagner, Mendelssohn, Rossini, and others.[2]

The Ringlings ordered a new pipe organ wagon for the 1903 season. Print Collection, CWM

Music in the Ringlings' Show

The talented musicians in the Ringlings' mounted parade band had to both play their instruments and handle their horses.
PRINT COLLECTION, CWM

the concert band expanded to thirty-eight members, and in 1904 it increased to fifty members.

Prior to the 1903 season, the Ringlings ordered a new pipe organ from the George Kilgen and Son pipe organ company of St. Louis. The organ was to have four keyboards and would operate by an "automobile steam engine, with coal oil for fuel, of ample power to blow the organ." Kilgen and Son promised to "build and deliver the organ at Baraboo, Wisconsin on or before April 1, 1903

and set up the wagon ready for use for the sum of $4,000.00."[3]

NOTES

1. Souvenir Program, Circus World Museum, 1995, CWM.
2. *The Circus: A Route Book of Ringling Bros.' World's Greatest Shows, Season 1902* (Chicago: Central Printing and Engraving, 1902), p. 12; *The Circus Annual: A Route Book of Ringling Brothers' World's Greatest Shows, Season 1903*, p. 54.
3. Charles G. Kilgen to Ringling Brothers, October 1, 1902, Fred Pfening III, private collection, Columbus, Ohio.

Otto also sent Henry a letter with a bill from Moeller & Sons in Baraboo. The Moeller establishment had long been building and repairing wagons for the Ringling Brothers, and now they were also doing some painting and repairing of Forepaugh-Sells wagons. Otto also instructed Henry about how to order blank paychecks for the working men:

> If you order the workingmen's pay checks, all you will have to do is to have the printers leave the heads off [the five Ringling Brothers images] and change the name. We have them put up in books of 50 each but you can have them in books of 50 or 100, just as you may decide. The first check will be dated as follows: May 6th for week ending April 29th. Number consecutively from No. 1 up. Have date of the last one dated November 18th. Otto.[16]

The Forepaugh-Sells show was still short of horses. On March 20 Otto wrote to Henry, "We have sent Delavan [Spencer Alexander, the boss hostler] to St. Louis to buy 15 Hippodrome horses. He will ship them to Columbus and he will pay for them by signing a draft on the Forepaugh-Sells Show for the amount which you will pay when presented."[17]

In that same letter, Otto told Henry that they were shipping to Henry the Parson concession wagon and a tableau wagon on a flatcar. He wrote that Henry should pay the freight and charge half of it to the Parsons. The paint shop in Baraboo had apparently planned to paint the Parson's concession wagon, but Otto wrote, "If we get time we'll paint his wagon if not you will paint it and charge to Parsons. Number eight [tableau wagon] is all painted and ready."

Although the Parson brothers had held the candy and lemonade concession at the Ringling Brothers Circus for many years, from the tone of Otto's letters he seemed less than pleased with the arrangement. In a March 25 letter to Henry, Otto wrote:

> I enclose the key for Parsons' candy wagon. . . . On account of taking so many out of our paint shop to paint the Forepaugh cars, we did not get time to paint Parson wagon. You do so and charge him. We are shipping No. 8 today and the Candy Wagon. Charge one-half of freight to Parsons. Otto.[18]

After the purchase of their half of Forepaugh-Sells, buying additional horses, and sprucing up that show as well as keeping their own huge show in top-notch form, the Ringlings were cash poor. Bank records from the Bank of Baraboo indicate that they took out three loans in the winter of 1905, one for $30,000 on March 3, another for $20,000 on April 3, and a third for $20,000 on April 20, all at 5 percent interest. The Ringlings paid off all three loans before the end of May 1905 with early-season receipts.[19]

Under Henry Ringling's management and with Otto's careful and detailed oversight, the Forepaugh-Sells show opened in Columbus, Ohio, on April 22, 1905. As the

Brothers had agreed with James Bailey, Forepaugh-Sells showed primarily in the Midwest and Texas.

Meanwhile, the big Ringling Brothers show opened as usual in Chicago and played there April 8 to April 23 before heading east, back to the Midwest, and then south. Following their success with the Jerusalem spectacle the past two years, the Ringlings mounted an even more elaborate and expensive stage show for 1905, "The Field of the Cloth of Gold." Their ads shouted:

> The most lavish, extravagant, largest, costliest amusement feature ever devised. 1200 characters, 300 dancing girls, a chorus of 200 voices, 2,500 magnificent costumes. A whole train load of armor, ancient weapons, paraphernalia, banners,

Sacred Ox Goes on Rampage

In late fall 1905, before the Ringling Brothers' show returned to winter quarters, there was excitement at the Case farm in Baraboo, where some of the animals that were not on tour were kept. The November 1, 1905, issue of the *Baraboo Evening News* included this headline: "Sacred Ox Makes a Wild Dash for Harrison Case, Jr." The story of excitement on Lynn Avenue followed:

> Ringling Bros.' sacred ox tried to take a toss out of Harrison Case, Jr. yesterday afternoon and gave him an experience that he would not care to have repeated every cold day. Harrison was loading dirt for his father near Hitchcock Street when his father called to him from across the meadow to come to him. Harrison started and was about half way across when his father motioned him back, and looking saw the ox, which had escaped from its pen at the Ringling farm on Lynn Avenue, coming full tilt. He ran for the wagon which he reached a fraction of a second ahead of the bull which charged the wagon but found it too heavy to overthrow. The bull backed off, made a survey and charged again, but succeeded only in throwing off some of the dump boards. By the time the third charge was made Harrison concluded it was capture the ox or be killed, so while the animal amused itself with tossing the boards and a duck coat into the air, Harrison slipped to the ground and succeeded in getting two fingers into the iron ring in the bull's nose.
>
> There was a fierce struggle in which the ox nearly tore him loose from his hold on the wagon, but happily Harrison Sr. now appeared on horseback and armed with a pitchfork, ready to battle as in war days when a member of the Third cavalry. They succeeded in passing a strap through the ring and then Harrison Jr. held the animal for another half hour while his father went to the barn got a team and heavy chain and returned. The absence of his coat all this time, subjected to the biting cold, did not improve matters very much.
>
> Together they brought the animal to the Ringling barns where he was put behind the bars in winter quarters. It was a lucky escape and a good capture.[1]

NOTES

1. *Baraboo (Wisconsin) Evening News*, November 1, 1905.

golden hangings, scenery and accessories. A whole city of people. Half a thousand gorgeously trapped horses. A dazzling picture of beauty, life, color and motion. The grandest spectacle ever devised.[20]

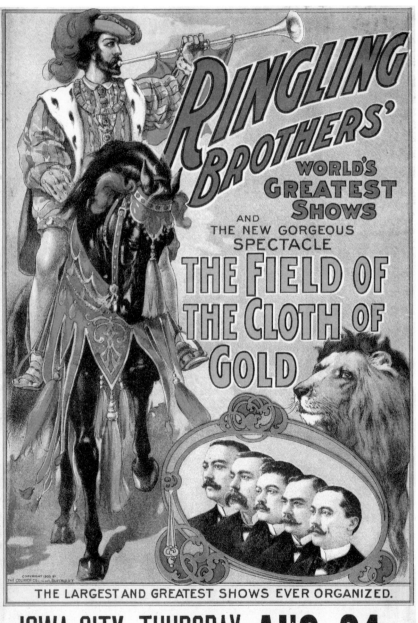

THE LARGEST AND GREATEST SHOWS EVER ORGANIZED.

IOWA CITY, THURSDAY, AUG. 24

While the Brothers' advertising clearly exaggerated the size and splendor of their show, there was no denying that Ringlingville had grown from a small town on the move to an elaborate, sophisticated, portable city of prestige and prominence.

But with all its power and position, the show was still at the mercy of the weather. While they were in Maryville, Missouri, on September 18, a storm struck, blowing down the Big Top with the performance in progress. About five thousand people were attending the show; three people were killed and many were severely injured. "The animal cages containing lions, leopards and tigers were overturned and the roars of the beasts added to the panic that ensued."[21]

In 1905 the Ringlings advertised their new spectacle, "The Field of the Cloth of Gold," as "the grandest spectacle ever devised." COURIER COLLECTION, CWM

By 1905 the Ringling circus parade was a truly spectacular event, attracting thousands of people. Here a twenty-four-horse hitch pulls the Swan bandwagon in the 1905 parade in Oneonta, New York. Print Collection, CWM

The Mechanical Stake-Driver

The Ringlings began using a mechanical stake-driver in 1904. It was powered by a gasoline engine and pulled by horses from location to location. Tent stakes were kept in the box on the wagon. Photo by Steve Albasing; Albasing Collection, CWM

rain. And the sheer volume of stakes to be driven—more than a thousand for the Ringling Brothers show in the early 1900s—made a mechanical stake-driver a welcome invention.

George Heiser, a long-time Ringling employee, wrote to the Ringling Brothers on January 9, 1904: "I have an idea for a machine that will drive stakes. . . . I would be pleased to go to Baraboo and explain it to you if you could send transportation."[1]

Heiser's invention proved to be a workable alterna-tive to strong young men wielding sledgehammers. Heiser applied for a patent on May 20, 1904. An ad for the machine proclaimed that the stake-driver would do the work of fifteen men. "Machine Strikes 65 blows a minute."[2]

By mid-July 1904 the Ringlings were using the stake-driver. According to a Ringling memo, it was a big labor saver:

Traditionally, husky farm boys who "ran off with the circus" hammered the hundreds of stakes necessary to guy the ropes for the Ringling tents. Stake driving was tedious work and required skill and dexterity as four, six, or eight men worked in a syncopated team, each man taking a turn hitting a four-foot-long wooden stake until it was pounded home.

Over time this rhythmic pounding of stakes became one of the traditions of the circus, and bystanders would gather to watch in awe as the crews worked to erect the tents on circus day. There were some attempts to develop mechanical stake-drivers, but for most circus people the response was "why bother when we can get plenty of cheap help" to do the work. But stake driving was also extremely hard work—especially when the ground was hard, the weather was hot, or it was pouring

The mechanical stake driver, a novel invention, is one of the interesting adjuncts of the big show this year. It is a sort of baby pile driver, and is perched upon a wagon which is also used for carry-ing the stakes. The apparatus is driven around the grounds, is operated by a four horse power gaso-line motor, which, together with one man, drives

The Mechanical Stake-Driver

all the stakes of the big shops, restaurants, cook tents, horse tents, dressing rooms, menageries, and all the smaller tents, and usually completes half the circle of the big tent before the sledge gangs are ready to perform their share of the stake driving.[3]

The Heiser stake-driver was not without problems. It took several years before the design was perfected, which may be why Heiser has received essentially no credit for its invention. Others also worked on mechanical stake-drivers, including Ringling employee Charles

Andress, who invented a driver that worked with compressed air. Some writers have credited Andress with inventing the device, ignoring George Heiser's contributions.

NOTES

1. George H. Heiser to Ringling Brothers, January 9, 1904, CWM.
2. Fred Dahlinger Jr., "The Circus Stake Driver: The Best, Simplest, and Most Economical Machine Ever Invented," *Bandwagon*, January–February 1999, p. 11.
3. Ibid.

Such accidents were always a risk for circus audiences, and until the turn of the century, people were usually satisfied in such instances when a Ringling employee known as "the Fixer" quickly offered them a cash settlement and had them sign a statement of release. Early in the 1900s, however, circus patrons who were injured or had their belongings damaged began seeking legal assistance. Considerable litigation followed the Maryville incident. The Ringlings hired John M. Kelley, a Wisconsin attorney and Portage, Wisconsin, native, to handle the lawsuits. According to circus historian Fred Pfening III, Kelley "did such a good job that they hired him full time. He was the first lawyer on their payroll; before that they used outside attorneys."[22]

The 1905 Ringling show closed in Meridian, Mississippi, on November 25 and then rumbled back to Baraboo for the winter. The Forepaugh-Sells show closed in Stuttgart, Arkansas, on November 23 and headed for winter quarters in Columbus, Ohio.

At the start of 1904, it appeared the Ringlings' options for keeping the lead among circuses were running out. They had increased the size of their circus about as much as they could without making it difficult for many smaller towns and cities to accommodate them. But by purchasing half of the Forepaugh-Sells show and mounting an even more extravagant spectacle with their main show, the Ringlings continued to increase their revenues and keep the lead. In 1906 they would discover opportunities to grow even larger.

Becoming Even Larger: 1906–1907

"The acquisition of the Barnum and Bailey properties has not been particularly sought after by the Ringling Brothers, but is simply the inevitable result of a superior fitness on their part, which it has not been possible for others to compete with."[1]

With their 1905 purchase of half of the Forepaugh-Sells show, the Ringlings again proved they were determined to keep expanding their circus. Perhaps this drive to keep growing resulted from a childhood spent in poverty. Perhaps it grew out of their competitive nature. Or maybe the Brothers simply felt as businessmen that there was no such thing as standing still: to succeed, they had to grow.

The Ringlings had once again signed a noncompete agreement with Barnum & Bailey for the 1906 season, giving Barnum & Bailey exclusive rights to show in Canada "and all of the southern states and territory lying east of the Mississippi River and South of the Ohio River, also all of the Eastern and New England States lying east of the Eastern Ohio State line except Pennsylvania."[2] The Ringlings would take their namesake show to Pennsylvania, the Midwest, and the South; the Forepaugh-Sells show would play the Midwest and the West.

The Ringling Brothers' main show opened April 5 in Chicago. Their ads claimed the show now had 650 horses, 1,280 people, 85 railroad cars, and daily expenses of $7,400.[3] The show took in $98,634.49 in gross receipts for twenty days in Chicago, an average of $4,933 each day. For the entire season (196 days), average daily gross receipts for the Ringlings' namesake show were $6,423.47.[4]

In truth, their average daily expenses could not have been anywhere near $7,400. If their expenses were that high, they would have lost money every day they were on the road. Just the opposite was true: they made money, and lots of it.

In mid-April 1906 the Ringlings faced another opportunity for incredible growth. James Bailey of the Barnum & Bailey Circus died on April 11. Bailey's widow, Ruth Louisa Bailey, sold Bailey's Forepaugh-Sells interest to the Ringlings for $100,000. The terms of the sale, which became official on June 5, 1906, allowed the Ringlings to pay $10,000 at the time of signing and additional amounts through August 1906.[5] The Ringlings now owned two huge circuses.

As usual, the Ringlings' namesake show was well received nearly everywhere it played. In August in Appleton, Wisconsin, a reporter wrote: "It was estimated that 20,000 people witnessed the show this morning and fully 12,000 people are witnessing the performance this afternoon, while at least 8,000 will see it to tonight, and everyone will say it is truly, 'the greatest show on earth.'"[6]

Some merchants tried to tie their reputations to the Ringlings' success. A feed dealer in Newark, Ohio, ran this ad in the local paper:

> Ringling Bros. Circus has purchased from C. S. Brown the feed man, 12,000 pounds of hay, 10,000 pounds of straw, 6,400 pounds of oats, 800 pounds of bran. Quality, fair prices and prompt delivery secures circus contracts for us—no matter how small may be your order you will receive the same attention. Give us a trial. C. S. Brown Feed Store.[7]

But not all was grand and glorious. Tragedy struck the circus while playing in Aurora, Illinois, on June 29. Frank Parson, manager of the candy and lemonade concession, wrote, "Bad storm struck us at 3 p.m., just as the elephant act was on. [The elephants] ran and people stampeded. Two people killed and several hurt. One candy butcher struck in the back by a pole. Tents did not go down but tore bad."[8]

A local newspaper reported the blow down and the terror that followed:

> The first gusts shook the canvas like a leaf and the next moment the center pole supporting it snapped near the top. Instantly the canvas sagged and the swaying of the guy ropes caused the hundreds of scantlings to swing about in the arena.
>
> Panic-stricken, the audience of 10,000 attempted to escape, but the women and children were unable to lift the canvas, which had become rain soaked and heavy. Egress was slow at the regular exits, and it was in the crush at these points that many were injured.
>
> Wild rumors that the whole menagerie had broken loose and was running the woods gained circulation and spread terror in several towns.[9]

No matter how large and successful a circus became, it couldn't outrun the weather. And while it was a rare exception that the tents did not go up on a scheduled show date, it happened several times in the 1906 season. In Sherman, Texas, on October 18, Frank Parson wrote, "Arrived here at 8:30 a.m. and it was raining and road to the lot was very

Employee Compensation, 1906

In 1906 the Ringlings' highest-paid performers received up to $350 a week. Thomas Cochran and his performing ostrich received $300 per week. As important as clowns were to the circus, their salaries did not approach those of name performers; longtime Ringling clown Jules Turnour received twenty dollars per week. (Turnour supplemented his income by being Ringlingville's postmaster).

In 1906 the ninety women classified as ballet performers were paid from seven to ten dollars a week. The ballet master, Professor Peri, earned forty dollars per week.[1]

The workingmen's ledger for 1906 listed 1,035 employees, but a large percentage of these did not work the whole season. For instance, of the 319 men listed as baggage horse men, 153 did not finish the season and were replaced with other workers. The Ringlings used a hold-back incentive in an effort to retain employees throughout the season. For example, baggage horse men's salary was on average fifteen to twenty-five dollars per month; the Ringlings would pay five dollars on payday and retain the remaining ten dollars until the end of the season. De-spite this incentive, only about 20 percent of the canvas-men (who had the backbreaking job of putting up and taking down tents every day, six days a week) worked the entire season from April to November. Some would work a few months; some would work a few days. It was grueling work in the best of weather, but rain and cold made the task miserable, as the men wallowed in the mud with freezing hands, slippery ropes, and unruly tent poles. Add wind to the mix, and putting up a tent was next to impossible.

Besides their salary, Ringling workers and performers received a bunk on the circus train and three meals a day in the cook tent. The value of three meals a day in 1906 was between forty-five and seventy-five cents (fifteen to twenty-five cents for each meal).[2] Many a country boy who "ran away with the circus" had never eaten so well.

NOTES

1. Ringling Brothers Performers Ledger, 1906, pp. 80–89, Pfening collection.
2. Candy Stand Book, Ringling Bros. Show, Season of 1906, Frank Parson, CWM, p. 82.

---

bad. No show. Just fed and layed here until night and went on to Bonham. It cleared in the afternoon."[10]

On November 17 at Little Rock, Arkansas, it "[r]ained hard all day. They put up everything but the rain kept up and it was so muddy they did not parade or show." Two days later, in Jonesboro, Arkansas, it "[w]as still raining and the lot was so muddy they just put up cook house and horse tents and did not try to show. Paid off the men and went home."[11]

Not all problems in 1906 were weather related. An altercation between two leopards while in Austin, Texas, on November 2 resulted in "such damage that one of the spotted attractions of the show went to the happy jungle." And a train wreck in Galveston, Texas, on November 5 demolished two cars and killed a horse.[12]

The Ringlings faced a string of problems in Duluth, Minnesota. After the Brothers paid the usual license fees to appear in that city, a city inspector found that the calliope had no steam boiler license, and the Ringlings were forced to pay another fee. Then the city sued the Ringlings for $1,000 for tearing up their "new macadam pavement" with their heavy circus wagons. "It was claimed by the city that the pavement was constructed to withstand all ordinary loads and traffic, but that the circus people drove over it with a large number of heavily loaded wagons with narrow tires. It is alleged that some of the loads were in excess of twenty tons."[13] The city held the Ringlings' Big Top tent as collateral until the lawsuit was settled. Finally, an agreement was reached, the Ringlings made a security deposit, and the circus was ready to pack up and leave for Superior, Wisconsin, the site of their next stand. As the Ringlings left the lot, the city's health inspector said the circus had left the park "covered with unsightly rubbish" and forced them to clean up the show grounds and the street in front before leaving.[14]

The Duluth experience had all the markings of a shakedown, a rather common occurrence on the road. Some city officials tried to get as much from the circus as they could. One way the circus handled the problem was to give certain city officials free tickets; this, too, was a problem, as the more free tickets that were handed out, the less room there was in the Big Top for paying customers.

Things weren't much better a few days later in Superior, just across a Lake Superior canal from Duluth. A Duluth newspaper reported:

> Ringling Brothers' circus has been sued in Superior because its heavily loaded wagons cut up the pavement in a number of places. Proceedings against the circus in that city were instituted yesterday when the city served summons on the proprietors to appear in court, July 20, and show cause why they should not repair the pavement or settle for damage done.[15]

The Ringlings were pleased to leave the shores of Lake Superior and be on their way to North Dakota, where fancy paved streets were still in the future.

The Ringling Brothers Circus closed its 1906 season in Pine Bluff, Arkansas, on October 16. The trip to Baraboo and winter quarters was uneventful except for the severe rains that had settled in the South. All of the equipment had to be loaded in the rain. While the circus was traveling between Madison and Baraboo, one of the old elephants died. A Baraboo newspaper reported, "She was an ancient animal said by Pearl Souder, a veritable encyclopedia on elephantology, to have been at least 80 or 90 years old [a considerable exaggeration as elephants seldom live beyond 50 years]. In her old age she had become petulant and testy, like some people."[16]

Some wag started a rumor that several menagerie animals escaped when the train arrived in Baraboo. The *Baraboo News* squelched the falsehood with these words: "The wild story that went the rounds of the press regarding the escape of ferocious beasts that afterwards infested the wilds of Juneau County, was a bungling piece of invention. There was not an escape nor an attempt at escape."[17]

Ringling Advertising

A 1901 Ringling ad proclaimed, "The only giraffe known to exist in the entire world. $20,000 was the price he cost. Not a million. Not a million times a million could buy another. He is the last, the only one, the single sole and lonely survivor of a once numerous race."[1] The actual cost of the giraffe was $4,042.65 ($3,462.95 to Carl Hagenbeck, the German animal dealer, plus $579.70 to the United States Express Company for shipping).[2]

Blatant hyperbole was but one of many marketing strategies used by the Ringling Brothers, who by 1900 had become masters of advertising. Their success in large measure depended on convincing thousands of people from near and far to see their circus, during good times and bad. Charles Ringling was in charge of advertising, and Alf T. was responsible for press relations.

Bill posters pasted multiple-sheet posters to the sides of buildings. The building owners were usually compensated with free circus tickets. Print Collection, CWM

Promoting a circus was a year-round effort. After the Ringlings returned to Baraboo each fall they immediately began planning marketing strategy for the coming season. By midwinter there was a flurry of activity in the advertising department at winter quarters. As soon as the Brothers knew which acts they would feature in the coming season, artists began creating the lithographs that would announce the show in vivid color. (From about 1880 to 1910 posted lithographs were the primary way that circuses advertised.)

Lithograph advertising paper was measured in sheets;

a single sheet was twenty-eight by forty-two inches, and larger posters were measured in terms of number of sheets. The lithographs could be quite detailed, because people riding in horse-drawn wagons or on horseback had time to read the content as they drove by. Red was the main color used in lithographs, expressing excitement and drawing attention. Lithographs included wonderful examples of exaggeration. Everything was bigger, heavier, the one and only, the smallest of the small, or the strangest of the strange. Large numbers of everything were proclaimed, from horses to elephants to the Ringling Brothers themselves, all lined up in a row.

Railroad circuses like the Ringling Brothers used railcars to distribute lithographs and other advertising material to communities several weeks before the circus arrived. In 1901 the Ringling show had three advance cars, also called advertising cars, and a "Special Brigade" car, whose purpose was dealing with competition. Gus Ringling served as manager of Advertising Car No. 1. Seventeen bill posters plus five lithographers and two programmers were assigned to Car No. 1, for a total of twenty-seven men. Tom Dailey managed Advertising Car No. 2, with Louis Knob as boss bill poster. Fifteen bill posters were assigned to Car No. 2. George W. Goodhart managed Advertising Car No. 3, with Joe H. Brown as boss bill poster and eleven more bill posters. In addition,

Ringling Advertising

The crew of the Special Brigade advertising car had the main purpose of confronting the advertising of competitive shows, making sure that Ringling posters and other advertising had not been defaced or removed. Sometimes broken noses and black eyes resulted when the men of the Special Brigade car challenged the men of a competing circus who had mutilated or covered Ringling advertising. PRINT COLLECTION, CWM

seven men were assigned to Car No. 3, with duties ranging from being in charge of lithographs and litho boards to handling banners and programs and making paste. All told, Advance Car No. 3 included twenty men. Finally, Special Brigade No. 4 was managed by W. H. Horton, with James E. Finnegan as boss bill poster and ten bill posters. Altogether, seventy-six men worked on the four advertising cars. Interestingly, these men worked as hard or harder than anyone associated with the circus, yet they never saw the Ringling show. By the time the show arrived in a town, they were from one to three weeks down the road, creating excitement and cranking up business.

A 1903 handwritten document states the duties of the Ringlings' advertising car manager:

> Make contacts for newspaper ads and supply newspaper with cuts and copy. Paste must be made at night. If have enough cans or barrels, can make two or 3 days supply paste at once. [Bill posters]

should telephone the livery man the hour they will arrive and when to have wagons ready to start for the country. Get as many hours in the country as possible. Manager must be sure to order [advance] car out early in morning by notifying station agent so in case of misunderstanding it can be adjusted and not lose a day.[3]

The railroad advance car became such an intrinsic part of the business that even after railroad circuses disappeared in the 1950s and the circus had become motorized, the trucks used by the advance were still called "advance cars."[4]

Each advance car was brightly painted silver or red, with large print proclaiming "Ringling Brothers, World's Greatest Shows." Advance cars were usually converted railroad baggage cars or passenger cars. Each one contained a small office for the manager, bunks for the crew, a boiler to cook paste, storage for wheat flour used in

(continued on page 132)

Ringling Advertising

(continued from page 131)

making paste, and piles of lithographs, banners, posters, and other advertising paraphernalia. The advertising cars were generally attached to the end of a regular passenger train. When the car arrived at the designated town, the train's engineer placed it on a side track to be hooked up again the following day for its trip to the next town.

Weeks before the arrival of the first advertising car, an advance man visited the town and made basic arrangements: securing a license for the show grounds and the parade, contracting for billboards, and ordering hay, straw, oats, wood shavings, coal, food for the cook tent, and meat for the lions and tigers (often from slaughtered broken-down horses). He also made sure of a ready source of water.

Imagine the effect on a small, rural, "nothing much happens here" community when it was invaded by circus bill posters. Their very presence in the community was itself an important kind of advertising. Advertising Car No. 1 usually arrived in a town three weeks before the circus's arrival. The bill posters fired up the boiler and soon had a cauldron of paste cooking, ready for other bill posters who had already rented teams at the local livery stable and set out on their routes in search of barns, fences, silos—anything on which they could paste a lithograph advertising the circus dates. Generally, there were country bill posters, some of whom ranged as far as forty miles on either side of the show town, and town bill posters, who pasted litho sheets on previously contracted billboards and the sides of town barns, livery stables, and stores. They placed posters in general store windows and barbershops, in hardware stores and blacksmith shops, in grist mills and harness shops. In every instance they asked for permission and usually exchanged free circus tickets for the privilege of pasting up a sign.

Bill posters had one of the most challenging jobs in the circus—and since they traveled several weeks ahead of the circus itself, they never got to see the show. PRINT COLLECTION, CWM

They carried contracts for the building owner to sign:

> I hereby agree to allow Ringling Bros. or their agents exclusive privilege to paste their bills on my [livery, store side, etc.] from this date until [the date of the circus], inclusive, the bills not to be covered up or defaced, and no other bills to be posted on said premises until after the date named above. In consideration of said privilege I have received an order for the admission of the number of persons as per coupon detached. . . . Signed (agent).[5]

The bill poster made a record of the agreement, how many tickets he gave out, and where the lithographs were placed. Later, a bill-posting manager, usually on horseback, did a spot check to make sure that bill posters had pasted signs where they said they had. If a poster had been torn down or, worse, covered over by one for

Ringling Advertising

There was great competition among circuses for advertising space; here signs for Buffalo Bill's Wild West and Pawnee Bill's Far East overlap those for the Ringling Brothers on a building in Manchester, New Hampshire, 1911. PRINT COLLECTION, CWM

(continued on page 134)

Ringling Advertising

(continued from page 133)

a competing circus, the person who received the free tickets would be denied admission to the show.

Just as circuses competed for audiences during the course of the season, bill posters competed for ad space. During the 1906 season the Ringlings often found themselves competing against The Carl Hagenbeck Greater Shows. The Janesville, Wisconsin, newspaper reported:

> According to former plans the Hagenbeck advertising car Number one arrived here today [June 1, 1906] . . . seventeen men were at work billing the city and surrounding country. . . . Though the Ringling show does not come until about fifteen days after the Hagenbeck circus it was necessary for the former's advance men to move quickly in order to secure facilities for a proper advertising campaign. Four [Ringling] billers . . . all of Chicago, arrived here at an early hour this morning. They called the same liveryman who was furnishing carriages to their rivals. They were out of bed at five o'clock and contracted for four rigs. These started out at six o'clock, just an hour before the Hagenbeck men began work. Very likely the Ringling agents secured the best and largest amount of billing space. This was bought at a high figure, while in some places it was bid for in competition. The Ringling men will continue their country work tomorrow and spend Sunday and Monday in the city. There is no doubt but that every available wall and fence will be hidden behind gaily colored bills and cloth and the decorations will be more profuse than when the Ringlings and Buffalo Bill carried on a similar fight several seasons ago.[6]

In the early 1900s circuses began tacking huge cloth

banners on the sides of buildings, usually high up. After the show the banners were removed and reused. The men who put up the banners, called "bannermen," wore coats and ties and were the highest paid of the bill posters.[7]

At day's end the bill-posting crew climbed back on Advertising Car No. 1, a passenger train backed up and coupled up with the advertising car, and the crew was off to the next town to do it all over again. This schedule went on six days a week, replicating the circus's schedule. (In those cases where the circus played in a town for more than one day, the advance car stayed for the same number of days the circus played in that town).

A week later Car No. 2 arrived. Workers checked to see if previously placed posters, billboards, and signs were still in good shape. They replaced any posters that were torn down, damaged by weather, or covered up, hung posters in new spots, and erected banners across streets.

One week before the circus arrived, Car No. 3 rolled into town. Bill posters again repaired damaged signs, continued to look for new sites, made sure businesses were showing their posters as agreed, and checked to see if the competition was making mischief. If competition in a given area was especially stiff, Car No. 4, the Special Brigade, was called into action:

> Every big show carries in advance what is known as an "opposition brigade" with no other duties save to fight the like brigades of other shows. As fast as one circus puts up a piece of billing, the "opposition" attempts to cover it. The result is flying paste brushes and buckets, faster flying fists, broken noses, black eyes, police, jail, bail—and the same thing over again until one side tires and quits, or circus day arrives to end the war of the opposition crews.[8]

Ringling Advertising

The Special Brigade car had no schedule. It went wherever it was needed and was usually alerted by telegraph reports from the managers of Cars 1, 2, and 3 as they did their work.

By the 1910s the advance man's job had become increasingly difficult. He negotiated license fees with city officials and was often in charge of "adjusting" any small claims made against the circus. The advance man often provided tickets to local police, elected officials, and other public figures as a way to try to keep license fees low and avoid unnecessary trouble when the circus arrived. Examples of license fees and ticket provisions in 1911 were one hundred dollars plus fifty reserve and twenty general admission tickets in Holyoke, Massachusetts; fifty dollars plus forty-five reserve and twenty-five general admission tickets in Poughkeepsie, New York; two hundred dollars plus twenty-five reserve and twenty-five general admission tickets in Spokane, Washington.

Sometimes local officials tried to shake down the Ringling advance man. When the show played in Bloomington, Illinois, in 1911, the local sheriff tried to collect an additional fifty-dollar county license fee beyond the usual fifty-dollar city tax. The advance man refused to pay the additional amount, telling the sheriff, "There is no law covering a county license fee." The Ringling journal does not say whether the advance man slipped a few reserved seat tickets into the sheriff's hand to avoid any trouble.[9]

As any good advertising person knew, people needed to see or hear about something at least twice, if not four or five times, before they acted on it. For the circus, local newspapers were the next front in the advertising war. In 1901 the Ringlings had five press agents, led by Alf T. Ringling. A couple weeks before the circus arrived in a town, a press agent visited the local newspaper, talked with the editor, took him over to the local saloon for a drink, bought him a good meal, handed him a clutch of canned news reports that lauded the virtues of the Ringling Brothers Circus, and even provided a ready-made display ad. The press agent gave the editor some free passes to the circus and agreed to meet him at the Big Top door and sit with him during the performance. From all this effort, the press agent expected to see an advance story in the paper and a positive review after the show pulled out of town.

Some editors were accused of running inflated stories about circuses and began preceding the press agents' stories with a disclaimer. A Newark, Ohio, editor wrote, "These notices are furnished this paper by press agents of the respective companies, and the Editor is no wise responsible for the statements made herein."[10]

With their immense popularity, the Ringlings received many requests for joint advertising efforts. For example, the advertising manager of a large clothing store in Allentown, Pennsylvania, wrote to the Ringlings:

> We enclose a copy of a special ad we propose to insert in over 32 newspapers covering a radius of 25 to 30 miles surrounding this city and which will reach a reading population of over 250,000. We should be pleased to promptly receive your best terms in furnishing us with a thousand or more tickets for your exhibition while in this city. . . . We think we should have better terms than fifty cents a ticket.[11]

A representative of the Ringling Brothers wrote in reply, "Must advise that we cannot furnish tickets in the manner you desire in any number whatever. Every ticket issued is licensed admission for the purchaser only and we must decline to provide the tickets requested."[12]

(continued on page 136)

Ringling Advertising

(continued from page 135)

Competition no doubt fueled the rampant exaggeration in circus advertising—every circus wanted to sound as good as or better than its competition. Circus advertising writers also became expert with alliteration.

Real and royal races for reward, huge heroic hippodromes, . . . superb struggles for success and supremacy between the short and the stout, the tall and the tiny, the fat and the frail, the mammoth and the midget. . . . [E]lephants in ponderous, pachydermic progress, camels in cross and comical cantering, horses in hurricane hustling for home, donkeys in deliberate, dragging, drone pace . . .[13]

NOTES

1. Ringling Bros. Circus ad in *Columbus (Ohio) Press-Post*, June 30, 1901.
2. Hagenbeck to Ringling Brothers, April 13, 1901; Hagenbeck to Ringling Brothers, June 15, 1901; invoice, United States Express Company, April 27, 1901, Fred Pfening III, private collection, Columbus, Ohio.
3. Ringling Bros. Business Records, Advertising, May 4, 1903, CWM.
4. Richard J. Reynolds III, correspondence with the author, December 6, 2002.
5. Outside billing forms, Ringling Brothers, Pfening collection.
6. *Janesville (Wisconsin) Daily*, June 1, 1906.
7. Reynolds, correspondence with the author, December 6, 2002.
8. Courtney Ryley Cooper, *Under the Big Top* (Boston: Little, Brown, 1923), p. 8.
9. Ringling Brothers, Standard Daily Journal, 1911, Pfening collection.
10. *Newark (Ohio) American Tribune*, April 24, 1904.
11. Koch Brothers Clothiers and Haberdashers advertising director to Ringling Brothers, May 17, 1910, Pfening collection.
12. Ringling Brothers to Koch Brothers, May 20, 1910, Pfening collection.
13. W. C. Thompson, *On the Road with a Circus* (Self-published, 1903), p. 236.

A poster advertising the Ringlings' Saxon Trio, "The Greatest German Giants of Strength," provides just one example of alliteration in circus ad copy. PRINT COLLECTION, CWM

Circus owners—and the Ringlings in particular—took advertising very seriously. They invested enormous amounts of time and money in getting the word out, and their efforts clearly paid off, with thousands of people enjoying circus day in their towns.

The Baraboo press continued to applaud and proclaim the virtues of the city's most widely known business.

All four sections of the Ringling Brothers' show are in Baraboo and the animals are safely housed for the winter. The arrival and unloading was devoid of incident and the denizens of the cages took to their permanent quarters as naturally as they would to their native jungle, if that luxury was again theirs.

This morning was all hustle and hurry to get the paraphernalia out of the wagons and into the store rooms; the dining hall was garnished, the tables set and life again reigns in Baraboo's greatest suburb, Ringlingville.

Out of an unbroken series of success, the season of 1906 stands as one of the most agreeable and prosperous.... The Baraboo product is of so high grade that the whole world strives to pay its tribute and admission fee.[18]

The Ringling Bros. World's Greatest Shows had one of its biggest seasons ever. Receipts for the 1906 season totaled about $1.3 million ($25 million in 2002 dollars).[19] Meanwhile, the Forepaugh-Sells show, which closed November 17 in Water Valley, Mississippi, had also had a profitable season, although the exact receipts are not known. For the two shows, the Ringlings cleared about $800,000 in profits.

At the end of 1906, another competitor, the Hagenbeck Circus, was coming up for sale. In December, the Ringlings struck a deal with the Hagenbeck people. But just before the deal was closed, the Ringlings discovered that ownership of the Hagenbeck name was in question, and the Brothers quickly called off the deal. In 1907 the Great Wallace Circus purchased Hagenbeck, and the circus became known as Hagenbeck-Wallace.

The question of whether the Ringlings would one day leave Baraboo was always present. The Brothers appeared well settled in Baraboo, with new homes, new buildings in winter quarters, and generally good feelings from the city (at least from the press's perspective). Nevertheless, a November 1906 news article reported that the Brothers had purchased fifty acres with the intention of buying forty more on the east shore of Lake Mendota, near Madison, for new winter quarters. They were purported to have paid six hundred dollars an acre for the property.[20] The article and others like it continually raised the question of the future of the Brothers and their connection to Baraboo. The five Brothers were quite tight-lipped about their plans and activities, and thus the press was left to speculate about what the Ringlings might do.

The year 1907 began on a sad note for the Ringlings. Their mother, Salome Juliar Ringling, died on January 27 at the age of seventy-four.

The Brothers had a fairly uneventful 1907 season. The Ringling circus opened in Chicago on April 4, 1907, and closed at Fulton, Kentucky, on November 15. The Forepaugh-Sells show opened in Columbus, Ohio, April 20 and closed November 16 in Pine Bluff, Arkansas. The bigger—much bigger—event of 1907 was the Ringlings' chance to make their biggest expansion ever.

Economic times had been good since the 1893–1898 depression. But the economy began to falter in late 1906 and took a nosedive in 1907. At first economists thought the country's banking problems would stay on the East Coast, but the trouble soon spread to the rest of the country. As one reporter noted:

> [T]here's nothing in the condition of general business to account for a panic, and so far, it is apparently confined to financial circles entirely. . . . Some people think that the gang down in Wall Street rocked the boat until they got scared themselves. . . . When things began to look squally in New York, Chicago and Milwaukee banks and all other centers that had balances in New York, began to pull them down.[21]

There was a run on the bank in Baraboo in the fall of 1907. Al Paschen, whose grandfather ran a grocery store across the street from the Bank of Baraboo, remembers his grandfather describing people lined up to draw money out of the bank. Charles Ringling was said to be in line with the others, carrying a large satchel. People thought he intended to stuff the satchel with all the money he hoped to draw out of the bank. But Charles Ringlings' satchel was already filled with money—which he deposited. As the story goes, this single action prevented an even more major run on the Baraboo bank.[22]

It was in the midst of these gloomy economic conditions that the Barnum & Bailey Circus came up for sale. The Greatest Show on Earth had been struggling since James Bailey's death in 1906. Otto Ringling, who by now had become one of the greatest businessmen in circus history, and John Ringling were in favor of purchasing the show. The other Brothers were less enthusiastic about borrowing money to buy what many still considered the number-one circus in the world. The Brothers argued long and hard before coming to an agreement; the deal became official on October 22, 1907.[23]

Soon after purchasing Barnum & Bailey, the Brothers decided to take the Forepaugh-Sells show off the road for the 1908 season so they could concentrate on managing two big shows. They would put Forepaugh-Sells back on the road for the 1910 and 1911 seasons before permanently closing the show at the end of 1911.

Once the Brothers agreed to buy Barnum & Bailey, Otto went looking for a loan. The amount the Ringlings needed surely exceeded the lending power of the Bank of Baraboo. After finding no success with St. Louis bankers, he finally convinced a New York bank to lend the Brothers $360,000. Otto, on a first-name basis with several bankers, agreed to accept $355,000 on account, with $5,000 to come later. Otto later explained the difficulty in obtaining a loan in 1907:

I do not know whether you have realized the true panicky condition that prevails here at this time. . . . [I]t will be a marvel if the country gets through without a crash. The depositors are like wild beasts and thousands who have nothing in a bank help the thing along. . . . [T]he bankers of all the big money centers like St. Louis were watching the private wires for news from New York and were no doubt badly scared. A demand for such a sum ($360,000) at such a time when they needed every penny [appeared nearly impossible].[24]

A Baraboo newspaper carried a short article, buried on an interior page, announcing the purchase:

Barnum sells to Ringlings. New York, October 23. The announcement was made at the Barnum and Bailey offices yesterday that it was Ringling Brothers of Baraboo, Wisconsin who had secured possession of the "Greatest Show on Earth," that henceforth it would be run in connection with other arenic enterprises. The sale was made in London yesterday. The transfer places Ringling Bros. at the head of the circus business in America and leaves them practically without a real rival in the world.[25]

Why the Baraboo paper did not run a headline story on the purchase of Barnum & Bailey remains a mystery. It was clearly a huge story in the entertainment world—the biggest story of the year, if not the decade. Was this an indication that the city of Baraboo was no longer as infatuated with its famous sons as it had once been? Had the city's perception of the Ringling Brothers shifted from "our boys" to "rich visitors" who had a business down on Water Street?

Billboard magazine carried a long article revealing that the Ringlings paid only $410,000 for the Barnum & Bailey show. The purchase included "all livestock, both horses and wild animals, and all real estate and buildings in this country and in England, owned by the company for show purposes."[26] The Ringlings apparently paid an unrevealed additional amount for the use of the Barnum & Bailey name. The sale also included the Barnum & Bailey holdings, the interest an English stock company held in Barnum & Bailey, and the physical equipment of Buffalo Bill's Wild West.[27]

A reporter for *The Show World*, a national entertainment magazine, summarized the impact of the Barnum & Bailey purchase on the circus world:

The extent to which the Ringling Brothers now dominate the circus world may be realized by a review of their various holdings. First, there is the circus enterprise which bears their name, with long trains, elaborate equipment, 658 horses, an extensive zoological collection and winter quarters in Baraboo, Wisconsin with great brick stables, training barns, hotel and animal houses; the Adam Forepaugh and

Al Ringling's Home

In December 1906 carpenters completed Al and Lou Ringling's new home in Baraboo. It was the largest and most imposing home in the city at the time, reflecting both the Ringlings' taste and their exposure to grand homes during their travels. Contractors Carl and George Isenberg managed the construction.

The house built of Superior brown stone from Port Wing, Wisconsin, was seventy-one by eighty-one feet and had a tower on the northeast corner. A reporter for the *Baraboo News* described the house:

The Isenberg brothers completed Al Ringling's Baraboo house in 1906. It was—and likely still is—the most palatial home in Baraboo. Photo by Steve Apps

The main entrance is upon Broadway and is at once imposing and beautiful. The vestibule is in English style with paneled wainscot on marble base with a tiled floor. The English effect is continued in the great hall with massive oak staircase and oaken pillars. On the walls the coloring is in dull yellow tones relieved by a floral frieze in shadowy blues. At the left of the entrance or at the southeast corner is the reception room. In design the decorations follow the French style the time of Louis XIV. The fireplace is of Mexican marble and the wood is finished in white enamel, with trimming of mahogany. The walls and ceiling are beautifully decorated; the French styling is carried out in the panels. . . . The rugs and furnishings for this room are all of French design and manufacture and harmonize perfectly with the mural decorations. The library is white oak. There is a beamed ceiling, a fireplace and scenic effects, all in keeping with the general design. The walls present an unbroken panorama of views in old Dutch days.

The stairs ascend at right angles to the hall and the conservatory is found slightly raised above the stair landing. Convenient seats are placed on the landing, the whole being in the design of an English staircase paneled in stained white oak.

On the second floor is found a red room at the northwest corner, a green room at the southwest, a yellow room at the northeast, and a green at the southeast. The bathrooms to all of the bedrooms are provided with sliding doors and the walls are of white enamel. . . . There is also a bathroom for the help. . . .

The floors throughout are of quarter sawed white oak, varnished. The walls bear three coats of adamant, a covering of canvas and made beautiful with the artist's brush. . . . In the attic there is an immense room and cozy quarters under the tower. In the basement is found a ballroom 30 by 50 feet, laundry, steam plant with Johnson regulator and other conveniences.[1]

NOTES

1. *Baraboo (Wisconsin) News*, December 12, 1906.

Sells Brothers circus with up-to-date equipment and extensive quarters; the Barnum & Bailey circus with main offices in New York, the leasehold for terms of years of the Madison Square Garden, vast winter quarters at Bridgeport, Connecticut, the trains, equipment and winter quarters at Stock-on-Trent, England, and lastly the owners of the physical equipment of the Buffalo Bill's Wild West which they have leased to Col. W. F. Cody.[28]

Immediately, Otto Ringling climbed on a train for Barnum & Bailey winter quarters in Bridgeport, Connecticut, to examine the Brothers' new holdings. In an October 26 letter to his brothers in Baraboo, he described the equipment and made many recommendations about how they should combine their three shows' inventories. He suggested selling some of the horses. "If we can dispose of the horses at good prices . . . it will save us lots of money. It will not be necessary to buy much of anything except canvas for Ringling Bros. and B & B," Otto wrote.[29] He also recommended selling several elephants.

Elephants are the most expensive luxury we have. I would sell some. If Bronx Park or other parks want the African elephants, I would let them have them at a good price of course.[30] They will sell best to parks. In dividing them I would sell all we do not need as they are expensive to feed.

After examining the railcars, Otto also concluded that some of the forty-thousand-pound-capacity cars were dangerous.

We can take the new ones Henry [Ringling] built and use them here and sell off the light ones. . . . The Forepaugh stock cars (old lot) are very bad being built too narrow, but they will do for Buffalo Bill.

Forepaugh harness is fine and I should think it advisable to put it away. Do not need it with Barnum show if it does not parade.[31] But it matches Ringling and is always available for that or if we should put out Forepaugh some other time.

Otto was already thinking about one day putting Forepaugh-Sells back on the road. As for the menagerie, Otto wrote:

Forepaugh show has some nice led animals and Ringling Bros. are short. Barnum is long on [led animals]. Forepaugh Hippo is a male breeder and there is room in Baraboo same as when we kept Pete. Barnum can use Forepaugh Eland also horned horses. Only two leopards here [Bridgeport] can use same. Only two tigers here, one of them 26 years old. Getting very thin and stomach gone. Three lions here. This show has very poor cages and only 21 [cages] besides giraffe cages. . . . The very best here is not in it with the poorest on the Forepaugh show.

He went on to describe in great detail the Barnum & Bailey equipment, often making negative comments:

> The Barnum coal oil ranges are all used up being five years old and the coal oil taints the food. Instead of refrigeration wagon they need car which takes tons of ice.
>
> The 18 tier reserve [seats] here are impossible from our stand point. It takes four men to carry the stringers and they twist so much they are dangerous. . . . [W]e need new stringers and plenty of planks and jacks. We will have to change the pitch of the grand stand as the risers here are only 6¾ while ours are eight.

Otto also wrote about the importance of a circus parade, which Barnum & Bailey had not offered in recent years. He made recommendations for decreasing the number of railcars "holding it down to 68 or 69 cars [for Barnum & Bailey] and 75 cars for Ringling Brothers."[32]

From Otto's lengthy letter of October 26, we learn not only about the rather sorry state of the Barnum & Bailey equipment, we also learn a great deal about Otto Ringling's gift for dealing with the minutest detail while seeing the bigger picture.

The Brothers suffered another loss in late 1907. August Albert "Gus" Ringling died of Bright's disease on December 18 in a sanitarium in New Orleans. He was only fifty-three years old. At the time of his death, he was manager of the advertising department of the Forepaugh-Sells show, although he still was not a Ringling partner. He left behind his wife, Annie, and three daughters, Mattie, Alice, and Lorene. The *Baraboo Republic* reported:

> The death of August G. Ringling is the first break in the Ringling ranks among the seven brothers. Although not a member of the firm his position was important and the salary large. . . . It is hard to find so many brothers who have spent so much of their lives together as these seven brothers. They have been brothers in every sense of the word, and his death is felt very keenly by them.[33]

Most businesses hunker down during financial panics, avoiding expansion or anything new or unusual. In 1907 the Ringling Brothers, with Otto and John taking the lead, once again proved their business skill and foresight when they bought the great Barnum & Bailey Circus. At less than a half-million dollars, the price was right, but to outsiders the purchase must have looked foolish and ill-advised, especially considering that the Brothers had to obtain a sizable loan at a time when banks were under financial pressure and the country was in a near economic crisis. But men like Otto Ringling and his brothers saw beyond the immediate. The Ringlings realized that this purchase was one more way for their enterprise to keep growing.

The Circus Parade

The Ringlings' fabulous parade dazzled people in rural areas and small towns, as seen in this photo taken in Algona, Iowa. No matter the size of the community, the parade was a powerful advertising tool for a circus. PRINT COLLECTION, CWM

Like the Pied Piper, the circus parade got people's attention—mesmerizing, entertaining, thrilling, astounding, and above all, attracting them to the circus grounds, where they would plunk down their quarters and fifty-cent pieces for a ticket to the Big Top. The parade was one of the circus's most powerful forms of advertising.

In 1882, when the Brothers put on their first Ringling Bros. Classic and Comic Concert Company shows, they marched down Main Street of the towns where they were scheduled to play, tooting their horns and pounding on a big drum. The parade of brothers and a few other would-be performers took five minutes or less to pass.

By the turn of the century, the Ringling Brothers' parade lasted an hour or longer. An ad for the 1900 Ring-

(continued on page 144)

The Circus Parade

(continued from page 143)

ling circus in a Columbus, Ohio, paper proclaimed: "Big new free street parade in 30 sections, every morning at 10:00. 1,000 people. 500 horses. 100 cages of wild animals. 25 elephants. 20 camels."[1] A writer for the same paper described the parade this way:

> The mounted band, the silver chimes, the clowned band; the couchee-couchee music and last but not least, the [clown] straw

Big cities turned out thousands of people to watch a circus parade, as seen in this photo taken in Detroit. When automobiles and streetcars began clogging the way, mounting the circus parade in larger cities became very difficult. PRINT COLLECTION, CWM

ride party at the end of the parade, caught the crowd.

There were numerous open cages of snakes, leopards, polar bears, hyenas, black bears and other "creepin" and "crawlin" things that were greatly admired by the spectators who lined the street wherever the toot of the calliope could be heard.

The parade started from the show grounds on St. Clair Avenue promptly on time. First came the route manager and Detective Sergeant Kelly; then a ten-horse chariot with a band. The band was different from other circus bands inasmuch as it played regular marches instead of the rump-tar-rarum of the grand entrée. The horses were

all white or gray, well fed and well groomed. The cages were all clean and neat and the parade did not seem to be in a hurry to get through. There were equestriennes in neat gowns; the mounted band led by outriders with the flags of America and England; Chasseurs and—well about everything new or novel in the circus line.

The hippopotamus had a mouth on him like the entrance to a mammoth cave; and in one of the cages, a black leopard "rubbered" out to see what kind of town Columbus was anyhow.

At the tail end of the parade came the rubes on their straw wagon. At each stop the [clowns] amused the throngs with acrobatic performances that were at once clever and comical. The camels,

The Circus Parade

of which there was a big caravan, were all nice appearing beasts and did not look as if they had to patronize some dandruff cure.

One of the most interesting features of the parade was the elephants' act. Each beast grasped the tail of the animal in front of him with his trunk and held on like grim death. Well ahead of the elephants a man on horse back rode by yelling "friends, secure your horses tightly the elephants are about to pass by."[2]

Both the sights and the sounds of the circus parade were something to behold, as C. P. "Chappie" Fox, long-time director of Circus World Museum, described:

The deep throated knock of the heavy wheels caused by the slight lateral motion of the wheel when it hit the axle [hub]; the soft shuffling sound as dozens of elephants slid their sandpaper-like feet on the pavement; the clopping of 40 shod hooves as a ten-horse hitch passed by; the rattle of chains on the eveners; the sudden roar of a lion.[3] Thousands of people turned out for circus parades. Many had come early to watch the crew unload the trains and set up the tents and now could get a glimpse of what to expect in the show. Circuses prided themselves in having colorful circus parade wagons. The decorations often included gold leaf, intricate hand-carved designs, mirrors, and pictures. Many wagons had beautifully painted sunburst wheels with painted wooden panels between the spokes. For many people the quality of the circus parade and its wagons was a powerful measure of the quality of the circus show itself.

NOTES

1. *Columbus (Ohio) Dispatch*, June 4, 1900.
2. Ibid.
3. Charles Philip Fox, *A Ticket to the Circus* (Seattle, WA: Superior, 1959), p. 79.

Managing Two Big Shows: 1908–1909

"The system of management is superb. Great things are accomplished with quiet effort, the results in many instances being nothing short of startling. An inspection of the Ringling Show in its entirety serves to impress one with its many exceptional features and above all its tone of elegance."[1]

The Ringling Brothers Circus would celebrate its twenty-fifth anniversary in 1908. By that year the Ringling Bros. World's Greatest Shows was a mammoth affair, with more than a thousand employees, upwards of six hundred horses, forty elephants, eighty-plus railcars, and a tent city that covered twelve acres. The Big Top had a seating capacity of twelve thousand people.

For the 1908 season, the Brothers added several acts, many imported from Europe. One new act, the "thriller," featured an automobile. An Ohio reporter wrote:

The "thriller" is nothing less than a double somersault in mid-air by a heavy automobile with Mlle. La Belle Roche, a young French woman, at the wheel. The car dashes down a steep incline from the dome of the tent. An abrupt up-curved terminal hurls the car high above the heads of the audience, where is accomplished two complete revolutions and then lands with a crash on a narrow speed way, exhausting its terrific momentum on the hippodrome track.[2]

Along with exciting new acts, the Brothers continued promoting traditional circus acts, the sideshow, and the menagerie because they knew these standbys attracted people to their tents. For 1908 they advertised sixty acrobats, sixty aerialists, sixty riders, fifty clowns, and "the tallest giraffe in the world."[3]

Another ad for the 1908 season sang the praises of both the show and the Brothers' reputation:

The "thriller" act, new for 1908, featured an automobile driven by Mademoiselle La Belle Roche, a young French woman. The car did a double somersault in mid-air. POSTER COLLECTION, CWM

The Gibraltar of modern circus development, rising high and mighty over all, an inspiration and glory to the business, stalwartly American, the substantiated, stupendous, supreme institution of the wide, wide world; and recapitulating back—back through the all the ages of tragedy and splendor to the days of Genesis.

The firm name of Ringling Brothers is known and honored wherever the dawn of civilization has risen. It stands for solidity and truth. It requires no decorative building or rhythm of worlds to invoke interest. Wherever the banner of Ringling Brothers flies, there is a vast dome beneath which is revealed the highest expression of the circus idea.[4]

The Ringlings continued their strict adherence to providing a clean, honest, family-friendly show free of pickpockets, short-changers, confidence men, and the other low-level crooks that plagued many other circuses. One newspaper reporter wrote in the summer of 1908:

Even from the time several years ago when the show was not nearly so large as it is today the people of Racine were impressed with the high moral tone of the Ringling Brothers' show and growth has not interfered with the morals about the Ringlings' tents. The circus is twice as big as it was fifteen years ago, but it is run with the same regard for the welfare of the people. The entire concern is policed and perfect order is maintained.[5]

Despite their size and power in the circus business, the Ringling Brothers never lost sight of their customers. They even policed their ticket sellers to make sure that there was no shortchanging of patrons. It was said that they had the ticket sellers wear aprons without pockets, so that a dishonest ticket seller had no place to slip money obtained from unknowing customers.

The Ringling Bros. World's Greatest Shows opened the 1908 season indoors in Chicago on April 2 and went under canvas on April 24, playing the Midwest, Pennsylvania, New York, and back to the Midwest, where they showed until late September.

To many people it was unbelievable that such a giant establishment could pick up and move each day and still put on two spectacular performances. A Duluth newspaper writer, no doubt with the help of a Ringling press release, described Ringlingville's kitchen and dining enterprise in 1908:

> The "flying squadron," by which term the first section of the four show trains is known, will arrive here shortly after midnight. It will carry the kitchen and dining tents, equipment and helpers, and by the time the three following trains are unloaded a steaming hot breakfast will be ready for the several hundred working people. In order to have a fresh supply of wholesome food for the small army of attaches, an agent was here yesterday contracting with grocer, bakers, dairymen, butchers and others for the immense quantities of food to be delivered at the show grounds early in the morning. [The contracting had actually been done several weeks earlier by the advance man.]
>
> Ninety gallons of fresh milk, twenty gallons of evaporated milk, 1,000 pounds of bread, 300 pounds of steak, Westphalia ham, young lamb chops and young veal cutlets, 90 pounds of butter, 45 bushels of potatoes, 18 bushels of spinach and young beets, 250 dozen eggs, 35 pounds of American cheese, 100 pounds of rice pudding, 300 pies of four varieties and 185 quarts of coffee and 65 gallons of tea are consumed each day. Nine cooks work under one chef to prepare the food.[6]

Barnum & Bailey, The Greatest Show on Earth, opened at Madison Square Garden in New York on March 19, 1908, and played there until April 18. That show then headed east to New Jersey and New York and later spent nearly all of September in California. The Brothers had to prevent their two big shows from competing with each other—

The Menagerie

People young and old were attracted to the Ringlings' vast collection of wild animals and birds. At the turn of the twentieth century, community zoos were just opening and were not yet common.[1] A circus menagerie provided people—especially those from rural communities—an opportunity to see exotic animals for the first time.

In 1901 a newspaper reporter proclaimed:

The Ringling Brothers purchased their first rhinoceros, Mary, in 1902. Print Collection, CWM

> The menagerie carried by the Ringlings this season must be even finer than Noah's. It is certain that Noah never had such a fine bunch of elephants, nor had he such magnificent lions. There is one particularly fine specimen in the lion family. His name is Prince, and he is a forest-bred beast. Another big feature in the animal display is the immense Royal Bengal tigers—quite the largest that ever traveled with a circus. There are yaks, zebus, zebras, ... ibexes, Philippine water buffalo, some handsome deer and antelopes, a large cage of kangaroos, and a hippopotamus weighing 4,800 pounds.[2]

Even in those parts of the country where some religious groups deemed the circus decadent or even immoral, their members could visit the menagerie because it was considered an educational show.[3]

The reputation of the menagerie was as important to a circus as the performance under the Big Top, and to be considered first-rate, a circus had to offer the "big four" animal attractions: elephant, giraffe, hippopotamus, and rhinoceros. In 1902 the Brothers had not yet exhibited any rhinos, which were scarce. Then in December 1902 the Ringlings learned of a rare Sumatran rhinoceros for sale by the Wildlife Conservation Society (formerly the New York Zoological Society at its Bronx Zoo). The zoo had acquired the animal in March of that year but had no place to house it properly. The Ringlings paid five thousand dollars for the animal, named Mary. She was the rarest animal ever housed at Ringlingville.[4]

The Brothers received very careful directions on how to care for the animal:

> In the morning, after giving her water, the following mash was prepared. Three loaves of graham bread cut in coarse cubes, 1/2 dozen medium sized carrots, 1/2 dozen potatoes, 1/2 head of cabbage, 1 pint of bran, 1/2 handful of salt. In the afternoon (about 4 p.m.) after watering her the second time

(continued on page 150)

The Menagerie

(continued from page 149)

for the day, she usually drinks about a pail and a half of water, we gave her a bundle of clover hay—about 16 pounds. We tried various ways of feeding her, and found she did best as stated above. She was given no hay in the morning and provided with peat bedding during the day as she would eat considerable quantities of ripe straw bedding when provided with the same. The mash given her in the morning, when well mixed, just filled a sixteen quart pail.

Hoping you will have good success in keeping her alive and in good health, and believing you will have no difficulty in doing so.[5]

Mary died in fall 1908 and at the time was the only Sumatran rhino in the United States.[6]

In 1904 the Ringlings valued their menagerie at $66,815.00, which included twenty-eight elephants ($1,200 each), a hippopotamus and rhinoceros ($3,000 each), and three "horned horses" (gnus) ($150 each).[7] By 1908 the Ringlings had acquired the largest and most varied menagerie of any circus in the world.[8]

NOTES

1. The nation's first zoo opened in New York's Central Park in 1861. The Philadelphia Zoological Society was organized in 1859 but because of the Civil War did not open its zoo until 1874. Richard J. Reynolds III, correspondence with the author, December 10, 2002.
2. *Ashland (Wisconsin) Daily Press*, July 27, 1901.
3. Milton J. Bates, "The Wintermutes' Gigantic Little Circus," *Wisconsin Magazine of History* 87, no. 1 (Autumn 2003): 10.
4. Receipt for $5,000 from New York Zoological Society, December 20, 1902, Fred Pfening III, private collection, Columbus, Ohio.
5. William T. Hornaday, Director, New York Zoological Society, to the Ringling Brothers, December 22, 1902, Pfening collection.
6. Richard Reynolds III, correspondence with the author, December 11, 2002.
7. Handwritten inventory of animals, 1904, Pfening collection.
8. "With the White Tops: Hippopotami at Baraboo," *Show World*, March 7, 1908, p. 16.

---

a complicated endeavor. Generally, a city hosted Barnum & Bailey one year and the Ringling show the next.

In 1908 the Ringlings also partnered with William "Buffalo Bill" Cody to put on Buffalo Bill's Wild West. The Ringlings provided the equipment, which they had obtained in the Barnum & Bailey purchase, and Cody provided the performance. The arrangement lasted but one season. As circus historian Fred Dahlinger noted, "After a season of dealing with Cody, the brothers wanted out."[7]

That fall the Ringlings—and financial genius Otto Ringling in particular—were keeping their eyes on the national political scene. It was an election year, with Democrat William J. Bryan running for president against Republican William H. Taft, President Roosevelt's chosen successor. Otto, no doubt recalling the trying times of 1907 when he observed firsthand the banking problems in New York, feared that a shift to a Democratic president would return the country to financial chaos and would threaten the Ringling fortune.

In a letter to Charles Ringling in October, Otto wrote, "In view of the remote possi-

With their purchase of Barnum & Bailey in 1907, the Ringlings also received the equipment for Buffalo Bill's Wild West. FROM THE J. E. STIMSON COLLECTION, WYOMING STATE ARCHIVES

bility of Bryan's election, which might start a flurry on Wall Street and tie up New York funds, I am writing checks dated November 2nd amounting to $250,000 for each member of the firm [$50,000 each], which will enable us all individually to place that amount on our responsibility."[8] Otto explained that he was putting aside enough money for winter expenses and getting the show on the road again in 1909. He then revealed this about Ringling operating funds: "Our balance last Sunday night . . . including $20,000 cash on hand was $482,000. Our interest on money in the bank is $850 per month.[9]

With two huge shows on the road, the Ringlings continued to make money—and Otto was planning deftly to ensure that they wouldn't lose any of it. When Taft won the presidential election, the Brothers breathed a little easier.

The Ringling Brothers show played the South in late fall, closing in Macon, Mississippi, on November 11 and returning to Baraboo. The Barnum & Bailey show ended its season in Clarksdale, Mississippi, and headed to winter quarters in Bridgeport, Connecticut.

In commemoration of the Ringlings' silver anniversary, a reporter for *The Show World* ran an article about the Ringlings' winter quarters:

> Baraboo, Wisconsin is the winter quarters of the great show which bears their name. Several hundred workmen are employed there during the cold months of the year, and a score of industrial buildings are ablaze with action. The equipment of the big circus running through every mechanical detail is manufactured there.
>
> A thrifty colony of circus people has grown up around these Wisconsin quarters. Most of them are married and have comfortable homes. The domestic instinct is strong in this class of showmen. Many of the men in this unique settlement have been in Ringling Brothers' employ from early days in their career.[10]

A young boy with the initials H. L. S. who also visited Ringling winter quarters, likely in winter 1908, wrote a letter to *Boys' World* magazine describing his tour:

> Ringlingville, as it is called, is situated on the banks of the Baraboo River, occupying so much space that it is a community of its own. When the show is here in the winter, it is exceedingly interesting to visit. Many like to do this, but it isn't easy. Some little "pull" is needed at headquarters to secure the pass . . . to the animal houses.
>
> The trip was, educationally, well worth many days in school, for Ringling Brothers' menagerie is the finest of any circus. An interesting study in contrasts was shown, in the case of the polar bears, panting and gasping with the heat, though the room was not heated, and at the other end of the same building, in a room heated carefully and guarded from all danger of drafts, were two melancholy-looking giraffes.

The youngster also saw the camels, which were kept outside much of the time in a yard behind the animal houses, and he was captivated by the elephants, which he saw being put through their daily paces in the ring. "They must go through with the tricks every day, so they may be in trim for the summer season. The trainers, deprived of their gaudy circus costumes, were ordinary mortals indeed."[11]

National writers enjoyed spoofing little Baraboo. That same winter a correspondent for *The Show World* wrote:

> According to our Baraboo correspondent, strange and curious specimens of zoology are quite numerous in that town. It is no uncommon sight to see a herd of elephants or camels driven through the streets as promiscuously as domestic animals in other communities. A curious sight was presented recently by a zebra hitched to a sulky. A report has reached us that the mayor is driven to his office every morning by a spanking team of camels and that social events are marked by waiting elephants at the doors, who usurped the places formerly occupied by automobiles and carriages.[12]

The Camel Hitch

The Ringlings' sixteen-camel hitch, circa 1905. Photo by Frederick W. Glasier; Print Collection, CWM

C. P. "Chappie" Fox, longtime director of Circus World Museum, told this tale about camel hitches and what happened one year at Ringling winter quarters:

It was the spring of the year, and the Ringlings were getting ready to go on the road. One new feature they had planned was a twenty-camel hitch. They lined up the camels four wide and five rows deep. It was some sight to see all those camels hitched up and strung out in a long line.

They piled some bales of hay on a wagon and hitched the team of camels to it. And they set off down Water Street, the driver of the team sitting on the hay bales. They got to a little rise in the pavement and they drove up it just fine, but going down the other side the driver discovered he couldn't reach the wagon's brake pedal because he was up too high on the hay. The wagon rammed into the rumps of the first camels, and they took

off—ran away down the street. Their harnesses became tangled, and one of the camels in the hitch broke free from the rest. This runaway camel headed for a little house where a retired circus man who couldn't walk sat on the porch.

The camel headed straight for that porch. The disabled circus man discovered that he could walk; in fact, he could run, as he hurried into the house with the freed camel trailing right behind him.

The remainder of the camel team entered a small wooded area off Water Street, where they became hopelessly tangled in their harnesses, and they stopped. It was quite chaotic for a time, but eventually all the camels were safely back in the camel barn. They never tried another twenty-camel hitch.[1]

NOTES

1. C. P. "Chappie" Fox, interview by the author, Baraboo, Wisconsin, August 20, 2001.

The Ringling Brothers' relationship to Baraboo seemed to become ever more complicated. The Brothers were from Baraboo, but not *of* Baraboo. They were on the road seven months of the year and thus were not seen as major contributors to the community. Yet when they were in winter quarters they made a major impact, employing dozens of residents, purchasing thousands of dollars in supplies, feed, and other goods, and of course, piquing the curiosity of locals.

Al, Charles, Alf T., and Otto spent considerable amounts of their off-season time in Baraboo. Al and his wife, Lou, seemed to have the strongest ties to the city and spent the most time there. All seven brothers and their father, August, were Masons and had received their degrees from Baraboo Lodge number 34 between the late 1880s and early 1890s.[13] John Ringling cared little for Baraboo and spent little time there.

Stories about the Ringling Brothers in Baraboo abound. Some are no doubt true, many contain elements of truth, and not a few are the products of someone's lively imagination. Al Paschen, a longtime Baraboo resident, recalled stories his grandfather, A. M. Rodems, told about the Ringlings. Rodems remembered the Ringlings, especially Al, Alf T., and Charles, as good customers of his grocery store. Rodems had a little truck he used for delivering groceries; a helper, Fred, drove the vehicle. On Saturdays Rodems hired out the truck and driver to haul horse and elephant manure from the Ringling winter quarters to nearby farmers. "Grandpa made more money delivering manure than he did delivering groceries," recounted Al Paschen. "[He]'d hose down the truck real good on Saturday night so it'd be ready for groceries on Monday morning."

A few automobiles began appearing on Baraboo streets by 1908, and Paschen recalled his grandfather's telling about Charles Ringling buying new cars for the five partners. Charles was never a flashy dresser, and anyone who didn't know him might take him for a farmer or a small-town businessman. When Charles approached a Milwaukee car dealer about purchasing five new Pierce-Arrow automobiles (about $450 each), the dealer didn't believe that he was a Ringling and showed him the door. Undaunted, Charles visited another dealer with the same story; they struck a deal, and Charles took $2,250 out of his pocket to pay the man.

The dealer had never seen so much money in one pile and thought it must be counterfeit. He sent an assistant to a nearby bank to check on the authenticity of the money—and upon finding it real, quickly agreed that the five cars would be ready in a couple months.

Upon returning to Baraboo, Charles ran an ad in the local paper asking for drivers to go to Milwaukee by train and drive the new autos back (he would pay their fare, overnight stay in Milwaukee, and a bonus when the cars arrived in Baraboo). Fred the grocery man and four other men applied—but unfortunately, only Fred and one other could drive, and they had to round up drivers. As Rodems always told the story, the cars arrived in Baraboo without incident.[14]

The Ringlings and the Unions

Ringling employees were not union members, but the Ringlings had to deal with many businesses that were unionized. For instance, the Ringlings ordered as much as a quarter-million dollars' worth of printing each year. Sometime before March 1908, they had evidently received a letter from the International Typographical Union about dealing with nonunion printers. Charles Ringling replied:

> In order that there be no misunderstanding as to our attitude toward the unions of the printing trade, we outline the same: We propose to confer with you on or about the first day of December, and place our typographical work with such concerns only as may have your approval.
>
> Concerning the union label: We have to say that we have no objection whatever to it but feel if it is used on any of our work it should be used on all of it, including lithographs and posters, as well as typographical work. Such general use of the label is not possible now.
>
> Concerning printing now on hand: Our season has now commenced. The plates are all prepared, and if we were now obliged to make new plates, our season would be half gone before we would be able to provide new advertising matter, and, therefore, we will use this printing with the understanding as to the future work outlined in the preceding paragraph. This applies to the Barnum and Bailey Show as well as to Ringling Brothers Show.[1]

Although not strictly a union, an International Alliance of Billposters and Billers of America was organized in 1908. There had been so much skullduggery among various circus bill posters—tearing down and covering up each other's posters—that several circuses signed an agreement outlining what was, and was not, appropriate behavior. The agreement specified bill posters' salaries, so that one circus would not try to buy off a competitor's bill poster. Salaries for first-year men were to be twenty-five dollars per month with a ten-dollar-a-month holdback, and they were to increase each year so the most experienced would receive forty-five dollars per month with a ten-dollar-a-month holdback. In addition, bill posters were to have a daily allowance of thirty-five cents for meals and fifty cents for lodging. Section 6 of the agreement stated: "It is agreed that the agents, managers or owners representing the undersigned circuses have the right to discharge men for violation of contract, disobedience, incompetency, misrepresentation and intoxication. However, sixty (60) days of continuous employment shall be regarded as evidenced of competency." Section 7 stated: "It is also agreed that unnecessary manual labor or advertising shall not be performed on Sundays, Labor Day, July 4th, or any legal holiday."[2]

Shows that signed the 1908 agreement were Hagenbeck-Wallace, Sells-Floto, Cole Brothers, Barnum & Bailey, John Robinson, and Buffalo Bill. The Ringling Brothers' show did not sign, although Barnum & Bailey, a Ringling property, did. Why the Ringlings did not sign the agreement for their namesake show remains a mystery. A writer for *The Show World* who visited the Ringling offices in Chicago asked Ralph Peckham, general excursion agent, "Is it true that the Ringling Brothers have refused to sign the agreement with the billposters and billers?" Peckham, good lieutenant that he was, answered, "Humph, I don't know."[3]

NOTES

1. Charles Ringling to James M. Lynch, March 28, 1908, Fred Pfening III, private collection, Columbus, Ohio.
2. Agreement with the International Alliance Billposters and Billers of America, January 25, 1909, Pfening collection.
3. "With the White Tops," *Show World*, January 2, 1909, p. 15.

While repairs and preparations for the 1909 season were taking place in Baraboo and Bridgeport, John Ringling was in Europe, scouting out new acts. In a letter he sent his brothers from the Hotel Athenee in Paris, John described several new acts he had recently seen or heard about. One involved a large Iberian sheep hound leading a pony and a donkey around the ring. John also wrote about the Fredianis, who rode three horses around the ring "very fast" while doing an assortment of flips and somersaults. And he described a lilliputian act "especially for the children" that involved ten midgets, five men and five women, the tallest only thirty-six inches. "I think it would be a good feature to bill [to contract] and will please. They ask $500 for the lot, but I think $400 or $450 will get them."[15] It is unclear which of these acts John signed up.

While the Ringlings spent considerable time scouting new acts, many acts also sought them out because of their national reputation. Late that fall they received a letter from John L. Sullivan, a heavyweight bare-knuckle boxer. Sullivan had been national champion in 1882 and fought until 1905, when he went on the lecture circuit. He wrote to the Ringlings about the possibility of appearing with them. "My monologue runs about twelve to fifteen minutes, and I can make it longer or shorter, as you may desire. I appear in full evening dress, and the stories told by me appeal to ladies and gentlemen, as well as the children. . . . My boxing exhibition with my sparring partner, Mr. Jake Kilrain, occupies eight or ten minutes."[16] The Ringlings turned down Sullivan's offer. (The closest they came to featuring John L. Sullivan was having a male Asian elephant with that name in the Forepaugh-Sells show. The elephant was trained to do a mock boxing match in the ring. Later he joined the Ringling elephant herd and was simply called John. He lived until 1932.)[17]

In December 1908 Otto Ringling contacted Gordon Lillie (known as Pawnee Bill), who was a part owner in Buffalo Bill's Wild West. Lillie managed the business operations while Buffalo Bill Cody, who was the featured performer, controlled the performance. Otto told Lillie that the Ringlings had limited room at the Barnum & Bailey winter quarters in Bridgeport, where the equipment for Buffalo Bill's Wild West had been stored. Otto said they wanted to sell the Buffalo Bill equipment and urged Lillie to buy it: "I will name you a price that is so low it will be almost like paying rent."[18] He suggested that Lillie offer $50,000 for the equipment and said the Brothers would discuss the proposition when they met for their annual Christmas gathering in Baraboo.

Lillie contacted Thomas Smith, who was interested in the Buffalo Bill and Pawnee Bill shows and who had inherited some money. Smith suggested offering the Ringlings $40,000, with the hope that $45,000 would be the final figure. "[Lillie] wired Otto in Wisconsin. 'Will you take $40,000 for the plant? Twenty down; twenty before we leave in spring. . . . [T]he reply came back the same day: 'We accept your offer. The Ringling Brothers.'"[19]

The Ringling Bros. World's Greatest Shows opened in New York's Madison Square Garden for the first time in 1909. COURTESY OF HOWARD TIBBALS

For the 1909 season the Ringling Brothers would open their two big circuses in new venues. (They would not put the Forepaugh-Sells show on the road that year, as the financial crisis of 1907 had made the national circus business soft.)[20] They debuted their Ringling Bros. World's Greatest Shows at New York City's Madison Square Garden on March 25 and played there until April 24. From there they moved to Brooklyn for their opening under canvas, as had been the practice of the Barnum & Bailey show in previous years. The Ringling show played in Brooklyn at Fifth Avenue and Third Street from April 26 to May 1. As circus historian Richard J. Reynolds III noted, "New Yorkers proved skeptical of the offering by these brothers out of bucolic Baraboo. The 1909 date at Madison Square Garden was a flop at the gate. It seems the finicky metropolitans preferred Barnum & Bailey for their Madison Square Garden. The Brothers never tried them again—not until they appended the Barnum & Bailey title to their own in 1919."[21]

After New York the Brothers toured eastern states and worked their way west, spending considerable time in California and Texas. They closed in Clarksdale, Mississippi, on November 13.

Meanwhile, Barnum & Bailey opened in Chicago for the first time and then toured the Midwest, played a few shows in Canada, and headed south to Tennessee, North Carolina, Virginia, Alabama, and other southern states. Barnum & Bailey closed in Okolona, Mississippi, on November 20.

After the shows returned to their respective winter quarters, newspapers (aided as always by Ringling press people) reported results of the Brothers' show season. An article in *The Show World* reported that the Ringlings cleared $1 million in 1909 (about $19 million in 2002 dollars). Before this their highest-profit years were 1905 and 1906, when they ran the Forepaugh-Sells show along with the Ringling show and cleared up to $800,000 each year.[22] According to the article, $600,000 in profit came from the Barnum & Bailey show and the remainder from the Ringling Bros. World's Greatest Shows.[23]

The Ringlings had never before cleared this much money—and they did it in a year that was not especially good for circuses. In late 1909 headlines in *The Show World* read: "Circuses Experience a Rather Trying Season: Most of the Tent Shows Fail to Make

The Ringlings and the Parson Brothers

For many years the Parson brothers leased concession sales from the Ringling Brothers. The Parsons sold pink lemonade, popcorn, peanuts, paper fans, Cracker Jack, cigars, and candy to circus goers. In 1909 the Ringling Brothers took back concession sales for themselves. Print Collection, CWM

The Parsons were farmers from Darlington, Wisconsin, and like many other young men of the time, they were interested in the circus. Joe Parson, the oldest of the brothers, worked in the late 1870s in a northern Wisconsin lumber camp during the winter months. On his way home from camp one spring, he supposedly saw a bison grazing in a farmer's field and traded one of his horses for the animal. He began showing his bison at carnivals, then added a few more animals and created the Great Palace Show. Al Ringling worked as a ropewalker in the Great Palace Show in 1881 (and probably in 1882, as well) and with Parson's Great Grecian Show in 1883.

When the Ringling Brothers organized their circus in 1884, they invited the Parson boys to participate. The Parsons signed on in 1887; Joe Parson performed on the high wire and did horseback-riding tricks, and Alfred E. "Butch" Parson managed the concession wagon, where he sold pink lemonade, peanuts, popcorn, Cracker Jack, cigars, paper fans, and assorted other items. Butch Parson paid a monthly fee to the Ringlings, hired his own help, ordered his own supplies, and kept any profits. The Ringlings stored and cared for the Parson concession wagon.

As the Ringling circus grew, Parson's business became more lucrative. The Parson brothers' income for the 1906 season was $66,612.50; their expenses, including labor (they had up to twenty employees), sugar, ice, lemons, and a weekly payment of $700 to the Ringlings, were $37,140.44. They cleared $29,472.06, for a 44 percent profit.[1]

The Ringlings and the Parson Brothers

In December 1907 Otto Ringling wrote to Butch Parson:

> My dear "Butch," Your letter received and in reply will say I have felt we ought to try the stands ourselves one season. . . . Regarding your wagon, you can leave it here until you have use for it or till the season after the coming one when we may be glad to lease you the privilege.[2]

By January 1908 Otto's tone was more formal. He wrote:

> Dear sir: Will you please write and give us full information and scale of wages and percentages you pay candy butchers. Thanking you in advance for your kindness in this matter, I am very truly yours, Otto Ringling.[3]

In November 1908 Otto wrote another letter to Butch Parson, making it clear that he was ending the relationship.

> On account of the Forepaugh-Sells stuff, Buffalo Bill's Wild West and Barnum and Bailey property, we are very short of room in winter quarters. We will run the candy stands with this show [Barnum & Bailey] same as last season. We find it much more profitable than to let the privilege. Your wagon takes up room which we need. Will you dispose of it in the near future? I think the freight to Baraboo, for instance, would be about $80. If you want to sell the wagon and take the freight cost into consideration, let me know your lowest figure.[4]

A final letter from Otto to Butch Parson, written in January 1909, includes this short paragraph: "In case anything should come up in the future, I would know whether it would pay to figure with you and if I think you are fair, I will bear it in mind and take the matter up with you when the opportunity offers itself."[5]

A. E. "Butch" Parson's career with the Ringlings ended, but he and his family had become wealthy selling pink lemonade and other concessions to circus customers.

NOTES

1. Candy Stand Book, Ringling Bros. Show, Season of 1906, Frank Parson, CWM.
2. Otto Ringling to Butch Parson. December 11, 1907, Fred Pfening III, private collection, Columbus, Ohio.
3. Otto Ringling to Butch Parson, January 29, 1908, Pfening collection.
4. Otto Ringling to Butch Parson, November 24, 1908, Pfening collection.
5. Otto Ringling to Butch Parson, January 6, 1909, Pfening collection.

Money."[24] Several factors had made it a difficult season: municipalities were increasing license fees, railroads were increasing their charges, and people had increasing opportunities for entertainment.[25] The Ringlings clearly had been able to overcome these challenges.

The Ringlings wanted their competitors and the show world at large to know that even in the face of difficult times, when others were showing losses, they could turn a profit—in fact, the largest profit they had ever made. At the end of 1909, each of the five Ringling partners received $200,000 ($3.8 million in 2002 dollars), according to their practice of dividing profits five ways.

That winter the Brothers' top priority was completing their new railcar shops, already under construction.[26] Earlier that year they had purchased nine acres of land known as the flats on the south side of the Baraboo River, north of the railroad and west of the Frank Herfort canning factory. In October, the Baraboo newspaper had reported, "The present plans of the circus men are to build a car factory on the middle of the property. Through this building the cars will be switched from the main track of the Northwestern. . . . Stone is being hauled there and the engineer to grade the place will arrive from Chicago Monday."[27]

The Isenberg brothers built the new sixty-four-foot by eighty-four-foot building. A November 4, 1909, news article stated that the new car shop "is well along toward completion . . . the first section . . . is nearly up and the grading for the tracks is being hurried along by contractor Isenberg and roadmaster, Leo Ryan. . . . The purpose now is to get the place ready for use this winter. . . . A large force of men is at work and no unnecessary delays are permitted."[28] Until this time the Ringling car shops had been on land they leased from the railroad, but the new car shops would be on their own land and under their full control. The old repair shops were to be torn down.

The Ringlings would use the new shops for railcar maintenance, repair, and painting; the cars, which the Ringlings bought rather than building themselves, were stored outside.[29] The new building straddled the railroad tracks, and the Ringlings had additional tracks built parallel to the structure. (By 1913 they would increase the length of the rail repair building to 260 feet.)

Always looking to the future, when the Ringlings gathered in Baraboo in December 1909 for their annual meeting, they discussed how to increase profits even further. They had increased the size of both the Ringling Bros. World's Greatest Shows and the Barnum & Bailey show as much as they reasonably could: each show had eighty-plus railcars, which filled to capacity the rail yards in many smaller cities. And they needed to fill the Big Top with enough customers to cover the enormous expenses associated with running such large shows; smaller cities simply could not turn out a large enough crowd.

One way to make a few thousand dollars more each year was to reclaim the concession privilege from the Parson brothers, a decision they had made late that fall. But they had bigger ideas in mind. It was time to put the Forepaugh-Sells show back on the road. Their experience managing two big shows had given them the confidence to do what no other circus organization had done: tour three circuses at the same time.

Doing the Impossible: 1910–1911

"Otto Ringling: Financial wizard of the syndicate forces."[1]

It seemed an impossible feat, but the Ringling Brothers put three large circuses on the road in 1910, leaving their circus competition far behind them. The Ringling show and Barnum & Bailey had eighty-four railcars each, and the Forepaugh-Sells show had forty-seven cars.[2] Never before or since has one circus organization had so many railcars on the road.

But the Ringlings were facing an ever-changing world and new competition that went far beyond that provided by other circuses. In 1903 the hand-cranked Victrola record player became available to music lovers. In 1904 the Chautauqua Institution of New York State began sending lecturers and tented stage shows to even the smallest towns in the country. Thomas Edison's silent moving pictures continued to attract thousands of customers. Even theater people were worried about the movies. An entertainment reporter wrote about the 1909 season: "That the moving picture business had made deep inroads in the theatrical business is a matter of record, and is generally acknowledged by theatrical powers."[3]

In 1908 Henry Ford began producing inexpensive Model T cars that sold for less than nine hundred dollars. He introduced the assembly line to speed production and by 1914 was paying workers five dollars for an eight-hour day, an unheard-of amount for a historically short workday.[4]

By 1910 automobiles were beginning to clog city streets, making it difficult to mount a circus parade and carrying people greater distances in search of entertainment. Vaudeville was attracting thousands of customers in the major cities and in the smaller ones, too, as communities built opera houses and traveling show troupes traipsed across the country entertaining huge numbers of rural and small-town people. The Ziegfeld

For the 1910 season the Ringlings had three shows on the road: their namesake show, Barnum & Bailey, and the Adam Forepaugh and Sells Brothers show. PROGRAM COLLECTION, CWM

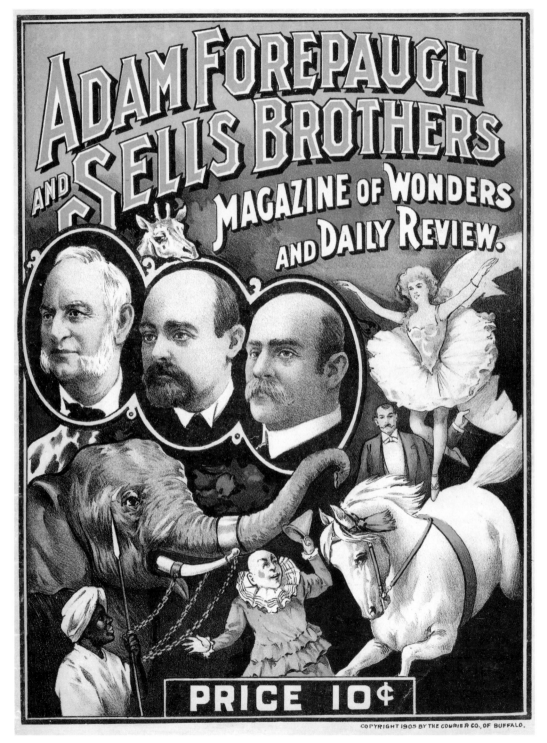

Follies began in 1907. Irving Berlin's *Alexander's Ragtime Band* debuted on Broadway in 1911 and was an immediate hit.[5]

In the midst of all these technological and cultural changes, the circus rolled on, much as it had since pre–Civil War days: horses and elephants, clowns and aerialists, ringmasters and Big Tops, trains and parades. And the crowds continued to come. Still, the Ringling Brothers, now the undisputed kings of the circus world, had to be highly concerned about the changes they saw going on around them.

Managing three circuses was a major task in every way, from staffing to equipment to, especially, routing. There was almost no way that the Ringlings could avoid competing with themselves. And there were nineteen other railroad circuses touring the country in 1910, all seeking a slice of the circus audience pie. Outside of the Ringling "big three," Hagenbeck-Wallace (forty-five cars), John Robinson (forty-two cars), and Sells-Floto (thirty-one cars) were by now the largest circuses on the circuit.[6]

By the early 1900s circuses faced growing competition from new forms of entertainment, such as the Ziegfeld Follies (pictured here are players in the show "Lady Godiva Rides Again"), vaudeville, silent movies, and hand-cranked record players. WISCONSIN CENTER FOR FILM AND THEATER RESEARCH

Early in 1910 the Brothers continued to negotiate with the Chicago law firm that had represented them in their failed attempt to acquire the Hagenbeck Circus. In a letter to attorney Allen Frost, the Ringlings acknowledged the fee they owed—$800 left on the Hagenbeck deal plus $1,400 for general law services. Otto convinced the firm to accept 10 percent less than they requested, for a total bill of $1,974.22. Otto Ringling was a master negotiator—always looking for a better deal, whether for a carload of corn or attorney fees. In a letter dated January 10, the Brothers informed Frost that they had now employed attorney John M. Kelley on a yearly basis and asked Frost to send Kelley "as much data as you think he should have on the matter which you have been handling for us."[7]

But Otto Ringling was ill. While in Chicago in February 1910, he wrote a note to Al saying:

> I am glad to hear everything is in fine shape for all the shows. Regarding myself, I have not attended to my business since I left Bridgeport. . . . Since I saw Dr. Herrick January 11th at his office, which occasion he informed me what I had to look forward to, I have made every effort to [word unclear] business entirely and train my thoughts in a different direction. How well I am succeeding I do not know. I know I am doing the very best I can. . . . I hope that you and Lou will retain your present good health and live long and happily. With regards to you both, Good Bye, Your Brother, Otto. P.S. Al, I know your feelings and every bodies concerning myself, and will ask you to refrain from writing me about my condition, which would be to no purpose.[8]

Otto was probably suffering from Bright's disease, the illness that had killed his brother Gus. From the tone of his letter, it was obviously serious.

From the very beginning of the Ringling Brothers' Circus, Otto had dealt with all things financial and myriad other details. Now his health was failing. It was a worrisome time for the Brothers.

Operating costs for the circus, especially licensing fees, continued to rise. In 1910 Denver passed a circus license ordinance stating that an eighty-car circus that charged fifty cents per ticket must pay the city four thousand dollars per day. (According to the ordinance, smaller circuses paid two hundred dollars per day.) The same year Kansas City, Missouri, instituted a fifty-dollar-per-railcar fee for circuses with eighty cars and fifty-cent admission fees (the result was the same fee as Denver charged). Both the Denver and Kansas City fees were likely instigated by Harry Tamman, who owned major newspapers in those cities as well as owning the Sells-Floto Circus, a Ringling competitor. The Ringlings had won a lawsuit against Tamman in 1909 for using the word *Sells* on Sells-Floto lithographs.[9]

Ringling representatives worked hard to convince the cities to lower these rates, without success. Regarding the Denver negotiations, a reporter for *The Show World* noted, "Mr. McCracken's [a Ringling representative] eloquence and persuasive power have availed him naught in this city thus far."[10]

For the 1910 season opening, the Ringling Bros. World's Greatest Shows would return to Chicago—a cheaper prospect than traveling all the way to New York for the opening as they had done in 1909. Likewise, Barnum & Bailey would go back to opening in New York. The World's Greatest Shows opened indoors on April 7 and then went under tents in Danville, Illinois, on April 28. The show slowly moved east and then played most of the summer in the Midwest.

Barnum & Bailey, The Greatest Show on Earth, opened March 24 in New York and played in the East and the Midwest until late July. Then it moved to the Northwest and then down to California for much of September. In late September Barnum & Bailey showed in Oklahoma, Arizona, Texas, and Mississippi.

The Forepaugh-Sells show opened April 28 in Springfield, Ohio. From Ohio the show moved on to Pennsylvania, New Jersey, Maine, New York, back to the Midwest, and then into the South.

The Ringling Brothers' shows continued to attract huge crowds in 1910. A reporter in Janesville, Wisconsin, stated: "The thousands of people who saw Ringling Brothers' big parade this morning thoroughly enjoyed the pageant that passed along the streets. From the great 24-horse band chariot in the lead to the tail end, nearly a mile away, it was one chain of excellent attractions."[11]

Some local merchants were not pleased when the circus came to town on a Saturday. In August 1910 an Illinois newspaper reported that "[i]f the Messrs Ringling will consult the merchants in Decatur they will not pull off any more circuses here on Saturday. The mixing of a circus with Saturday trade is not a good thing for the trade. . . . Many people went to the circus instead of coming down town to make their usual purchases."[12]

Many forms of entertainment didn't even try to compete with the circus. For instance, baseball games were sometimes postponed when the circus came to town, as happened in Janesville that August: "Today's games in the Commercial League have been postponed owing to the fact that there is a counter-attraction in town, the circus, and it was felt by the board of managers of the league that the attendance at the games would not be large enough to make it worth while for the players to engage in the contests."[13]

Even the barbers in some towns were unhappy:

"Circus day was not a good day for barbers," said a barber last night. The people kept too busy trying to see that show. The parade was late and they were afraid that if they went to the barber shop to have work done the parade would get by them. After the parade they had to rush for dinner and after dinner they had to rush again to the circus grounds. It was a continual rush. It was not a big day for the barbers.[14]

Occasionally, local writers put a cynical twist on a circus's arrival in their town, especially if other circuses had preceded it:

> Today is circus day in Columbus . . . Ringling Brothers, who themselves are numerous enough to put on a pretty fair show all alone, are the visitors today, and theirs is the third big show to visit the Arch City this season. . . . Lizzie, the snake charming lady, sat in a glass cage with a beautiful, slimy cobra where some man's good right ought to be, and the hippopotamus wagon was hauled through the streets to the great delight of everyone who has X-ray machines to look through the wooden sides.
>
> There were tigers, lions, cougars, wolves and a few other pets exhibited during the parade, however, there was positively something new. There was a sixteen "horse" hitch of camels pulling a beautifully painted wagon full of beautifully painted ladies representing something or other in some other country. The parade was witnessed by many thousands of people.[15]

The hippopotamus and rhinoceros were major attractions, so the Ringlings kept them concealed in parades. They expected customers to pay to see these animals.[16]

The Barnum & Bailey show ended its 1910 season in Mississippi on November 5 and headed back to winter quarters in Connecticut. The World's Greatest Shows closed in West Point, Mississippi, on November 9, and Forepaugh-Sells closed in Sardis, Mississippi, two weeks later; those two shows would winter in Baraboo.

When the Ringlings made their decision to house both the World's Greatest Shows and Forepaugh-Sells in Baraboo, they knew the strain on winter quarters would be great. They had built new car shops in late 1909, but the space problem went well beyond storage and maintenance facilities for the railcars. Between the two circuses, there was a need to house thirty-seven elephants.[17] That fall the Ringlings had the Isenbergs construct a thirty-three-by-sixty-foot addition at the rear of the brick elephant house.[18] Although it is not easily confirmed, elephants may have been housed in other facilities in and around Baraboo, as well. The Rooney farm north of Baraboo was the apparent burial site of several Ringling elephants.[19] And the present owners of the Lynn Avenue property, Jan and Duane Neuman, reported that elephants were once housed in the basement of the barn still standing on their property in 2002.[20] Jan Neuman pointed out a mound of ground back of the barn where she said an elephant was buried. "It's why the trees grow so well there," she said.

The Ringlings would also need additional stables for horses after the 1910 season. At the Lynn Avenue farm, the Isenbergs built a new horse barn with a capacity for seventy-five horses. They also built a new brick paint shop, sixty-six by one hundred feet and with enough room for fifteen large wagons, on land the Ringlings had purchased from George M. Reul in December of 1909.[21] An adjoining building was constructed to house the heating plant.

According to a local news article, the Ringlingville buildings constructed in 1910 had the following values: car shops: $7,000; elephant house addition: $2,600, paint shop: $5,800; and horse barn: $2,000.[22]

Otto Ringling (1858–1911) was the first of the five partners to pass away. Behind that assertive look was a gentle, mild-mannered bachelor who enjoyed classical music and good books.
PRINT COLLECTION, CWM

After another winter of training and preparation, the Brothers were ready to take their three shows on the road again in 1911. The Barnum & Bailey show opened at New York's Madison Square Garden on March 23. The Ringlings' namesake show was scheduled to open in Chicago on April 1, and Forepaugh-Sells would open in Vincennes, Indiana, on April 26. But not long after the Ringling trains rumbled out of Baraboo and Bridgeport, tragedy struck. Otto Ringling, the financial wizard of the Ringling enterprise, passed away at John's home in New York.

A Chicago newspaper reporter described the circus pulling out of Baraboo just as it had for many years:

But this year something happened. Hardly twenty-four hours had passed when there was a returning stir of excitement. One of the leaders of the departed army had died suddenly. And on the returning trains of the next few days little groups of sober-faced men came back, one of the trains bearing the remains of the dead leader.

The funeral of Otto Ringling was simple. In three great cities of the country three huge amusement enterprises were at a standstill. At Baraboo a handful of quiet men listened to the reading of a brief service. Then they went back to work.[23]

As always, Otto had anticipated future events and planned carefully. His will, which he had prepared on January 18, 1910, included a cover note that read:

Dear Brothers, Rather than have any contest over this will in case it should be attacked, I believe you will have no trouble in fixing up by a reasonable settlement as I believe there are only four who would dream of trying and I hardly think they would and they have not been ignored. We have labored together successfully for a long time. Good bye, Otto.[24]

Otto's will gave Henry one-fifth interest in the Ringling business, making him a full

Otto Ringling was one of the most visionary of the five Brothers. The circus was never the same without him. MILWAUKEE SENTINEL, APRIL 1, 1911; WHS MICROFILM P76-4572

partner. To carry out the other mandates of his will, the Sauk County Court would have to inventory Otto's estate. The total value of the three circuses was determined to be $348,193 (about $6.5 million in 2002 dollars): $129,513 for the Ringling Bros. World's Greatest Shows; $144,285 for the Barnum & Bailey Circus; and $74,395 for the Forepaugh-Sells show. These were extremely low figures. The actual value of each circus was several times these appraised values. (The Ringlings had purchased a worn-out Barnum & Bailey Circus in 1907 for $410,000. Later in 1911 they would put Forepaugh-Sells on the market at an asking price of $200,000.)[25]

Nevertheless, the court based the value of Otto's estate on these figures. His portion of the business amounted to $69,639.[26] Otto Ringling hadn't taken the time to spend much of the money he had accumulated over the years, and in various bank ac-

Otto Ringling's Will

On January 18, 1910, Otto mailed his will to his brother John, with an accompanying letter. "The enclosed envelope addressed to you all contains my last will and testament. You will please open it in the presence of the rest, and I hope you will take every legal step possible to carry it out." (Otto obviously trusted John. More so than any of the other Brothers, John had a broad, less hands-on approach to the circus holdings.)

Otto also wrote:

As the original members of the firm are still accumulating more worldly goods than they really care for, I have made no effort to leave anything to them except in your case and Alf's which unimportant bequests I have made for convenience sake as it disposes of the two cases without any trouble being held in your name and Alf's and the furniture, books, billiard table etc. being in Alf's home.

(Otto was probably referring to his bequests to John of his "entire investments in the Orient Railway Company. Construction bonds and the Smith Valley Land Co." and to Alf. T. his "books, furniture, billiard table, etc. and interest in the lots I am joint owner with him in.")

Otto had never married. He bequeathed the following to family members and associates: To sister Ida: $75,000 in a trust; nephew Richard Ringling, Alfred's son: $250,000 in a trust until he reached twenty-five; nephew Robert Ringling, Charles's son: $25,000 in a trust until he reached twenty-one; nephew Henry Ringling Jr., Henry's son: $25,000 in a trust until he reached twenty-one; niece Hester Ringling, Charles's daughter: $50,000 in a trust until she reached twenty-five; sister-in-law Mrs. Gus (Annie) Ringling: $15,000; niece Lorene Horton (Gus's daughter): $15,000; niece Martha Ringling (Gus's daughter): $15,000; niece Alice Ringling (Gus's daughter): $15,000; Ralph Peckham (official with the Ringling circus): $10,000; Sam McCracken (official with the Ringling circus): $10,000; Spencer Alexander (Ringling boss hostler): $10,000; John Snellen (previously in charge of Ringling tents): $10,000; brother Henry, $100,000 beyond the one-fifth interest in the firm; brother Al: Renault automobile; brother Charles: $10,000 "to buy and equip a launch of any kind desired." Finally, he willed his nephew Richard Ringling, Alfred's son, "all the residue over and above the amount required to properly wind up my affairs and personal indebtedness . . . to be held in trust until his twenty-first birthday."[1]

As to the portrait of the five brothers that was widely used in their advertising, Otto wrote, "I believe my portrait should be taken from the billing as soon as possible and replaced with that of Henry." (The surviving brothers did not make this change; after Otto's death they simply ceased using the five brothers portrait.)

With his usual foresight, Otto was worried that someone might contest his will. He closed the letter with the following:

In the remote possibility of someone making such attempt, I believe there are enough directly interested that can afford to fix the matter up . . .
I know you will not misunderstand me John, in this I trust you all and implicitly. God bless you. May you each and every one live long and happily. Otto.[2]

NOTES
1. Last will and testament, Otto Ringling, January 18, 1910, CWM.
2. Otto Ringling to John Ringling, January 18, 1910. Copy from original owned by Sally Clayton Jones, CWM.

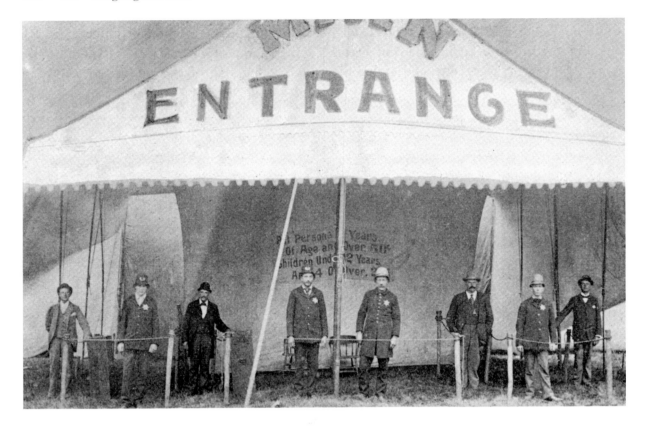

Henry Ringling, third from right, became a full partner upon Otto's death in 1911. ALF T. RINGLING, BENEATH WHITE TENTS: ROUTE BOOK OF RINGLING BROTHERS, 1894 SEASON, CWM

counts in Baraboo and Bridgeport, Connecticut, he had $402,902. His furniture and personal effects were valued at $1,809. In total his estate was worth $479,243.32 (about $9 million in 2002 dollars)—less than the amount he had bequeathed, $635,000, to relatives and others.

Before the court determined how to handle this discrepancy, Gus's three daughters challenged the will, stating that it was not a will but merely a letter indicating how Otto wanted his property divided. Unsatisfied with the amount Otto had left them, they each asked for $100,000.[27] Although the decision took several years, all parties involved reached an agreement on June 23, 1913. Lorene Ringling Horton (age twenty-eight), Martha "Mattie" Ringling (age twenty-six), and Alice Ringling Coerper (age twenty-three) received together $75,000—$30,000 more than Otto had bequeathed to them—to end the matter.[28]

Even with the Brothers' great loss, their shows went on. The Barnum & Bailey and Forepaugh-Sells shows continued as scheduled. The main show opened on April 1 and played indoors in Chicago until April 23. While there the Ringlings received twenty-three zebras from Nairobi, the largest shipment of African zebras ever sent to a single buyer in America. Seven of the animals arrived dead, leaving a total of sixteen to add to the four the Ringlings already owned.[29] From Chicago the Ringling Brothers' show moved first east and then west, again spending most of the fall in California and Texas.

After Indiana, Forepaugh-Sells traveled the East, Midwest, and West, and then headed south. It was the first time the Ringling Brothers sent one of their shows to Florida; Forepaugh-Sells had its biggest stand of the season in Tampa, grossing $10,372.85.[30]

In the course of the 1911 season, the Ringlings dealt with the usual claims of damage to property or injury. By this time the Ringlings employed an "adjustor" to deal with such claims. In 1911 the adjustor recorded the following incidents: "Buggy upset. Lady's arm broken. Adjusted $2.50 plus two tickets." "Mrs. J.D. Maxon fell from seats during matinee and injured her leg. Adjusted for $5.00." "Horse frightened by elephant. Lady thrown out, but nothing serious. No claim." "Mrs. Kennedy and child was thrown out of buggy, horse being scared by elephants. Were carefully warned [before occurrence]. No claim."[31]

More serious accidents did occur. While the Ringling show was in Stockton, California, on September 13, a band member, late for the parade, ran alongside the bandwagon, slipped, fell beneath the wagon, and was run over. He died instantly. The adjustor took the names and addresses of several witnesses and recorded them in his diary. Then he wrote, "Sent body home to Hot Spring, South Dakota, $105.50."[32]

As circus historian Richard J. Reynolds III noted, "Circus history is replete with similar incidents. Hardly an issue of *Billboard* went by without a similar tale. People, both patrons and circus employees, were killed or seriously injured with hardly a blink of the eye in the press and little resort to the judicial system. . . . [This] casual attitude also applied to all sorts of industrial accidents and deaths."[33] The claims settled by the Ringling Brothers for the Ringling show in 1911 totaled $2,720.56.[34]

Just before the end of the season, on October 29, another tragedy occurred: Spencer "Delavan" Alexander died unexpectedly following a banquet for circus people at the Hotel Main in Fort Smith, Arkansas. The Ringling Brothers' Circus would play Fort Smith on Monday and Fayette, Arkansas, on Tuesday before returning to Baraboo. Alexander had just entertained several of the circus staff in his hotel room, and everyone had left except for the circus physician and a circus superintendent. Alexander slumped in his chair and died instantly.[35]

A Ringling employee since 1889, Alexander was considered one of the best boss hostlers in the world of the Big Tops. He had cared for the Ringling horse herd with meticulous attention. During the winter months, Alexander lived with his wife and children at the Lynn Avenue farm where many Ringling horses were housed. He was well respected among both circus people and the residents of Baraboo. During his funeral services in Baraboo, all the businesses in town closed in his memory.

The three shows ended their seasons and returned to their respective winter quar-

ters. Back in Baraboo, the five partners, now including Henry, decided that operating three shows was just too much, especially after the loss of Otto. Reality had set in. The year 1911 had challenged and stretched them. For 1912 they would stick with two big shows. The loss of financial wizard Otto likely had some part in this decision. Even though the Ringlings employed financial managers, none could come close to the skill and knowledge Otto had possessed. Besides, Otto had been a leader in making important and often far-reaching decisions, such as influencing his brothers to purchase the Barnum & Bailey show.

Late that fall the Ringlings put the Adam Forepaugh and Sells Brothers Circus up for sale, asking $200,000. William P. Hall, a horse and mule dealer from Lancaster, Missouri, expressed an interest, and the closing for the transaction was scheduled for November 11, 1911.[36] But for reasons unknown, the sale fell through, and the once famous and well-respected circus was sold piecemeal.

Tax Woes: 1912–1914

"All taxation is an incubus, a handicap upon productive energy, and every dollar taken out of productive channels to go to public running expenses is a dollar gone."[1]

W hen Robert M. La Follette became governor of Wisconsin in 1901, he had reform on his mind. He sought to stop governmental corruption and throttle big-business influence peddling. The governors who immediately followed La Follette (James Davidson, 1906–1911, and Francis McGovern, 1911–1915) had similar agendas. These years became known as the Progressive Era in Wisconsin.

One element of reform that grew out of this political climate—though some argued it was not reform but a drag on progress—was a state income tax. On January 27, 1911, a state income tax bill was introduced in the state legislature. After considerable debate in both houses, Governor McGovern signed the income tax bill into law on July 14. Wisconsin's new graduated income tax levied a 1 percent tax on annual incomes over $1,000 ($18,500 in 2002 dollars) and 6 percent on incomes over $12,000. In 1911 most people did not earn even $1,000 per year and thus would be exempt from the tax. Nevertheless, "[t]he new tax was subjected to brutal attacks even before it went into effect, but it survived all tests in court."[2]

The Ringlings, of course, would be subject to the 6 percent tax, and they were furious. They considered the income tax grossly unfair because they earned most of their income outside the state, and they quickly began voicing their unhappiness. A *Chicago Tribune* reporter described the Brothers' financial situation:

The progressive legislation of Wisconsin includes a graduated income tax ranging up to 6 percent. The Ringlings, who winter their [Forepaugh-Sells] and Ringling circuses in Baraboo are thus called upon to contribute somewhere between $30,000

The Ringling Brothers de-
tested all forms of taxes.
They were especially ap-
palled at Wisconsin's new
income tax, arguing that
they earned only a tiny
portion of their substan-
tial income in Wisconsin.
MADISON DEMOCRAT,
JULY 14, 1911; WHS
MICROFILM P43429

and $40,000 (approximately $525,000–$700,000 in 2002 dollars) on an income derived almost entirely outside the commonwealth. This they consider unfair. They said so to the legislature, to the governor, and to the tax commission with no appreciable effect.[3]

The Ringlings suggested they would not return to Wisconsin at the end of the 1912 season. Once again, rumors spread about the Ringlings leaving Baraboo.

The *Chicago Tribune* story fed the fire. The reporter penned his article as if the circus was leaving Baraboo in the spring of 1912 for good.

No more will the unwieldy elephant his lithe proboscis swing upon the picturesque streets of Baraboo, Wisconsin; no more will the tiger's fearful symmetry inspire the casual admiration of the inhabitants of that sophisticated town. Gone are the red chariots, following in the wake of many sleek and plumed coursers; gone the yellow railway cars, the blithe calliopes, the bright band wagons, and all the arenic glory that once was Baraboo. In short gone are the Ringlings, taking with them everything from snakes to spangles—the reason being that they have found it cheaper to move than to pay taxes.[4]

Over the years there were several times that it seemed the Brothers would leave Baraboo. In 1888 the *Milwaukee Sentinel* reported, "The Ringlings have lately purchased a tract of land here [Waupaca, Wisconsin] to accommodate their circus and menagerie and will winter here in the future."[5] In 1896 the Ringlings seriously considered moving to the old Forepaugh winter quarters in Philadelphia.[6] In 1897 the Ringlings had apparently considered a move to Whitewater, Wisconsin: "There has been considerable talk about Ringling Bros. changing their headquarters from Baraboo to Whitewater, but Baraboo will continue to be the home of the 'World's Greatest Shows.'"[7] Such rumors surfaced again in 1906 and 1909.

This time it seemed like a move was a sure thing. But during the winter and early spring of 1912, the Brothers continued to make improvements on the buildings at Baraboo winter quarters. In March Al Ringling purchased the old Wisconsin House in downtown Baraboo (across the street from the courthouse park) with the intent of razing it and building a new twelve-hundred-capacity theatre at the location. The *Baraboo Weekly News* proclaimed, "The playhouse will give Baraboo a building not equaled in other cities in its class as no expense will be spared. . . . It will no doubt be known as 'The Ringling' and should be so called for the ones who have done much for Baraboo and who are willing to keep the good of the city at heart as the years go by."[8] In April the Isenberg brothers began tearing down the old ring barn, at that time the oldest of the Ringlingville buildings, built in 1888.[9]

It's possible that the Brothers believed that the new income tax would be amended

Suffrage and the Ringlings

In early 1912 the women's suffrage movement was gaining momentum across the country, and on April 1 of that year the Illinois Equal Suffrage Association wrote to the Ringlings:

> You are perhaps aware that on April 9 the question "Are you in favor of the extension of suffrage to women?" will be submitted to the men of Chicago on a preferential ballot. This is the first time the matter has ever been presented to the voters of Illinois, and the women are very anxious that the attention of as many as possible shall be called to this opportunity. . . . We would very much like to put some advertising features in your circus. Of-course, this will be widely noticed in the papers to your great pecuniary advantage we hope and believe. . . . [T]o save time may we hear from you by telephone, Harrison 3856.[1]

The Ringling Brothers replied on April 2: "Esteemed Madam. . . . [I]t has been an inflexible rule with this company to avoid giving publicity to anything in the way of either religious or political movements, and we are sorry to say it will be impossible for us to introduce any advertising features in our circus."[2]

_____

NOTES

1. Mary R. Plummer, Secretary, Illinois Equal Suffrage Association, to the Ringling Brothers, April 1, 1912, Fred Pfening III, private collection, Columbus, Ohio.
2. Ringling Brothers to Mary R. Plummer, Secretary, Illinois Equal Suffrage Association, April 2, 1912, Pfening collection.

to exempt firms that did much of their business out of state. Likely, they had not yet made any real decision about their future winter quarters. But Al put his downtown Baraboo theatre plans on hold, and the Brothers continued to let the public believe they would not return to Baraboo in the fall of 1912.

The deadline for the income tax payment was April 1. On March 6 Al wrote from Baraboo to his brother Charles, wintering in Sarasota, Florida: "It is getting time we should send in our tax list. I understand people around here are filling out their lists and sending them in. We do not know what to do in this matter. Will you be here soon, or will you suggest to us what you think we should do in the matter as the time will soon be up when we are supposed to have our list filled out and sent in."[10]

When people across the country read about the Ringlings' apparent plans to leave Baraboo at the end of the 1912 season, offers for new winter quarters poured in. Most came from Illinois, Indiana, and Ohio. The offers included a three-hundred-acre farm one-quarter mile from a "steam railroad" (Ravena, Ohio), an abandoned woolen mill plant (Peru, Indiana), a cement works (Kimmell, Indiana), fifteen acres and nine buildings with three railroad spurs (Kankakee, Illinois), an "old race track grounds" (Joliet, Illinois), and an old fairgrounds (Adrian, Michigan). By July 1, 1912, the Ringlings would receive fifty such offers.[11]

Wisconsin newspapers carried several stories about the possibility of the Ringlings leaving the state. One article began, "Baraboo is receiving one bad commercial blow after another; recently the Northwestern road changes affected a number of families causing their removal to other points, now comes the statement that the Ringlings are leaving the place on account of the effects of the income tax."[12]

Some people weren't sympathetic to the Ringlings' plight. To someone making less than a thousand dollars a year, hearing that someone earning two hundred times more had to pay income tax, the likely response was, "Tax them, they can afford it. After all, wasn't that what the so-called progressive income tax was all about?"[13] Charles apparently had been hearing comments to this effect, and on April 19 he wrote a letter to the editor of the *Sauk County Democrat:*

> I am advised that there is a decided misunderstanding as to the taxes the Ringlings have been paying the past years at Baraboo. I believe statements made by some of our friends have created a wrong impression, and in order to correct same I wish to state that the Ringling families, including taxes paid on homes and personal property, as well as on circus property, have been paying about ONE TWENTIETH of all taxes collected in Baraboo, a city between six and seven thousand inhabitants. This of course does not include taxes paid by employees of the circus. As this is a matter of record the above statements can be easily verified by anyone interested enough to inspect the tax records.[14]

Not everyone in Baraboo thought well of the Ringling Brothers. A Chicago reporter wrote about their apparent departure:

> So Baraboo is perturbed. Not demonstrably so, for I saw a Northwestern locomotive pull forty Forepaugh cars out of the shops the other day and start east with no one in Baraboo looking on. It was deemed expedient, however, to apprise the tax commission of the catastrophe and Mr. Haugen . . . a Progressive, was none too tactful, and he told Baraboo quite candidly that Mr. Otto Ringling, deceased, had not paid his fair share of the expenses of the state.[15]

Nevertheless, a group of business and professional men of Baraboo, no doubt recognizing the Ringlings' economic contributions to the city, offered the Brothers their support and made a plea for them to stay in Baraboo. Mayor G. T. Thuerer, chairman of the group, declared, "Some step should be taken to keep the show in Baraboo and that the present conditions came about as the result of the income tax law."[16] The group drafted a resolution that read in part:

> The business men and citizens of Baraboo on this 23rd day of April 1912, at a mass meeting assembled, hereby resolve: That it is the sense of this meeting that the citizens of Baraboo as well as the citizens of Wisconsin feel a just pride in the success of the Ringling Brothers. . . . Their success is chiefly due to their integrity, their

loyalty to their home town, their manly methods, their devotion to business, their fidelity to each other and their high ideals. They have materially assisted in building up our city, have built beautiful homes and in addition to the annual amount of money they spend, they have added greatly to real estate values and the general prosperity of the place. . . . We pledge our loyalty and offer our undivided support to Ringling Brothers and express the hope that their business interests may not be antagonized to any extent that will necessitate the removal from Baraboo of their permanent winter quarters. Adopted, George T. Thuerer, Chairman, T. F. Risley, Secretary.[17]

The Brothers, still having made no firm decision about a new winter quarters location, continued planning and preparing for the 1912 season. As usual, John Ringling spent much of the winter in Europe seeking new acts. During one trip he learned about a stage show featuring Joan of Arc. He described it in a letter to Al:

When the spectacle of "Joan of Arc" was done at the Hippodrome in Paris it was the biggest success of any spectacle every produced in that city. . . . One feature in this spectacle amounted to a sensation and was the talk of Paris; in the spectacle they burned Joan of Arc, and as the smoke and flames came up around Joan, she made her getaway into the bottom of the funeral pyre, and in her place there was a very finely gotten up dummy, dressed like Joan of Arc, and two angels came down from the top of the building on wires . . . This could easily be done at the Coliseum in Chicago and would be a great effect.[18]

Al was not especially impressed with the Joan of Arc idea. He wrote back to John:

Your letter of recent date received and note what you say concerning Joan of Arc. Yes, I believe that the burning of Joan the way you say would be well as far as the flash and spectacular work is concerned, but we all thought to keep away from that part of this: finishing the "Spec" with the coronation of King Charles. I doubt whether the burning scene would take so well with a big majority of our patrons. It might perhaps be looked on as sacrilegious.[19]

John, obviously exasperated with his older brother, wrote back, "Regarding the burning of Joan of Arc, I think you will make a big mistake if you don't put this on. It certainly will make a big hit and will create a lot of talk. No one could look upon this as being sacrilegious—in fact it will be considered the opposite."[20]

Later that spring Charles, now back in Baraboo to help with the tax payment, wrote to John in New York City:

With reference to the Joan of Arc matter: Al says that we will try to work this ascen-

The Ringlings featured the spectacle "Joan of Arc" in 1912. The Brothers had some disagreements about how it should be staged. The press later applauded this new spectacle, proclaiming it a "welcome change from dangerous thrillers." COURIER COLLECTION, CWM

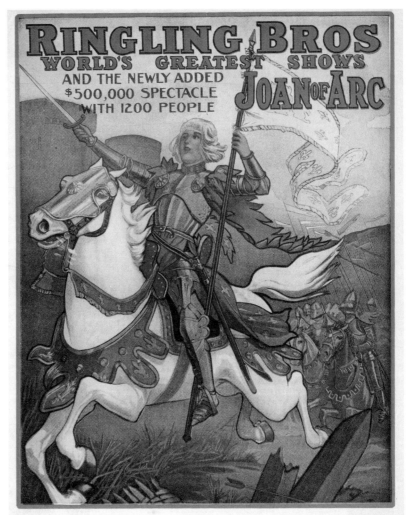

sion if we can. Of course you know that our drop curtain at the coliseum comes out to the edge of the balcony, and we would have to work this from a position in front of the drop curtain as we cannot draw her up through the balcony floor. However, I believe this can be worked out all right and shall try to assist Al in getting away with it, which he seems agreeable to.[21]

With regard to the 1912 season opening in Chicago, Charles wrote, "Do not know whether I will be able to come down to the opening or not. Wisconsin state tax matter has got us going here, and it must be attended to before the first of April."[22]

In the wardrobe department at Ringlingville Baraboo, "Joan of Arc" (Elizabeth Rooney) tried on costumes for the spectacle, assisted by equestrienne Edna Curtis. Charles Ringling, second from right, was actively involved in the smallest details. PRINT COLLECTION, CWM

Amid rumors and speculation about the Ringlings' future winter home, the two shows opened their 1912 seasons. The Barnum & Bailey show, with John and Alf T. Ringling in charge and featuring the spectacle Cleopatra, opened in New York's Madison Square Garden in March. The show played East Coast towns into July and then moved into the Midwest and the West.

The Ringling Bros. World's Greatest Shows and the new spectacle Joan of Arc opened at the Chicago Coliseum on April 6, 1912, and played there for thirteen days before going under canvas in Danville, Illinois, on April 26. The show moved east and by June was in eastern Canada, where it played from June 10 to June 22.

The 1912 Ringling parade featured a twenty-camel team, with five camels walking abreast, a team of eight zebras, six elephants driven tandem, and a "great golden band chariot with a team of 30 horses."[23]

The Ringlings billed their new Joan of Arc show as a "$500,000 magnificent spectacle."[24] Reviews were positive. The *Toledo Blade* (no doubt with help from a Ringling press agent) reported, "The addition to the regular performance of the wordless spectacle of 'Joan of Arc' has given Ringling day a double significance. In one big scene, the coronation of Charles VII, 1,200 characters are within view of the audience."[25]

Another Midwest newspaper declared, "Joan of Arc Spectacle Welcome Change from Dangerous Thrillers." The story went on to applaud the spectacle:

> The gorgeous pageant of Joan of Arc was perhaps the most unique and impressive feature of the entire circus. About 300 took part in this magnificent spectacle, arrayed in the brilliant and elaborate costumes that were peculiar to the French court life of that day. It was a beautiful feature, and a welcome change from the harrowing "loop the loop" or "dive of death."[26]

New safety laws began affecting the Ringlings' shows in 1912. Before the namesake show's opening in Chicago, an official from the Coliseum wrote to John Ringling: "This is to remind you that some provision is necessary for light on wagons with the show in some of the states, which will required a light showing both forward and backward on all vehicles."[27]

As in every season, the Ringling circuses had their share of problems in 1912. While the Barnum & Bailey show was playing in New York City, a sheriff attempted to claim the entire menagerie because of a bareback riders' suit against the show seeking $25,000 in damages. "A score of deputies accompanied the sheriff to Madison Square Garden. When the sheriff found it would cost the city $3,500 a day to feed and care for the animals he agreed to permit the circus managers to exhibit the animals."[28]

A serious fire on August 22 in Sterling, Illinois, destroyed the Ringling Big Top— a loss estimated at $25,000. An Ohio newspaper recounted:

> There was no one but circus employees in the "big top" when sparks from a barn burning near the show ground ignited the oiled canvas, but so rapidly did the flames spread that one man was seriously burned before he escaped. There was panic among the animals in the menagerie tent but they were quieted when great canvas covers were drawn over their cages.[29]

By August the Brothers still had not decided where they would take their circus at the end of the season. On August 8 Charles wrote to Al from Lincoln, Nebraska:

> I wrote to Henry today telling him I would like to leave the show by the end of August and asking him to telephone you and see whether either one of you could care to come on at that time. . . . I am also suggesting to Henry that you and he decide upon the wintering of the show. I believe I have not been fully informed as to what you propose to do on this matter at any time and I am satisfied to step aside and have you and Henry decide it regardless of my opinion at all. Only a decision should be reached at once so that the show can be routed accordingly as Wilson [Ringling railroad contractor] is now ready to close up contracts and must know whether the show goes to Wisconsin or Connecticut or where it goes. Hope you will let me know about these things very soon.[30]

Brothers Disagree

For the most part the Brothers got along well. But disagreements happened occasionally, and some rifts developed, often involving the sometimes arrogant John Ringling. For instance, in early January 1914 Al wrote to Charles:

> Sam McCracken [a Ringling official with the Barnum & Bailey Show] was here the other day. . . . In talking to him I asked him to let me see the list of side show people they had engaged for the coming season. He did this. In his list I see that he had a contract with Mlle Gabriel, the Living Half Lady, so I told him that we had her engaged and showed him the contract we made with her through Mr. Pitrot last August. He said that he did not know anything about it only that John gave him this contract and told him that she was to be with the Barnum Show.
>
> John Ringling knew she was to go with our show for he talked with me about her and said she was the greatest freak in the world, and so she is, and John said we ought to let the Barnum Show have her. I told him "No," that it was hard work for me to get her to sign a contract to remain in this country and I was fully three weeks in arranging with her and that we needed a strong attraction for our side show, as she would be a drawing card wherever she is placed. The only way I figure this is that John went and cancelled our contract with Pitrot and then got Pitrot to make a contract with him for her to do with the Barnum Show. I am writing to Pitrot today that we have signed this lady to go with the Ringling Show and will expect her to fill her contract with us. . . . Now if John has made any other arrangements with any the rest of you, let me know, but this Living Half Lady is a great feature.[1]

Clearly, John had done an end-run around his brothers—behavior that did not sit well with them, particularly Al and Charles.

NOTES

1. Al Ringling to Charles Ringling, January 2, 1914, Fred Pfening III, private collection, Columbus, Ohio.

Charles, an avid sportsman, most likely wanted to go on an extended fishing trip, which he often did. So it was up to Henry, the new partner, and Al to decide on where to winter the Ringling show in 1912. John and Alf T. were with the Barnum show, and they apparently were not directly involved in the decision.

In his letter to Al, Charles also listed the World's Greatest Shows' daily gross income from ticket sales from July 25 to August 7, which ranged from $5,399 in Sheldon, Iowa, to $14,501.70 in Sioux City, Iowa. The average daily ticket sales for twelve days in Minnesota, Iowa, and Nebraska were $8,540.[31]

The two Brothers made their decision, and without fanfare, the Ringling show returned to Baraboo in the fall of 1912, quieting those who "knew for sure" that they had left their old winter quarters for good that spring. The Barnum & Bailey show returned once again to Bridgeport, Connecticut. In true Ringling fashion, the Brothers had left the decision about returning to Baraboo in fall 1912 an open question until the last minute, or so it seemed. It appears that Al and Henry made the final decision and it really didn't matter to the other Brothers where they wintered. Al had the strongest connections to Baraboo, and as the oldest brother, his opinion likely had considerable influence on Henry, the youngest. And the Brothers were still hopeful that a change would be made to the new income tax law, exempting their out-of-state earnings.

In April Charles had had the Isenbergs build him a new home in Sarasota, and by late December he and John were back in Florida. Charles picked up his new sixty-foot launch in Tampa on December 10. As a Baraboo paper reported, "It is magnificently appointed and reported to be one of the finest and swiftest in American Waters."[32]

Alf T. and Henry Ringling spent winters in New York City, where they could be close to the Barnum & Bailey winter quarters. Only Al remained in Baraboo.[33] The typical flurry of activities took place in Baraboo during the winter of 1912–1913. As usual, the staff at Baraboo was busy ordering necessities for their winter work—disinfectant by the barrel; sandpaper, varnish, and shellac; dry white lead, lamp black in oil, imitation gold, turpentine; and hardwood lumber—necessities for the winter work.[34]

They also ordered new tents that winter, as they did nearly every year. John Snellen, superintendent of canvas, sent a letter at Charles's request to Al Ringling, outlining details for the new dressing room and trapping room tents:

> Dressing Room: A fifty foot round top with one forty and one twenty foot middle piece, made with four widths of cloth between the side poles, and an eleven foot side wall of khaki cloth. . . . Trapping Room: A fifty foot round top with one forty and one twenty foot middle piece, made with four widths of cloth between the side poles, and an eleven foot regular wall as used in all other tents.[35]

The Ringlings were always looking for horse meat to feed their lions, tigers, and other carnivores. They advertised in area papers and received many interesting replies. One display ad in winter 1912 read: "Wanted to buy old useless horses in good health to be used for animal feed. Apply to Charles Smith, Ringling Brothers Winter Quarters, Baraboo, Wisconsin."[36]

A fellow from Hancock wrote the Ringlings:

> I could pick up a few horses in this section, and ship you dressed horse meat, mostly rather thin. If you are in need of anything in this line, kindly write me and I will dress some in good shape and ship to you. Let me know whether you want them examined by a horse doctor before butchering. The manner of shipping, whether boxed or wrapped and all particulars including price. Hope to hear from you, I am, Harry Humphrey, RFD #1, Hancock, Wisconsin.[37]

Even with all their wealth and prestige, the Brothers themselves continued to work

Ringlingville: A Portable City

The more the Ringlings' circuses grew, the more people marveled at how Ringlingville's twelve hundred residents could move from town to town, day after day. An example of this incredible accomplishment was recorded by a Pittsfield, Massachusetts, observer in June 1913:

By 1915 Ringlingville on the road had grown to the size of a small city, its tents requiring about fourteen acres. With few exceptions, the show moved to a new town each day. PHOTO BY STEVE ALBASING; ALBASING COLLECTION, CWM

Ringling Bros. Circus arrived this morning from Holyoke, Mass., at 3:30 a.m. and the first section started to unload at 4:30 a.m. First section consists of 21 cars: 17 flats, 2 horse cars, 2 sleepers, 56 wagons of which 30 are cages.

Second section came in at 7 a.m. and consists of 21 cars: 19 flats, 6 horse cars, 5 sleepers, 25 wagons and 3 small wagons.

Third section came in at 7:30 a.m. and consists of 20 cars: 14 flats, 5 horse cars, 1 stock car, 38 wagons, 2 chariots.

Fourth section came in at 8 a.m. and consists of 20 cars: 7 horse cars, 4 stock cars, 9 sleepers.

Twenty horses are loaded to a car so there are over 400 horses, 27 elephants, 20 camels, 5 zebras.

Stock cars are painted yellow and the ends red. Flats are yellow. Sleepers are red and the wagons are red and yellow. Some have gold lettering. Advance cars No. 1 and No. 2 are red and advance car No. 3 is blue and yellow.

All tents were put up Sunday morning except the big top [the Ringlings had no shows on Sunday]. There are 17 tents—big top, menagerie, side show, dining tent, colored dining tent, private dining tent, cookhouse, 3 horse tents, 1 pony tent, 2 dressing tents, ballet tent, wardrobe tent, candy stands and small tents. All of the wagons are unloaded by 10:30 a.m.

A large crowd was watching the unloading and also on the lot. Sunday afternoon the horse tents were open to the public. A large crowd was on the street Monday watching the 10:00 a.m. parade which was the best circus parade ever seen here.[1]

NOTES

1. Unpublished notes by Isaac Marcks, Pittsfield, Massachusetts, June 22–23, 1913, CWM.

on the minutest details. That winter Al was concerned about the need to replace the Number 3 advertising car and wrote in a detailed letter to Charles, "[The car] is not as strong as the number one and number two cars but the only fault of the number three car is that the roof is in bad shape, but this could be easily fixed." He went on to say that John was looking for a new Number 3 advertising car.

Most of the Brothers' letters are solely business related, but Al ended this one a bit more personally:

> Everything here going good but the weather is very cold, in fact we are having the coldest weather of the season. I hope that you are well and putting in a nice winter. Henry was here a few days last week. He and his family are going to Florida—I think they left Chicago last night for the south. The weather and climate does not agree with little Henry so this is the reason for them going south.[38]

That winter Al also took care of awarding the 1913 balloon privilege. During the 1912 season the balloon contract (which included the privilege of selling "toy balloons, whips, canes, beads and badges") had gone to Thomas Zingaro of Jersey City, New Jersey. Zingaro had paid the Ringlings $150 each week in advance. The Ringlings furnished transportation for four balloon sellers and paid a twenty-five-cent meal allowance.[39]

Al assured Zingaro that he would have the privilege again in 1913. In December 1912 Thomas Zingaro sent Al Ringling two kegs of wine, one white and one red, and a letter asking about the contract Zingaro's brother had signed. Zingaro wrote, "What my brother signed is all right. He told me he didn't leave no deposit if you want it I will send it to you."[40]

Al replied, "Your letter as well as the wine arrived here alright. I surely thank you very much for same. . . . In regards to the deposit for your privilege: It is alright, you can suit yourself. . . . The privilege is for you and we will look for you to handle the balloons with the Ringling Bros. show next season."[41]

That winter the Brothers were also concerned with larger matters. They had been considering taking one of their shows to Europe, and in December 1912 Al wrote to brother John:

> You ask me to let you know what I think about the London proposition. Would it be the Ringling show that would go over? If either of the two shows goes over I should think it should be this show for the simple reason that this show would be new over there while the Barnum show would not be a new attraction for them. Besides, the B & B show may not stand so well over there on account of the stock being sold at a loss and perhaps the show had quite a lot of newspaper notoriety on that account. But I don't think much of any of them going over. Surely we can do plenty of business without running those chances and going to all that trouble.[42]

Al's downtown Baraboo theatre project had been on hold since 1912, and in February 1913 the architect for the project, George Rapp of Chicago, wrote to Al:

> We have not heard from you for quite a while, but judge that you will be ready to go ahead with your theatre proposition now within a few weeks. Your plans and specifications, of course, have all been completed and figures have been in for some time.[43]

When the Ringlings returned to Ringlingville in Baraboo in the fall of 1912, they were aware that the Wisconsin legislature was considering income tax exemptions. In reply to Rapp, Al Ringling wrote:

> Our state legislature is now in session and I hope that legislation will be so that I can go ahead with the construction of the theatre building. From what I can learn the conditions are favorable and I should be in position to let you know concerning this within a few weeks.[44]

The legislature had considered the Ringlings' complaint of unfairness and debated whether to give the Brothers a reprieve from the new state income tax. An April 1913 news item in the *Baraboo Weekly News* detailed the legislature's discussion. "Most of the argument against the bill to exempt the Ringlings and other shows from the income tax on business done outside the state was that it was an entering wedge for other lines of business to ask the same favor."[45]

Assemblymen Andrew Gulickson and George Carpenter explained that the Ringlings paid monthly license fees of $13,000 while on the road, meaning that they were already heavily taxed. After considerable debate, the bill to exempt the Ringlings from state income tax passed sixty-nine to sixteen.[46] The exemption would save the Ringlings up to $40,000 a year ($700,000 in 2002 dollars). Their income tax nightmare was over.

No doubt feeling the sting from their hassles over state income tax, the Ringling Brothers agreed in 1912 to come under the provisions of Wisconsin's new Workmen's Compensation Act without complaint.[47] A labor newspaper in Duluth reported:

> The Ringling Circus has over 1,000 employees who are on duty practically 24 hours a day when the show is on the road. All are included in the number coming under the protection of the act. Twenty-eight other concerns [businesses] have elected to come under the act so far this month.[48]

The Ringling Bros. World's Greatest Shows, again featuring the spectacle Joan of Arc, opened in the Chicago Coliseum on April 5 and played there until April 20. The show moved east until late June, when it returned to the Midwest. From there it continued on to California and then south, closing on November 1 at Okmulgee, Oklahoma. Mean-

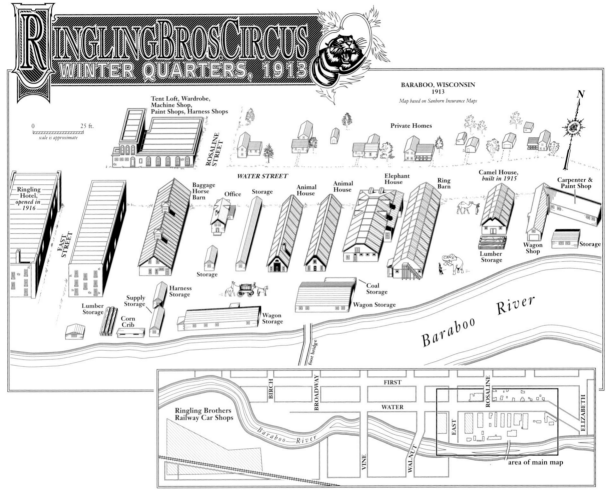

RINGLINGBROSCIRCUS
WINTER QUARTERS, 1913

BARABOO, WISCONSIN
1913
Map based on Sanborn Insurance Maps

N

Private Homes

Tent Loft, Wardrobe,
Machine Shop,
Paint Shops, Harness Shops

0   25 ft.
scale is approximate

ROSALINE STREET

WATER STREET

Camel House,
built in 1915

Carpenter &
Paint Shop

Ringling
Hotel,
opened in
1916

EAST STREET

Baggage
Horse
Barn

Office   Storage   Animal
House

Animal
House

Elephant
House

Ring
Barn

Lumber
Storage

Wagon
Shop

Storage

Storage

Supply
Storage

Harness
Storage

Coal
Storage

Wagon Storage

Lumber
Storage

Corn
Crib

Wagon
Storage

Baraboo   River

foot bridge

BIRCH

BROADWAY

FIRST

ROSALINE

ELIZABETH

Ringling Brothers
Railway Car Shops

WATER

Baraboo   River

EAST

VINE

WALNUT

area of main map

MAP BY AMELIA JANES

while, Barnum & Bailey, The Greatest Show on Earth, with the spectacle Cleopatra, played at Madison Square Garden from March 22 to April 19 and then played in Brooklyn for the week of April 21. Barnum & Bailey moved on to the Midwest and then played in eastern Canada until the end of June. Then it was back to the Midwest, including dates in Milwaukee and Madison, west to the Dakotas, and then into the South. The Barnum & Bailey show closed November 3 in Louisville and returned to winter quarters in Bridgeport, Connecticut.

Ringling Winter Employees 1913–1914

Baggage horses: 23	Blacksmith shop: 5	Harness shop: 3	Wardrobe: 5
Ring stock: 7	Car shop: 16	Wagon shop: 1	Watchmen: 2
Animals: 8	Paint shop: 16	Repair shop: 8	Office: 1
Elephants: 10		Boarding House: 12	

Average weekly salary for workers was $3.50; car shop workers earned sixteen dollars each week and blacksmiths and harness-makers earned about fifteen dollars. Meals (worth about seventy-five cents per day) and lodging (about fifty cents) were also furnished to the working men.

Salaries for superintendents ranged from a little over fifteen dollars per week for Charles Rooney, who was in charge of baggage horses, to seven dollars per week for Howard Anderson, superintendent of wardrobe.[1]

_____

NOTES

1. Ringling Brothers 1913–1914 Winter, Working Men Time Book, CWM.

Even with excellent leadership in all departments, the Brothers maintained their hands-on management approach. In August 1913 Charles wrote a detailed letter to Al about plans for the 1914 season:

With reference to the Saxons. In my opinion the act is good, but hard to place in a number with other acts and a lot of stuff to carry; but outside from this I would not reengage them because they demoralize things in the cars. They had been bringing tubs filled with beer into the sleepers and breaking all the rules. I have had this stopped, but I would not reengage them under any condition. . . .

Regarding the spectacle: I think we should have it next year. I believe it is a necessity, but I would do as you say—have one scene only, one change of costumes only and a ballet of fifty instead of sixty. I would open same with a fanfare of twenty trumpeters, the musicians in the band, then the band and tournament followed by an assembly and ballet, and confine the slow pantomime work to the least possible. I would put it away up high so that everybody can see it. Our spectacle this year is not put up high enough and the people on the back side of the blues [bleacher seats] cannot see it. It will be easy to arrange a spectacle of this kind and it will advertise as well as before and give better satisfaction.

With reference to Detective Brice. In my opinion he is the deadest detective we have ever had since we have been in show business. He is a good fellow personally, but no good on the job, and I would positively not reengage him. I have one other reason besides this which I will explain to you later.

With reference to the Roeders: Mrs. Roeder pretty near put an end to the Martinettes [a "heavy-juggling act," meaning they juggled heavy objects]. She broke a plate in the cook house and with the raw edge of one piece cut a hole in Martinette's head, cutting a principal artery. He has not been able to work since, as the cut is right where he balances on his forehead. The Roeders should not be reengaged. I assessed a heavy fine against both for fighting, etc. I suppose I should have let them go.[49]

The Ringlings and the U.S. Army

In 1912 the Ringling Brothers' incredible efficiency caught the eye of the United States Army. That year two army officers from Washington, D.C., spent two weeks traveling with the World's Greatest Shows. According to the *Baraboo Weekly News*, "They will study the methods by which a circus moves so smoothly and rapidly. It has been estimated that taking into consideration the total number of people with the circus, nearly 1,300, and the fact that it carries about 1,000 animals and 650 horses, besides all the necessities of a moving village, the machinery of the thing must be worth observation. No army detachment in action has ever pitched camp and moved each day with such rapidity."[1]

NOTES

1. *Baraboo (Wisconsin) Weekly News*, May 23, 1912.

In 1913 the Ringling Brothers replaced all their gas lighting with electricity. The Brothers had used light plants as early as 1903, but their new General Electric generators were more reliable than anything they had used before.[50] Electric lighting also lessened the danger of the Big Top's gas lamps causing a fire.

Unfortunately, fire remained a fearsome threat to the circus. While the Ringling Brothers circus was playing in Cleveland, Ohio, on May 25, 1914, a fire broke out in a nearby lumberyard. Although the Big Top was five blocks away, embers soon began falling near the circus grounds. Circus officials stopped the performance, and the crowd of thirteen thousand customers left the tent. The tents were spared, but the circus railcars, which were spotted on sidings in the midst of the fire, did not fare as well. Forty-three cars were lost—twenty-three flats, nineteen stockcars, and one baggage car. Al Ringling was the only brother in attendance at the time, but working with his brothers he soon acquired replacement cars so the show could be moved to Marion, Ohio, for its May 27 engagement. The Brothers rented cars from the Frank P. Spellman circus, moved some from the Barnum & Bailey show, which was playing in Buffalo, rented others from the Palace Car Company, and obtained still more from the New York Central Railroad.[51]

In 1901 a fire in the Kansas City Exposition Building, across the street from the circus grounds, threatened the Ringling tents. Circus tents were treated with waterproofing material that made them highly flammable; even a spark from a nearby fire could set them ablaze. DON S. HOWLAND CIRCUS COLLECTION SCRAPBOOK, CWM

It is unlikely the Brothers had insurance to cover their loss, and the fire had considerable economic impact. They contacted the Barney & Smith Car Company of Dayton, Ohio, to build twenty-eight new railcars (eighteen flatcars and ten stockcars). The stock cars would cost $1,175 each and the stockcars $1,400 each, for a total cost of $35,150 ($614,530 in 2002 dollars).[52] They also hired Barney & Smith to repair seven flatcars damaged in the fire, repair costs unknown.[53]

In the fall of 1914, with the Ringling show safely back in Baraboo and the Barnum & Bailey show at winter quarters in Connecticut, the Brothers looked to the coming season with confidence, despite the horrific fire that had destroyed more than half their namesake show's railcars. The Wisconsin income tax was no longer a major threat to their continued success.

But little did they know how the events of June 28, 1914, in faraway Sarajevo, Bosnia, would effect them and their circus. They would soon find out.

The Effects of War: 1915–1918

"It was Al Ringling's success in show business that influenced his four brothers to join him in the circus venture. Although he had given up the active management of the shows some time before he died, his was always the guiding spirit. More than any of the other brothers he was beloved of his associates and friends the world over."[1]

On June 28, 1914, the assassination of Austrian Archduke Ferdinand ignited World War I. It was soon obvious to the Ringlings that their business—which had withstood economic depression, formidable competition, and the death of one of its founders—would not escape the war's impact.

The Ringlings had for many years relied on circus acts they imported from Europe. With the onset of war, it became difficult to obtain acts—or even to contact them. In fall 1914 the Brothers were trying to locate the Eretto Trio, a performance act. They sent a letter to an address in England that read:

> For sometime past we have made every effort available to locate you, but without success. We have cabled, written and otherwise inquired. We are wholly without information as to your whereabouts, and at a loss to understand why, as is customary, you have not communicated with us. . . . We are anxious that you respond immediately.[2]

There is no record as to whether the Eretto Trio ever joined the Ringlings' shows.

The Ringlings were also unable to obtain new wild animals for their menagerie. According to circus historian Richard J. Reynolds:

> The war devastated the [German] Hagenbeck firm, which depended heavily on shipments of African animals from its German colonies. That source was soon cut off.

The Ringling Brothers
opened the 1915 season
at the Chicago Coliseum.
Print Collection, CWM

The firm of Louis Ruhe was somewhat less affected because it had a subsidiary in America and continued to send animals from Alfeld, Germany, via Dutch intermediaries and Dutch ships, the Netherlands having remained neutral.[3]

Not all troubles the Ringlings encountered during the 1915 season could be blamed on the war. Because of an outbreak of hoof-and-mouth disease in the country, the U.S. Department of Agriculture banned the interstate shipment of cloven-hoofed mammals. This ban prevented circuses from carrying camels, giraffes, water buffalo, bison, deer, antelopes, and warthogs. Thus, when the World's Greatest Shows headed to Chicago for its April 15 opening at the Coliseum, it left those animals behind in Baraboo. A writer for the *New York Clipper* commented: "The hoof and mouth quarantine has curtailed a good deal in the circus menagerie. A herd of ostriches has taken the place of the giraffes with the Ringling show and none of the cloven footed hay-eating animals were brought to Chicago for the Coliseum engagement. The youngsters missed the camels."[4]

The Ringlings played in Chicago until the end of the April and then went under canvas in Zanesville, Ohio. A highlight of the 1915 show was the remarkable aerialist Lillian Leitzel, who became known as one of the finest female performers of all time. Fred

A highlight of the 1915 show was the remarkable aerialist Lillian Leitzel. Poster Collection, CWM

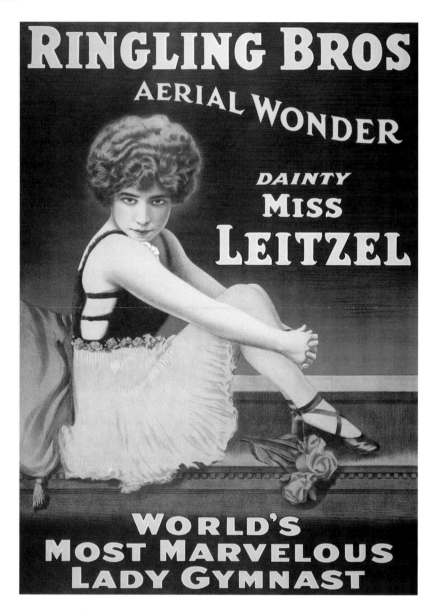

Bradna, equestrian director with the Barnum & Bailey show in 1915, believed that Lillian Leitzel was the greatest circus star of either sex: "Her showmanship, her artistry, [and] the management's ballyhoo of her act are without parallel. And the way in which she, alone in the tent top, twisted her dainty body over one arm seventy-five to hundred times in a feat of endurance, was unique."[5]

Barnum & Bailey, The Greatest Show on Earth, opened its 1915 season at Madison Square Garden in New York on April 1. With their two big traveling shows, the Ringlings continued to dominate the circus business. That year there were twenty-one railroad circuses on tour, most of them tiny shows compared with the Ringlings'. The Brothers' namesake show had eighty-five rail cars; the Barnum & Bailey show had eighty-two.[6] The next-largest show in 1915 was the Carl Hagenbeck-Wallace Shows, with fifty-three railcars.

Even with the threat of the United States becoming a part of the conflagration in Europe, the Ringlings did well in 1915. They attracted large crowds, even some turn-aways, and by season's end the Ringling Bros. World's Greatest Shows had grossed $1,347,452 ($23.3 million in 2002 dollars). The Ringling circus showed 172 days, with an average gross income per day of $7,834. The biggest days were in Washington, D.C. ($15,732); Hartford, Connecticut ($13,774); Boston ($16,359); and Dallas ($14,656). Unbelievably, they took in $10,849.50 in little Postville, Iowa, population 972, proving that their Iowa roots remained strong.[7] For the matinee and evening performances in Postville on September 3, 1915, the Ringling Brothers attracted 18,000 people. A local German-language newspaper reported:

> The likes of the mass of humanity, which the Ringling Brothers Circus attracted last Friday evening, has never before seen in Postville nor is it likely to be seen again. Beginning Thursday evening every road leading to Postville was alive with traffic carrying those wishing to watch the unloading of the circus.
>
> The [passenger] trains were filled beyond capacity and the morning train to St. Paul, which had extra cars, had to [go] back to Monona to pick up all of those there and in Luana, for whom there was no room on the regular train and bring them to Postville.[8]

The Ringling circus closed in Memphis, Tennessee, on November 1 and returned to Baraboo for another winter. The circus was an escape from the worries of the day, and the circus business had once again proven its resilience during difficult times. That winter each of the Brothers drew $55,000 in profit sharing from the business's account ($949,000 in 2002 dollars). On January 1, 1916, the Ringlings had $93,560.26 in the bank.[9]

After their threats and indecision about leaving Wisconsin earlier that decade, the Ringlings now seemed content at Ringlingville Baraboo. They even added to their holdings there, having purchased during the previous December thirteen and one-eighth acres from Theron and Lucy N. Case for $1,800.[10]

But the Ringlings were shocked when Al, the oldest brother, died on January 1, 1916, at sixty-three years of age. It is impossible to say which of the original five brothers had made the greatest contribution to the Ringling Brothers' shows. But there probably would not have been a Ringling Brothers Circus without Al Ringling's enthusiasm and experience.

Al Ringling (1852–1916), the oldest of the Ringling Brothers, was largely responsible for starting the Ringling Brothers Circus. PRINT COLLECTION, CWM

Al, for many years the show's program director, knew how to keep a circus show moving and to keep an audience interested. He was also well respected by his peers. *The Show World* had once written:

> The debut of the five Ringlings in the Northwest some twenty years ago marked the beginning of an evolution in the performance. The father of this evolutionary idea was Al Ringling, who today is beyond the shadow of doubt the greatest director general of circus programs ever known. He is the wonder of the age at collecting and putting together acts and stunts that hold audiences spellbound.[11]

Al was the glue that held the confederation of five together. Without a written contract, the Brothers shared equally the decision making and the profits. Of all the brothers, Al seemed to enjoy living in Baraboo the most. While his brothers sought homes in other places, Al made his home in Baraboo with his wife, Lou, spending most of his winters there, looking after activities at winter quarters. After Al's death, his sister Ida's son, Henry Ringling North, wrote that "Al Ringling had the sweetest disposition of all the brothers; he was the one whom the circus people really loved. When the news reached Winter Quarters, clowns and cooks, hostlers and equestrians, wept for 'Uncle Al.'"[12]

Although they had lost their leader, John, Charles, Alf T., and Henry were committed to continuing their shows. They went on with planning the 1916 season and looking for new ways to attract people to their tents. In early 1916 Charles Ringling had heard about a big snake that was available for sale. "We want the big snake if it is nearly 30 feet long. I take it F. O. B. France might mean 'before the duty is paid.' Make sure about it as it would make a big difference in price."[13] There is no evidence that they acquired the big reptile.

That season the Ringlings would debut a new spectacle, advertised as "Ringling Brothers Circus and Fairyland Spectacle Cinderella," with "1250 characters, 300 dancing girls, 735 horses, 100 musicians, 108 cage zoo, 400 arenic artists, 60 clowns, 89 railroad cars. One fifty cent ticket admits all. Children under 12 half-price."[14] The performer who played Cinderella was from Europe, and the Ringlings had some difficulty in contacting her and arranging her safe transportation to the United States.

Winter Quarters Expenses, February 1916

A circus earned income during its show season, usually from April through November, but it spent money all year long. The Ringlings' departure from Baraboo clearly would have a huge economic impact on that community.

By the winter of 1915–1916 the Ringlings had to feed about five hundred horses and ponies, twenty-nine elephants, and fifteen camels, plus an additional twenty or so other hay-eaters, from antelope to zebras. In February 1916 the Brothers purchased 159 tons of hay, for $1,848.62, and eighteen bushels of carrots, for $9.40.[1] They bought eight old horses from neighboring farmers ($58.00) to feed the carnivores, which included tigers, lions, leopards, and hyenas.

As usual, preparations for spring included purchasing equipment for the coming season. That February they bought 162 sixteen-foot tamarack tent poles ($24.30), 100 twelve-foot poles ($6.50), and 55 seventeen-foot poles ($8.25). Paint for the poles cost $47.04, and new ropes cost $1,110.47. They purchased an "electric engine" for $2,375 and electric light supplies, bulbs, and the like for $322.98. In addition general hardware, lumber, and paint cost $1,017.36.

The payroll for the approximately 120 employees for the month of February 1916 was $3,205.65 ($52,552 in 2002 dollars). Other expenses that month included flowers for Mrs. Gollmar's funeral ($35) and for Al Ringling's funeral ($80), the telephone bill ($59.87), the gas and electric bill ($341.05), postage ($11), and freight cost to the railroad ($31.08).[2]

NOTES

1. Inventory, estate of Al Ringling, October 11, 1918, CWM.
2. Winter Quarters Ledger, February 1916, Fred Pfening III, private collection, Columbus, Ohio.

Fire once again struck the Ringling show in fall 1916. On the afternoon of October 28, in Huntsville, Alabama, a fire started in one of the baggage horse tents just before the afternoon show was to begin. Before the horses could be cut loose, more than one hundred were lost to the flames.

The Hagenbeck-Wallace Circus had just closed for the season and was back at winter quarters in West Baden, Indiana, some 375 miles north of Huntsville. The Ringlings quickly acquired one hundred Hagenbeck-Wallace horses, which joined the Ringling show at Clarksdale, Mississippi, on October 30 and stayed with the show until it closed on November 4. Even though circus people competed vigorously, in times of disaster they were quick to help each other.[15]

By the end of 1916 World War I continued to pose international problems and threatened to drag America into the fray, but the Ringlings had nevertheless had another successful season. During the week of May 20, in Ohio, the Ringling show took in $76,825.60; in Illinois, Tennessee, and Kentucky during the week of September 30, they earned $54.567.55; and in Mississippi and Louisiana, during the final week of the season, the show took in $61.684.87. The Ringling show's gross earnings for 1916 were $1,613,150 ($25.6 million in 2002 dollars).[16]

During the 1916 season the Ringling show was out 204 days with 177 show days.

This Ringling Hotel, on Water Street in Baraboo, opened in fall 1916.
PRINT COLLECTION, CWM

They put on 353 performances, visiting 152 towns and 23 states. And they traveled 12,974 miles, not including miles to and from winter quarters in Baraboo. They closed on November 4 in Baton Rouge, Louisiana, and made their way back to Ringlingville Baraboo.[17]

That winter the "European war" continued to rage, but the remaining Ringling Brothers stayed optimistic. They built a new hotel for their employees on Water Street in Baraboo. "The new hotel, the pride of the employees, and in the construction of which Henry Ringling had had the supervision during the summer months, is the best equipped circus hotel in the country. It has been designed and constructed for the peculiar purpose for which it is planned, and is a revelation in the circus world."[18]

The heating plant was located in the basement of the hotel, along with quarters for "colored help." The first floor was a lobby/reading room. The second floor held dining and sleeping rooms, and the third floor was a large dormitory, designed to be used in the spring, when the circus was preparing to go on the road and employee numbers increased.

There is no record of it, but the Ringlings likely bought horses before the start of the 1917 season to replace those killed in October in the fire. By this time they had from seven hundred to eight hundred horses, and they routinely bought and sold them in very large numbers.

By the following spring, America was at war. President Wilson presented a war message to Congress on April 2, 1917, and it immediately passed both houses with large majorities. The federal government, through the War Industries Board, assumed control of many facets of the U.S. economy, including the railroads. There were "meatless" Mondays and "wheatless" Wednesdays. With the draft the army swelled from one hundred thousand to five million within the year.[19] Able-bodied men who could work for the circus became scarce. Normally, the Barnum & Bailey show employed 250 canvasmen; when the show went under tents in 1917, it had only 80.[20]

The Ringlings intended to feature the Cinderella spectacle again in 1917. But Jeanne Rae, the performer who played Cinderella, had spent the winter in Europe. Could she safely return to the United States for the show season? On April 5 a Chicago newspaper reported her safe arrival in that city:

> Cinderella flits past submarine danger zone. Cinderella does not fear the submarines. Under convoy of the very best fairies, Cinderella, otherwise Miss Jeanne Rae, care of Ringling Brothers' circus, sailed across the danger zone and yesterday arrived in Chicago. She spent the winter doing hospital work in Belfast. Her father and two brothers are in the trenches. Irregular sailings delayed other performers, but the management had a special train to bring them from New York. All have reported and a dress rehearsal will be held tomorrow evening.[21]

The 1917 show also included the Clarkonians, consisting of three Clarke brothers. Their contract specified that the act should consist of the following:

> Clarkonians Big Aerial Act by Ernest and Charles Clarke. Jockey Act (In Highland Costume) by Clarke Brothers and others to be supplied by Ringling Brothers. Principle somersault act by Percy Clarke. Principle somersault act by Ernest Clarke if required. Juggling Riding act by Charles Clarke if required. Clarke Brothers to furnish stock for above acts. All to take part in tournament or entry. Ringling Brothers to furnish state room in sleeping car.

The Ringlings also paid the three Clarkes $325 per week.[22]

With the costs of war and lack of labor, circus operating expenses soared. In 1917 there were eighteen railroad circuses on tour in the United States, down from twenty-

Coining a Phrase

On May 8, 1916, President Woodrow Wilson attended the Barnum & Bailey Circus in Washington, D.C. As Equestrian Director Fred Bradna escorted President Wilson across the arena to the music of "Hail to the Chief," the president took off his hat and threw it into the middle of the center ring. The press picked up on the stunt, announcing that Wilson had "thrown his hat in the ring" for the 1916 election. The phrase, of course, continues to this day.[1]

NOTES

1. Fred Bradna, *The Big Top* (New York: Simon and Schuster, 1952), p. 118.

one in 1915 and 1916 and twenty-five in 1914. The Ringling Brothers, with eighty-five railcars, and Barnum & Bailey, with eighty-four cars, were the largest.[23]

Despite their worries people flocked to the circus in 1917. In Chicago the Brothers had turn-away audiences on April 14 and April 15 and took in more than $10,000 each day. There would be turn-away audiences throughout the season and across the country. The Ringling show was out 212 days in 1917, with 184 show dates and 356 performances in 145 towns and 28 states including the District of Columbia. The show traveled 18,115 miles.[24] Gross receipts for the World's Greatest Shows were $1,792,475, an average of $9,742 per show date.[25] The Ringlings closed the 1917 season in Memphis, Tennessee, on November 5 and returned to Baraboo.

The year 1918 would be one of transition for the Ringlings. The war continued in Europe. Labor shortages were rampant. Business expenses were rising to unbelievable levels, and certain essential supplies needed for circus operations were simply not available. In a July 1917 letter, Charles Ringling wrote:

> With reference to next year, we have been rather uncertain as to what we might expect after the control of foodstuffs is established. I am afraid that we will not be allowed to use flour for paste. Starch is a poor substitute for our use as it can not be carried thick for country use and thinned as used. Starch, too, may be subject to regulations for food conservation.
>
> We might be obliged, if this war continues, to resort to advertising matter that can be tacked up—cloth, cardboard, etc.—and window work to a far greater extent than in the past and so not be able to post the quality of wall work we do at present. . . . [C]osts are way beyond anything ever experienced before and difficulties of transportation are serious. We would be satisfied for the present year and the next to be able to keep our business running on the same plane as in past years without anticipating any very large profits.[26]

Nevertheless, while the world's major powers battled in Europe in March 1918, peace and tranquility seemed to prevail at Ringlingville Baraboo. A reporter for *Billboard* wrote:

> The snow lies deep among the Wisconsin hills and the rivers are choked with ice, but at Ringling Brothers Circus winter quarters in Baraboo there is such activity and many signs of the approaching spring opening. All talk of war and rumors to the contrary have not retarded the work nor delayed the preparations for the coming season. The world's "greatest shows"—the "biggest thing that moves"—will go out this season bigger, better and grander than ever. The big show will carry a mes-

sage of cheer and brighter things to every point the itinerary touches, taking the people's thoughts from serious subjects and relieving the nervous tension occasioned by troublesome times. Along the muddy streets of "Ringlingville," that portion of Baraboo that lies near the river bank and has been so designated by the show folks as well as natives, there are many indications that the show is about to start.[27]

By the 1918 show season, only thirteen railroad circuses were on tour. The Ringling Brothers' show and Barnum & Bailey were clearly the largest, with eighty-five railcars each.[28] European acts were now impossible to acquire, and wages were soaring, making it difficult for the Ringlings to keep help. That year the Brothers presented the spectacle "In Days of Old," a show written by Charles Ringling that depicted times of "Romance and Chivalry" and featured ballet dancers. The Ringlings increased the price of general admission tickets to 60 cents ($8.12 in 2002 dollars), which included a war tax.[29]

The Ringlings' spectacles, such as 1916's "In Days of Old," featured dozens of ballet dancers. PRINT COLLECTION, CWM

Then, just before the Ringlings left winter quarters in April 1918, a force nearly as deadly as the war began taking shape. An army private at Fort Riley, Kansas, went on sick call on March 11 with a sore throat, fever, and headache. By noon of that day, one hundred soldiers had come down with the flu; by the end of the week the number had soared to five hundred.[30] By summer the great flu epidemic of 1918 was sweeping the country, killing people by the thousands.

The Ringlings opened their 1918 season in Chicago and moved east to Pennsylvania, New York, and then back to the Midwest, where they played most of the summer. Daily receipts were modest, especially during the rainy early season. By midsummer attendance improved; they took in $16,684.47 on July 9 in Milwaukee, one of their biggest

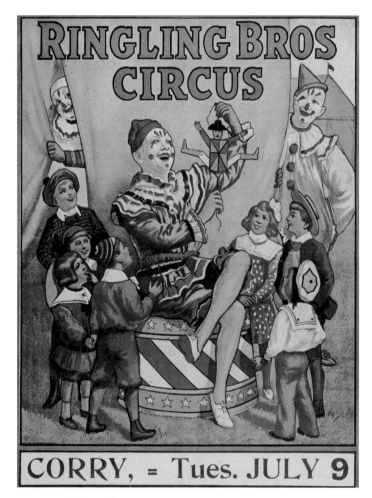

RINGLING BROS CIRCUS

CORRY, = Tues. JULY 9

A 1918 Ringling Brothers courier. In 1919 they would combine their show with Barnum & Bailey. COURIER COLLECTION, CWM

days ever. The crowds in Birmingham, Alabama, on September 23 were enormous, producing daily receipts of $21,298.28. Still, the deadly flu (known as the Spanish influenza because it had devastated Spain) swept across the United States like a Great Plains windstorm. By fall cities were canceling events, including parades, sporting events, and church services. On a single day in October, 851 persons died in New York City. All told, the pandemic killed an estimated 20 million persons worldwide, with the U.S. death toll at 548,000.[31]

The Ringlings were forced to close the show early, on October 8, 1918. "Quarantine regulations made necessary by the epidemic of Spanish Influenza at one swoop brought the circus season to a close last week. Nearly all of the circuses still on the road were playing Southern territory and were caught in the first restrictions regarding amusements that were issued. Both the Ringling Bros. and Barnum and Bailey circuses closed Tuesday, October 8."[32]

The Ringling Brothers managed only 158 show dates and 302 performances in 1918. Total receipts for the namesake show were $1,385,984; average daily receipts were $8,772, about a $1,000 less per day than in 1917.[33]

After the early closing in Waycross, Georgia, the Ringling trains headed northeast rather than northwest. Without any warning to the citizens of Baraboo, the Ringling Brothers hauled their circus to the Barnum & Bailey winter quarters in Bridgeport, Connecticut. They had at last abandoned Ringlingville Baraboo, which they had called home since 1884.

Then on October 10, 1918, Henry Ringling died from heart disease at his home in Baraboo. He would have been fifty years old on October 27. He had been ill much of 1917 and had spent the winter of 1917–1918 in Florida, returning to Baraboo in the spring. Henry's wife, Ida Belle Ringling, was not interested in owning part of the business, and the surviving brothers purchased Henry's share of the circus, probably paying the share's value to Henry's estate.[34]

For the first time in thirty-four years, Ringlingville Baraboo was quiet. No strange animals called in the dark of night, no elephants trumpeted, no great loads of hay lumbered up Water Street, no Ringlingville winter quarters employees kicked up their heels on Saturday night in Baraboo bars.

Earlier in the season there had been some conjecture that the opposite might happen—that Barnum & Bailey would winter in Baraboo along with the Ringling show and that the Bridgeport winter quarters would be used by a manufacturer producing war goods.[35] After the Ringlings' 1912 decision to stay at Baraboo, very few people anticipated their abrupt departure.

On October 17, 1918, the *Baraboo Weekly News* carried this story:

> Arthur N. Buckley received a telegram from his brother, Thomas B. Buckley, which stated that the show had closed in Georgia and would go to Bridgeport for the winter. The plan was to return to Baraboo but on account of the war conditions and the influenza it was decided to move to the eastern city. In case the war should continue it might not be possible to take the shows on the road next summer. Davis and Cooley had filled the bins with coal at the winter quarters here and other work was done to make the place ready for the show to return soon. . . . On account of the scarcity of help and disease the attraction has been laboring under difficulties. Baraboo will miss the presence of the elephants, red wagons and men whose families reside here.[36]

The details of the Brothers' decision remain somewhat of a mystery. According to Chappie Fox, Mrs. Henry Ringling believed the decision was made on the train after the Brothers left their last stand in Georgia on October 8. The vote was tied—Henry and Charles voted for Baraboo and John and Alf T. voted for Bridgeport. Finally, they agreed to return to Baraboo. But, as the story went, Henry died while they were en route, and now the vote was two to one in favor of Bridgeport. The train changed direction and headed for Connecticut.[37] This story persisted around Baraboo for many years—but there is no truth to it, as Henry died on October 10 in Baraboo, and the Brothers made their decision to head to Connecticut before the train left Georgia on October 8.

On October 5, three days before the circus left Georgia, *Billboard* magazine reported that the Ringlings would leave Baraboo:

> It is currently reported that the Ringling Brothers will depart from their time-honored custom of wintering the Ringling Brothers' World's Greatest Shows at Baraboo, Wisconsin and that Bridgeport, Connecticut will be the winter quarters this season of that show as well as the Barnum and Bailey.[38]

The story gave wartime labor shortages as the reason for the move.

As usual, the Brothers had kept their decision a secret, not informing anyone in

Baraboo or anywhere else of their intentions. They saw no need to tell the employees until just before they left for Connecticut. *Billboard* reported that on October 8, Charles had spoken to the Ringling employees while they were still in Waycross, Georgia. He informed them that the Ringling show would winter at Bridgeport with the Barnum & Bailey show and said that there might be a consolidation of both shows. If they were fortunate enough to put out a show the next season, it would be a combined Ringling and Barnum & Bailey circus.[39]

Henry Ringling North, Ida's son, later wrote about the move to Connecticut and the consolidation of the two circuses. According to North, the move had nothing to do with wartime shortages. John and Charles Ringling had concluded that the American people would no longer support two big circuses. North also noted that "[o]ne or more of the partner-brothers had always been on the trains to make instant decisions, quell revolts, or meet emergencies with the full authority and confidence of all the others behind him."[40] With only three partners left (and Alf T. was sick), there were no longer enough brothers to maintain their usual level of control over their enterprise.

Some speculated that property taxes were another reason the Ringlings left Wisconsin. The October 1918 issue of *Billboard* reported: "As far as can be learned the State authorities of Wisconsin have taxed the Ringling Brothers so heavily on their property that the Brothers decided that inasmuch as the quarters at Bridgeport afforded ample shelter and convenience for both of their shows, their interests might profitably be concentrated there."[41]

Another major factor—perhaps the primary one—in the Brothers' decision was the start of new restrictions on the number of railroad locomotives they could use. Under the authority of the Army Appropriation Act, President Wilson, by Presidential Proclamation 1419, had established the United States Railroad Administration (USRA) on December 26, 1917. The USRA took over the operation of U.S. railroads, steamship lines, inland waterways, and telephone and telegraph companies in the name of national defense. Among other things, the USRA would now determine locomotive usage and routes. By 1918 the Ringlings needed eight locomotives, four for each circus, to take their shows on the road.[42]

Historian Richard Reynolds III interviewed the late Raymond "Sabu" Moreau, whose father had worked for John Ringling, mostly handling John's personal business. According to Reynolds, Moreau's father had told his son about the situation:

> The government controlled the railroads. . . . In mid-1918, when the war was at fever pitch and the end not in sight, the government told the surviving Ringling Brothers that for 1919 they could not make but four locomotives available to them. Since both the Barnum and Ringling shows each operated four sections, this meant that one or the other of the shows would have to stay in the barn. Of course, neither

The Al Ringling Theatre

Al Ringling hired Chicago architects C. W. and George Rapp to design his theatre; the project's general contractors were the Wiley Brothers, also of Chicago. The theatre's construction took eight months COURTESY OF THE AL. RINGLING THEATRE FRIENDS, INC.

Construction of the Al Ringling Theatre began in March 1915. By then Al Ringling's health was failing, and friends and family feared he might never see the building. The city of Baraboo held a "day of tribute" for Al Ringling on June 24, 1915, on the courthouse grounds, across the street from the theatre project. Thousands attended. On that day Baraboo Mayor G. T. Thuerer declared:

> We have assembled on this day to acknowledge our deep sense of gratitude to a man who, by his generosity and public interest, has endeared himself to the people not only of Baraboo but the entire surrounding neighborhood. In the construction of the an opera house Mr. Ringling is supplying a long felt want that he should build same of such magnificent proportions, is the strongest evidence of his unselfish nature.[1]

The theatre, originally with seats for 874, cost about $100,000 to build and was patterned after the Opera

(continued on page 204)

The Al Ringling Theatre

(continued from page 203)

The theatre's lavish interior (shown here in the 1920s) boasts seventeen curved box seats, candle-fixture chandeliers, gold-trimmed draperies, ornate carvings and columns, and elaborate murals including cherubs that represent "joy, pleasure, delight, and varying pleasurable emotions." COURTESY OF THE AL. RINGLING THEATRE FRIENDS, INC.

House of the Petit Trianon in the Palace of Versailles. One writer described the theatre this way:

> Like a gem in our midst, the Al Ringling Theatre is a treasure of rare quality. Magnificent and richly designed in the style of grand French Opera

houses, the Theatre is a masterpiece of European architecture. Fine plasterwork, tasseled draperies, intricate ceiling frescos and decorative lighting create an atmosphere steeped in the artistic pleasures both exuberant and serene.[2]

The theatre's grand opening, on November 17, 1915, featured the comic opera *Lady Luxury*. Al was in attendance that night, although by then he was nearly blind, and his wife, Lou, whispered to him throughout the show to describe the event. The next day a *Baraboo Weekly News* reporter proclaimed, "It must be a source of gratification to Al. Ringling to know that his efforts in providing a playhouse in Baraboo is so much appreciated by his fellow townspeople. Every seat in the house was sold in four hours and hundreds were disappointed in not being able to be present at the first performance in order to show their appreciation to the one who made possible this fine building." The theatre would go on to showcase everything from opera to vaudeville to first-run films.[3]

After Al Ringling's death seven weeks later, Lou Ringling was not interested in owning the theatre, and the control of the building passed to the surviving brothers. They tried to give the theatre to the city of Baraboo in 1917, but because of certain legal restrictions connected to the offer, several locals opposed the gift, and the brothers withdrew the offer in 1918. The theatre was passed on to several Ringling heirs and eventually came under the control of Henry Ringling Jr., who operated it until his death in 1952, at which point the theatre was sold outside the family. It was placed on the National Register of Historic Places in 1976. In 1989 ownership of the building passed to the Al. Ringling Theatre Friends, Inc., a community-based group that continues to maintain and restore the building.[4]

The Al Ringling Theatre

The Al Ringling Theatre was completed in 1915 and was described by one writer as "a gem in our midst." It probably was the Ringling Brothers' greatest legacy to the Baraboo community. Photo by Steve Apps

NOTES

1. "The Al. Ringling Theatre," http://www.alringling.com/.

2. Ibid.

3. Ibid.

4. Ibid.

the government nor the show knew at the time that the war would end suddenly and well before the 1919 season started. Moreau said that the decision to combine the shows was made around June or July of 1918. By the time the war was actually over, they had already started painting "Combined Shows" on some of the equipment. The 1919 combination was not a "now and forever more" decision. Moreau said it was done initially as an experiment, but they made so much in 1919 in the Garden and later on the road, that they decided to stick with the combination.[43]

Richard Thomas, John Ringling's biographer, wrote about a meeting the Brothers had in the summer of 1918: "Before the meeting adjourned . . . the Railroad Administration notified them that two large circuses could not be transported during the war. . . . The long postponed decision to consolidate the two shows into one was made. . . .

With the decision to combine the two big shows into a super-colossal circus, one circus era died and another was born."[44]

The USRA decree brought a long-simmering decision to a boil. But other evidence suggests that the boys had been considering consolidation of the two shows at least a year earlier.

Barnum & Bailey employee Fred Bradna wrote that he, Charles Ringling, and Charles's son, Robert, went on a swimming party in Lake Erie on a hot day in summer 1917. (Fred Bradna was with the Barnum & Bailey show in 1917.)[45] "As we relaxed on the sand, Charlie said to no one in particular, 'We could get around all these shortages [brought on by the war] if we combined the two big shows. Then we'd have help enough, and acts enough, to go on. What a show *that* would be!'"[46]

Although conversations leading to the Brothers' move out of Baraboo will likely never be known, the result remains the same. The glory and spectacle that once breathed life into Ringlingville were gone. Ringlingville on the river in Baraboo became a ghost town. On quiet winter nights, many residents thought they could still hear the lions' roar and the hyenas' wail. When the snow began melting in spring, they imagined hearing the sounds of horses' shod hoofs echoing along the streets as they pulled multi-colored circus wagons. Some missed the parade of huge elephants, ears flopping and trunks swinging as they walked the side streets and thoroughfares for exercise.

The economic loss to the Baraboo community was considerable. Using 1916 winter quarters figures and assuming five months in winter quarters, the salary losses alone amounted to $16,028 (about $294,000 in 2002 dollars). Add the money spent on feed ($9,533), utilities ($2,000), and materials for repairs ($5,086), and a conservative estimate for the economic loss to Baraboo would be $18,247 ($311,000 in 2002 dollars)—for just one winter season. A less-obvious loss was railroad business in and out of town. But perhaps more important than economic losses, and largely overlooked or even unknown by the community, was the prestige of having the largest circus in the world wintering in their midst. Circus historian Fred Dahlinger said it well: "Baraboo lost the highest international image enterprise that it's ever had."[47]

Some Baraboo residents were angry that the circus had left Baraboo so abruptly. The late Robert Barnes, who was born in 1914 and grew up in Baraboo, recalled, "A common belief among many Baraboo people at that time was that circus people were scalawags, always out to get people."[48]

Indeed, some in Baraboo felt relieved with the circus gone. Over the years the affectionate reference to the Ringling Brothers as "our boys" had slowly shifted to "those circus people"—words often spoken with disdain.

But no one could deny that Ringlingville, both on the road and in Baraboo, was a unique part of the entertainment business not replicated anywhere in the country. And now, abruptly, Ringlingville had become history.

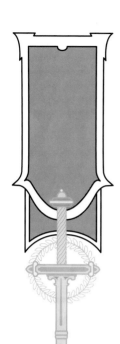

EPILOGUE
After Ringlingville

"There had never been anything like it before; and I am willing to prophesy that there will never be again."[1]

In early fall 1918, when the Ringlings took both the Ringling Brothers and the Barnum & Bailey shows to winter quarters in Bridgeport, Connecticut, nearly everyone believed that World War I would continue for some time. But not long after the Brothers arrived at Bridgeport, the Armistice was signed on November 11, 1918, and the war abruptly ended. The Treaty of Versailles was signed on June 28, 1919. Government control of the railroads would continue until 1920.

That winter the remaining Ringling Brothers—Alf T., Charles, and John—merged their two huge circuses into one colossus. They called it Ringling Bros. and Barnum & Bailey Combined Shows, The Greatest Show on Earth. Hundreds of employees, from laborers to managers, lost their jobs in the consolidation. Alf T., who lived at his estate in New Jersey, was ailing and had little involvement with the circus in 1919. John and Charles would manage the new show, John finding acts, planning routes, and working with the railroads, and Charles managing personnel, arranging the program with the equestrian director, and supervising press agents. They spent the winter scurrying to combine the two shows, repaint wagons and cars, and line up help. The show debuted at New York's Madison Square Garden on March 29, 1919.

The Ringling Bros. and Barnum & Bailey Combined Shows closed on November 21, 1919, in Savannah, Georgia. Alf T. Ringling had died three weeks earlier in Oak Ridge, New Jersey, on October 29 at the age of fifty-five. He was not a flamboyant man, like his brother John, but he made a unique contribution to the Ringling success with his writing skill and promotional savvy. Since the acquisition of the Barnum & Bailey show in 1907, Alf T. had worked with John in managing that show.[2]

John and Charles continued to expand their enormous show and add new acts. In

One of first advertising posters announcing the combined Ringling Bros. and Barnum & Bailey shows. POSTER COLLECTION, CWM

1920 the combined show had ninety-two railcars. (In 1921 the Brothers had ninety-six cars, and from 1922 through 1928 they had one hundred cars.)[3] By 1928 it truly was the Greatest Show on Earth—exaggeration no longer required.

But by the early 1920s John and Charles were not getting along well. Al had been a stabilizing force among the Brothers. Without him, John and Charles bickered. Their personalities were just too different. According to Henry Ringling North and Alden Hatch, authors of *The Circus Kings:*

> [W]hen Charles and John were left to divide their world between them, a ground mist of jealousy rose to cloud their relationship. This did not affect their management of the circus. . . . But in their outside business ventures and their social life, the rivalry between them became more acute, even bitter. . . . [T]hey carried this competition to ridiculous lengths. If Uncle John got a yacht, the *Zalophus,* Uncle Charles had to have an even bigger one, the *Symphonia.* Because John had formed the Bank of Sarasota, Charles founded the Ringling Trust and Savings Bank. Sarasota of that time needed two banks considerably less than a dog needs two tails.[4]

John had many interests outside the circus. Over the years he bought railroads and land from Oklahoma to Montana, and he came to love Sarasota, Florida, where he bought considerable real estate. With a business associate, Owen Burns, John Ringling financed the Ringling Causeway and bridge to St. Armands Key, which he donated to the City of Sarasota in 1928. He also donated 130 acres of land on Longboat Key to the city for a golf course development.[5]

In 1901 Alf T. Ringling (1863–1919) purchased a farm east of Baraboo, where he built a European-style chalet. An avid angler, he enjoyed fishing in the stream that ran through his property. PRINT COLLECTION, CWM

Charles, who had a fine home in Evanston, Illinois, also bought waterfront land next to John's in Sarasota. By 1926 both of the brothers had built multimillion-dollar homes in Florida, and both owned two yachts. Charles and Edith Ringling's marble mansion on Sarasota Bay was built in 1925. Marshall Field and Company of Chicago did the interior decoration, and many of the furnishings were imported from Europe. The cost of the home was estimated at $880,000 (about $9 million in 2002 dollars). Charles also built a home for his daughter, Hester, on adjoining property; both buildings are now owned by the New College of Florida.[6]

John and Mable Ringling's mansion, Ca d'Zan (house of John), was built in 1925 and 1926. The palatial home is the largest Sarasota has ever seen, with thirty-one rooms and servant quarters in one wing. It was later proclaimed to be "among the most charming products of the 1920s fashion for new historical mansions for the rich and famous."[7] A restoration of the home, which is open to the public, was completed in 2002.

By the late 1920s John Ringling had collected more than 625 paintings and hundreds of other pieces of art. In 1927 he and his wife began construction of The John and Mable Ringling Museum of Art, also on their estate, to house the collection. "It is the largest art museum south of Washington, D.C. and has been authoritatively called 'the most important collection of Italian baroque art, and Flemish artist Peter Paul Rubens in the United States.'"[8] Unfortunately, Mable Ringling died on June 8, 1929, and did not see the completion of the museum.

Charles Ringling, age sixty-two, died on December 3, 1926. He left his interest in the circus to his wife, Edith.[9] As Richard J. Reynolds III noted:

John Ringling (1866–1936) was disliked by some but loved by many. He was a railroad routing genius and was largely responsible for the Ringling Brothers' shows finding success in out-of-the way places. Print Collection, CWM

Charles Ringling (1864–1926) was an accomplished musician and was loved by nearly all the Ringling employees. He was responsible for the behind-the-scenes operations of the circus moving smoothly. Print Collection, CWM

John Ringling would regret not having pressed brothers Alf T. and Charles to make a formal written partnership agreement. . . . [E]volving business principles argued for an agreement. [An agreement] usually provides that in the event of a partner's death the survivors have the option to purchase his share before it goes to his heirs. Since the Ringlings had no such agreement, John wound up a minority owner of the circus. He had a third of it but the two women . . . Edith Conway Ringling had one-third, inherited from her husband, Charles; and Aubrey Ringling—later Aubrey Haley—had one-third, inherited from her husband, Richard, who had inherited his father Alf T.'s share. Despite his minority position, the imperious John operated the show as though he alone owned it.[10]

With Charles's death, flashy John Ringling was the last remaining of the original seven brothers. The Bridgeport winter quarters lease would expire on January 1, 1928, and in 1927 John moved the circus winter quarters from Connecticut to Sarasota, where he had purchased a former fairgrounds. It proved to be a good business decision: thousands of visitors came to the Sarasota winter quarters, making it one of the top tourist attractions in the state and providing winter income for the circus. Many circus performers also made their winter homes in Sarasota, bringing a considerable diversity to the area.[11] Many people today associate the Ringlings with Sarasota, not with Bridgeport or Baraboo.

In 1928 the Greatest Show on Earth's most serious competition was the American Circus Corporation, headquartered in Peru, Indiana. On September 10, 1929, the Associated Press carried this surprising news item:

> John Ringling, who started as a singing clown, rules as supreme master of the circus world Tuesday by purchase of five of his foremost competitors. The last of the famous Ringling brothers has acquired control of the largest group of tent shows in the world, including their talent, menageries, equipment and winter quarters. The shows which have been added to the Ringling group are Sells-Floto, Hagenbeck-Wallace Animal Show, John Robinson's, Sparks, and Al. G. Barnes Wild Animal Show. The properties were purchased from the American Circus Corporation in a transaction which friends of the showman said, involved several million dollars. The exact figure was not disclosed. There are about 3,000 persons employed in the newly acquired shows, as compared with 1,600 in the present Ringling Bros-Barnum & Bailey organization.[12]

Of course, even John Ringling, who had fame and fortune and considerable luck, could not predict the devastating stock market crash that occurred but a month after his purchase. The crash of October 29, 1929, launched the worst depression in the nation's history. And the devastating economic times took their toll on the John Ringling empire. Circus attendance was down so much in 1931 that the Greatest Show on Earth closed on September 14, the earliest closing in its long history.[13]

John eventually was not able to meet an interest payment on a loan, and at a 1932 meeting with circus creditors and his partners, Edith Ringling and Aubrey Ringling, he was voted out of control of the Ringling Bros. and Barnum & Bailey Circus. By this time John was very ill, having suffered a stroke in 1931. Although he was now no longer general manager of the show, John would retain one-third of the stock in a new stock company that was formed in 1932. That fall John suffered another stroke, from which he recovered only partially.[14]

Sam Gumpertz became general manager. Gumpertz had no experience in circus management, but he had considerable circus experience, having begun his career as an acrobat at age nine. Before managing the Combined Shows, he was a producer of kinetoscopes, early motion picture projectors. According to Henry Ringling North, Gumpertz allowed the circus to deteriorate. Wagons remained unpainted. The quality of performances declined. The circus was losing money "like a broken hydrant gushing water."[15] (Henry North's statement may have been a bit of an exaggeration; in 1937, still under Gumpertz, the Greatest Show on Earth once again became profitable.)[16]

Circus World Museum

In 1959, thanks to Ringling attorney John M. Kelley's vision, a statewide fund-raising drive, and $10,000 provided by the Baraboo City Council toward the purchase of the old ring barn at Ringlingville, Circus World Museum was born.

Karen DeSanto, an education coordinator at Circus World Museum, introduces some young friends to the thrills of the circus. Photo courtesy of Circus World Museum Foundation, Inc.

According to Robert Ott, a longtime Baraboo resident who was a city council member at the time, Baraboo people didn't think much of museum organizer John Kelley. "About everyone in town avoided John M. Kelley when he came down the street because they knew he was going to pitch his vision for the circus museum to them again."[1]

The land and the buildings were deeded to the State of Wisconsin debt free. Since the museum's opening on July 1, 1959, it has been owned by the Wisconsin Historical Society. It is operated by the nonprofit Circus World Museum Foundation, Inc. The museum site was listed as a National Historic Landmark in 1969.

Charles P. "Chappie" Fox was an original Circus World Museum board member. He became director of Circus World Museum in January 1960, at which time the museum owned only two of the historic winter quarters buildings, the camel house and the ring barn. Since then the museum has acquired the baggage horse barn, two animal houses, the former office building, and the car shops. Two other former winter quarters buildings, the 1916 hotel and the paint shops, still stand but are privately owned.

In addition to acquiring the historic buildings, the museum maintains an extensive library and research center that attracts circus researchers and historians from around the world. The museum preserves more than eight thousand circus posters and has collections of handbills, business records, personal papers, old newspapers, films, photographic prints totaling more than one million items. In 1996 the museum established an artifacts department.

Chappie Fox conceived the idea of a historic circus parade. Circus World Museum presented the first horse-drawn parade in downtown Milwaukee in 1963, and the parades continued each year until 1973. In 1985 the circus parades in Milwaukee began once more, continuing through 2003. The colorful circus wagons were loaded onto train cars in Baraboo using horses and following historic loading techniques. Then the train rumbled from Baraboo to Milwaukee, stopping at several communities along the way. Tickets were sold to those who wanted to experience an old-time circus train ride. Tickets were also earned by donors who supported museum programs and

Circus World Museum

In preparation for the Great Circus Parade, Circus World Museum staff loads railcars by traditional methods, using horses to get the job done. PHOTO BY STEVE APPS

operations. In 2004 the Great Circus Train did not run, and the circus parade was held in Baraboo on July 3.

John Kelley acquired the first of Circus World's historic wagons before the museum opened, and in 1969 the museum constructed a pavilion to house some fifty restored wagons. In 1998 the C. P. Fox Wagon Restoration Center opened on the museum grounds.

Circus World Museum is open year-round; the library and archives are open to researchers by appointment. During the summer visitors to Circus World can take in a live circus performance under the Big Top, with elephants and other circus animals, a ringmaster, aerialists, and clowns. It's an incredible chance for older people to relive the circus experience and for youngsters to learn what circuses were like when the big tent shows traveled the country. Programs are also offering during spring, fall, and winter, along with holiday programs and several special events. For anyone interested in the circus, whether researcher or fan, Circus World Museum is truly a national treasure.

In 2004 Circus World Museum employed about 20 full-time people, 80 to 105 seasonal employees, and 30 to 40 volunteers assisting with everything from library research to summer programming.

NOTES

1. Fred Dahlinger Jr., correspondence with the author, August 28, 2001.

John Ringling died on December 2, 1936, a sick, defeated, and crushed man. He had lost much of his fortune and no longer controlled his beloved circus. John Ringling North, Ida Ringling North's son, took over management of the circus in 1938, two years after John's death. In 1956 the circus quit showing under canvas; it continued to show in arenas, coliseums, and auditoriums, booking throughout the winter.[17]

On November 11, 1967, the Irvin Feld family purchased the Ringling Bros. and Barnum & Bailey Circus. Successful rock and roll concert promoters, brothers Irvin and Israel Feld were familiar with the new arenas popping up around the country and saw them as a venue for their newly purchased circus. Irvin's son, Kenneth, joined the Ringling Bros. and Barnum & Bailey show in 1970. When his father died suddenly on September 6, 1984, Kenneth took control. The Feld family continues to operate the show, sending out three different "editions" to different communities, playing indoors.[18] The Ringling Bros. and Barnum & Bailey, The Greatest Show on Earth, is the last remaining railroad circus.

◈

When the Brothers didn't return to Baraboo in winter 1918, it was like someone leaving for a short trip but intending to return. But the Ringlings didn't come back, not even to retrieve their business records, which remained in the little gray office on Water Street. According to Richard Reynolds, "Property that didn't go aboard the circus trains when they left in the spring of 1918 stayed there. Some properties were sold, but a lot of it seems to have been left to rot, not least a treasure trove of business files."[19] Also abandoned were such items as wagons, blacksmith equipment, lumber, and show props.

Many of the records were stored in an underground vault, where they got wet and mildewed. The records remained in the vault until the 1930s, when the office buildings and other properties were sold. The new owners freely gave Ringling records to circus fans who wanted them. Madison attorney Sverre Braathen obtained a considerable amount of the records, and he eventually gave them to Illinois State University in Normal. Braathen, for reasons largely unknown, was not fond of Circus World Museum and chose Illinois State University because it had a modest circus history collection.[20]

William Kasiska, member of a prominent Baraboo family and known among circus historians as "Baraboo Bill," obtained even more Ringling office records. When Kasiska died in 1978, a circus collector bought Kasiska's material at auction. Other people acquired additional Ringling records. Over the years, through donations and purchase, a large amount of material has returned to the Circus World Museum Library in Baraboo.[21]

The several buildings that made up Ringlingville in Baraboo sat empty for years, receiving little if any attention as attorneys and the courts debated who owned what after all the Ringling boys had died. Baraboo native Robert Barnes recalled playing at the abandoned winter quarters as a child in the 1920s. "We played in the elephant house. It was all boarded up, but we got in anyway. There we found African shields and spears. We tossed spears at old dried elephant dung. It was great fun."[22]

Finally, in 1933, after considerable negotiating, local judge Adolph Andro and businessman Fred J. Effinger completed the agreement to purchase the Ringlingville property, which had an assessed value of $37,000.[23]

The new owners began repairing the Ringlingville buildings, which had stood vacant since 1918. They leased several of the buildings and began selling them in 1939. Schwartz Farm Equipment purchased the horse barn. The Baraboo Chick Hatchery bought the menagerie building; a second menagerie building was sold to L. R. Carpenter for storage. The W. C. Fullmer Transfer Company bought the elephant barn for use as a garage and storage building. The City of Baraboo bought the former paint shop, and the Deppe Lumber Company purchased the middle portion of the paint shop to use as a machine shed. Several of these new owners had previously leased these buildings from

Ringlingville, Water Street, Baraboo, 2002. Now part of Circus World Museum, these are several of the original buildings that made up the winter quarters for what became the largest and most profitable circus in the world, the Ringling Bros. World's Greatest Shows. PHOTO BY STEVE APPS

Andro and Effinger.[24] In June 1939 Andro and Effinger sold five more buildings—the ring barn, giraffe and zebra barn, blacksmith shop, a storage building, and a building used for drying tent poles—to a Mr. Liss.[25]

It was attorney John M. Kelley, the Ringlings' general counsel for more than thirty years, who first dreamed of a museum honoring the golden age of the railroad circus. In 1954 Kelley incorporated the Circus World Museum. The museum opened to the public on July 1, 1959, at the site of the Ringlings' Baraboo winter quarters. The museum and its Robert L. Parkinson Library and Research Center, established in 1965, help preserve the legacy of the Ringling Brothers and their great circus.

APPENDIX I

1903 Ringling Brothers' Official Program

Ringling Brothers' Official Program.

Two Performances Daily. ◊ ◊ **Commencing at 2 and 8 P. M.**

Doors open One Hour Earlier for Inspection of Menagerie.

ALBERT RINGLING, Equestrian Director.

RHODA ROYAL, Assistant Equestrian Director.

RINGMASTERS:

G. St. Leon.   John Carroll.   John Rooney.   John Agee.   George Wood.   Jno. Mercer.

RINGLING BROTHERS' MILITARY BAND.—GEO. GANWEILER, Conductor.   Popular Concert preceding each performance.   Numbers will be rendered from the following repertoire and announced by placard displayed from band stand, corresponding with numbers of selections, as below:

GRAND MARCHES.

1. La Reine de Saba..............................Gounod
2. Tannhäuser..............................Wagner
3. Welcome Polonaise..............................Hecker
4. Wedding (Midsummer Night's Dream)..............Mendelssohn
5. Coronation (The Prophet)..............Meyerbeer
6. Invocation to Battle..............................Wagner

OVERTURES.

7. Tancred..............................Rossini
8. Poet and Peasant..............................Suppé
9. William Tell..............................Rossini

CHARACTERISTIC, ETC.

10. Antony and Cleopatra (Suite de Ballet)..............Gruenwald
    No. 1..............................In the Arbor
    No. 2..............................Dance of the Nubians
    No. 3..............................Solo Dance, Minuet
    No. 4..............................Antony's Victory
11. Benediction des Poignards..............................Meyerbeer
12. Providence (Sacred Fantasia)..............................Tobani
13. Southern Memories..............................Hecker

COMEDY-OPERA.

14. Chinese Honeymoon..............................Talbot
15. The Prince of Pilsen..............................Luders
16. Foxy Quiller..............................DeKoven
17. The Wizard of Oz..............................Baum and Tietjen
18. Little Duchess..............................DeKoven
19. The Sultan of Sulu..............................Ade and Wathall

Ring No. 1.	Stage No. 1.	Ring No. 2	Stage No. 2.	Ring No. 3.

DISPLAY No. 1.—Grand Introductory Spectacle:

JERUSALEM AND THE CRUSADES.

By JOHN RETTIG.

Under the Direction of ALBERT RINGLING.

Ballet under the Supervision of SIG. MARQUETTI, assisted by B. PERI.

Ringling Brothers' Spectacular Production of the Salient Dramatic and Thrilling Episodes of the Momentous and Romantic Story of Jerusalem and the Crusades, vividly portraying in Characteristic and Radiant Costumes, Athletic and Picturesque Pastimes and Chivalric Types the Days "When Knighthood was in Flower." The Prodigal Extravagance and Voluptuous Revelries of the Oriental Court shown with Historic Accuracy in Festal Gaieties and Dancing Divertisements.

DISPLAY No. 2.—The Three Greatest Herds of Performing Elephants in the World.

A Company of Highly Educated, Unwieldy Brute Actors in an Unique Exhibition of Elephantine Sagacity. **Mr. Christian Zeitz.**	A Quintette of Elephant Comedians in a Medley of Unquestioned Funny, Ludicrous, Button-Bursting. Terpsichorean, Athletic, Musical and Bacchanalian Revels. **Mr. Pearl Souders.**	A Company of Intelligent, Agile Giants in Picturesque Pyramids and Displays. **Mr. Geo. Kealey.**

DISPLAY No. 3.—A Series of Mid-Air Performances of Exceptional Skill, Daring and Endurance.

Laughable Antics and Grinning, Freakish Mad-Cap Frolics on the Revolving Suspended Ladder. **Plamondon & Amondo** Exploits on Two Swaying Aerial Swings. **The St. Leon Sisters.** Flying Ring Specialty and Fearless Midair Evolutions. **Miss A. Forepaugh.**	Astonishing Evolutions, Somersaulting, Swings, Drops and Exhibitions of Strength and Daring upon the Aerial Bars. **The Three Alvos.**	Incomprehensible High-Air Divertisements upon a Slender Wire, held by the Teeth, showing the Possibilities resulting from Physical Culture. **TY BELL SISTERS.**	Absolutely First American Appearance of Europe's Most Famous Horizontal Bar Champions in an Entirely New Comic Conceit. **The Three Fortuns.**	A Convulsing Performance on Revolving Ladders, Suspended in Mid-Air. **Kelly Brothers.** Novelty Diversions, Graceful Posing and Muscular Exercises on the Flying Rings. **Miss Reta TATALI.**

DISPLAY No. 4.—Coterie of the World's Most Famous Equestriennes and Equestrians.

Double Vaulting Equestrian Exhibition. Two Peerless Champions Alternating Mounting and Dismounting. Riding Simultaneously upon a Single Horse. **Mr. John Rooney Mr. Fred Ledgett.**	**Forty Clowns** Bubbling over with Fun and Frolic. Forty "Merry Andrews" to please the Old and Young.	Double Vaulting Equestrian Exhibition. Two Peerless Champions Alternating Mounting and Dismounting, Riding Simultaneously upon a Single Horse. **The Hobsons.**	**A Potpourri of Comic Fellows** In an ever-changing Medley of Funny Situations, Laughable Antics and Ludicrous Maneuvers.	Double Vaulting Equestrian Exhibition. Two Peerless Champions Alternating, Mounting and Dismounting. Riding Simultaneously upon a Single Horse. **Miss May Davenport & Mr. Reno McCreen.**

Ring No. 1.	Stage No. 1.	Ring No. 2.	Stage No. 2.	Ring No. 3.

DISPLAY No. 5.—New Astonishing Diversified Trained Animal Display.

A Troupe of Diminutive Shetland Ponies in an Exhibiton of Especial Interest to the Children, performed by **Mr. John Carroll.**	The Most Unique Display of Animal Training Ever Attempted. Unquestionably the Most Wonderful Act of the Kind in the Known World. **Capt. Webb's Companies of Awkward Looking, Deft Juggling, Wonder Working Seals.** Performed by **Prof. Frank Barnes.**	The Wonderful Acting Pony, "Dandy," performed by **Mr. Jno. Agee.**	The Most Unique Display of Animal Training Ever Attempted. Unquestionably the Most Wonderful Act of the Kind in the Known World. **Capt. Webb's Companies of Awkward Looking, Deft Juggling, Wonder Working Seals.** Performed by **Prof. H. J. Reichert.**	A Splendid Group of Trained Icelandic Ponies, introduced and exhibited by their trainer. **Prof. George Woods.**

DISPLAY No. 6.—International Exhibition of Famous Saddle Horses.

A Duo of Perfectly Trained Saddle Horses in an Exposition of the Haute Ecole. Ridden by **Miss Etta Jordan and Mr. John Rooney.**	A Peerless Exhibition of Special Horse Accomplishments. Four Distinguished Prize-Winners appearing together in One Ring Ridden by the famous Masters and Mistresses of the Saddle **Mr. and Mrs. Rhoda Royal. Mr. Michael Rooney Miss Ida Miaco.**	Superb Double High-School Equestrian Display. Two Superb Perfectly Trained Menage Horses. Ridden by **Miss Savoy and Mr. John Agee.**

ON THE HIPPODROME TRACK—A Thoroughbred Horse showing all gaits in harness. Driven by Mr. Al Thompson.

DISPLAY No. 7.—Highly Skillful Medley of Contortion Specialties, Hand Balancings and Unique Performances on the High Wire.

Highly Interesting Feats of Equasion on a Single Swaying Strand of Wire. **Miss Addie Nelson.** An Immensely Clever Acrobatic Duo in a Pleasing Double Contortion Act, showing the flexibility of the human form, the direct result of physical culture training. **The 3 Nelson Sisters.**	A most Remarkable Exhibition of Muscular Dexterity—on the Roman Rings. Feats of Muscular Rigidity Unsurpassed — The most Marvelous Act of the Kind in the World, performed by a Trio of Past Masters in Athletic Excellence. **The 3 Rio Brothers.**	Peculiar Quintal Display of Dexterity, Skill and Agility in Rapid Juggling by the Deft Japanese Expert **M. Ando.**	Agile, Flexible, Nimble Bodies in a Peerless Double Contortion Act. Confusing Tangles of seeming Boneless Beings. The Marvelous **Genaro and Theol.**	The European wonder contortionist. A performance in which the flexibility of the human body is shown in a most astonishing degree. **Master Tatali.** Specialties of a Thrilling Nature, ably executed on a Slender Wire by **Miss J. Dollard.** Marvelous Feats of Contortion by **Mamekichi & Moto.**

DISPLAY No. 8.—The Unquestioned Champion Bareback Riders of the World.

Incomparable High Class Bareback Somersault Riding Act, Introducing a Complete Somersault from one Horse to another while both Rapidly Circle the Arena. A Splendid Exposition of Perfect Equestrianism. **Mr. Michael Rooney.**	**THE CLOWNS' HOLIDAY. A FAMOUS LOT OF FOOLS ON A LARK.**	The One and Only Lady Somersault Rider, the Unquestioned Champion Equestrienne of the World. **Miss D. Julian.**	**A COMPANY OF FAMOUS FOOLS IN FROLIC AND FUN.**	Exceptionally Great and Artistic Equestrian Bareback Somersault Act, Introducing the Marvelous Feat of Throwing a Backward Somersault, Starting from one horse and alighting upon Another while Galloping at Full Speed. **Mr. John Rooney.**

DISPLAY No. 9.—A MARTIAL CONCEIT.

A Poem in Graceful Marching Figures, Feeding the Eye with Exquisite Conceptions in Costume and the Inspiring Suppleness and Daintiness of Youth, and Delighting Every Sense with Exceeding Charms of Rhythm, Beauty, Music and Novelty. A Priceless Pastel of Terpsichorean Genius.	**THE SAVOYS** In an Uproaring Laughable Skit.	A Poem in Graceful Marching Figures, Feeding the Eye with Exquisite Conceptions in Costume and the Inspiring Suppleness and Daintiness of Youth, and Delighting Every Sense with Exceeding Charms of Rhythm, Beauty, Music and Novelty. A Priceless Pastel of Terpsichorean Genius.

DISPLAY No. 10.—Ringling Brothers' Great Creation, the Wonderfully Successful, Original Arenic Feature, 61 Beautiful Specimens of the Perfect Horse, Gayly Caprisoned with Costly Trappings. Obedient to the Trainer's Call, Moving in Harmony in the Most Complicated, Intricate and Difficult Maneuvers. Performed by MR. RHODA ROYAL.

DISPLAY No. 11.—A Potpourri of Phenomenal Performances by Artists of Skill and Diversified Talent.

Dexterous and Difficult Feats of Hand Balancing. **The Three Tatalis.** Marvelous Equilibristic Performances upon a Frail and Lofty Framework of Bamboo, with Breakaway Finish. **Mamekichi and Moto.**	Artistic Evolutions and Graceful Performances on a Skilfully balanced Breakaway Ladder. **Velette & Julian Ty Bell.**	Oriental Pastimes on the Rope, concluding with a Sensational and Daring Slide for Life. **Little All Right.** A Wonderful Exhibition of Posturing by the Japanese Artist, **M. Okeo.**	Nationally Characteristic and Intensely Interesting Exploits on the Vibrating Bamboo Perch, presenting Unusual Feats of Equilibrium. By **Ando, Mitso & Ohana.**	An Elastic, Mobile, Plastic Miss, Bending, Twisting and Turning her Flexible Form in remarkable Contortion Feats. **Miss Ida Miaco.** Deft and Dexterous Exercises on a Frail and Swinging Wire. **Miss Dollard.** The Latest Conceits and most Elite Novelties—Statuesque Acrobatiques by the Australian Experts. **The 5 St. Leons.**

| Ring No. 1. | Stage No. 1. | Ring No. 2. | Stage No. 2. | Ring No. 3. |

DISPLAY No. 12.—A New Big Aerial Number.

Sensational Long Distance Mid-Air Leaps and Somersaults, by America's Remarkable Aerial Meteors, **THE FLYING FISHERS.**	"The Upside Down Man" in an Accurate, Unusual, Balancing Trapeze Act—The Performer Executing Equations Requiring Minute Accuracy—Head down—Feet up. **MR. FRANK SMITH.**	An Absolutely New and Original Aerial Display, Dazzling, Brilliant Sextuple Return Act, Double Mid-Air Somersaults Across the Entire Arena. Particular attention is called to the Wonderful Double Somersault and Half Twister performed in this act. **THE SIX AERIAL POTTERS.**

DISPLY No. 13.—A Series of International Athletic and Acrobatic Sensations.

A Troupe of European Artists Executing the Most Hazardous Feats—An Acrobatic Divertisement both Unique and Novel. A Remarkable Display of Muscular Dexterity. First Time in America. **THE DOLLARD TROUPE.** (6 in number.)	The Unquestioned Premier Acrobats of the World, in the Most Marvelous Display of Grace, Dexterity and Skill ever Attempted. The Undisputed Champions. **THE FAMOUS NELSON FAMILY.** (11 in number.)

DISPLAY No. 14.—A Number of Thrilling and Varied Equestrian Specialties.

Beautiful Double Carrying Act on the Backs of Two Fast Running Horses. Artistic Poises and Pictures and Graceful Transitions. **Mr. & Mrs. Homer Hobson.**	Statuesque Double Riding. An Exhibition of Unusual Grace and Beauty in Equestrianism. **Mr. Reno McCree and Miss May Davenport.**	Artistic Double Carrying Act. Exceptionally Clever Equestrian Feats. **Mr. S. St. Leon and Miss Daisy St. Leon.**

DISPLAY No. 15.—A Novel Burlesque Equestrian Conceit.

A Terrible Scramble by a Nimble Clown who does not know how to stay on his Mule's Back, while the latter swiftly circles the Arena. **Mr. F. Schadle.**	The Inimitable Peer of Comic Riders. The Whirlwind Equestrian Clown and his funny Mule "Thunderbolt." **MR. ALBERT CRANDALL.**	A Merry Andrew on a Long-eared Companion who insists on running too fast and bumping too hard. **Albert Thompson.**

GRAND HIPPODROME SENSATIONS. Hotly Contested Trials of Speed and Skill.

FIRST EVENT.—Gentlemen's Jockey Race. (Three times around the track.)
HORSES HAZARD—TORNADO—THUNDERBOLT—FIRE FLY.
RIDERS—AL THOMPSON, Green.—JOHN MERCER, Red.—RAY THOMPSON, Blue.—GEO. COLE, Black and Yellow.

SECOND EVENT.—Tandem Over Hurdles.
Four Thoroughbred Horses, ridden and driven by one man—MR. JOHN CARROLL.

THIRD EVENT.—Shetland Ponies, ridden by Monkey Jockeys. (Twice around the track.)

FOURTH EVENT.—Ladies' Jockey Race. (Three times around the track.)
HORSES—SALAMANDER—BEN HUR—STALKER—SAM COX.
RIDERS—MISS ETTA JORDAN, Purple and Gold.—MISS MILLIE SAVOY, Red and White.
MISS DAISY ST. LEON, Red and Blue.—MISS FANNY JENKS, Black and White.

FIFTH EVENT.—Roman Standing Race. (Three times around the track.)
HORSES—DANGER AND SULTAN.   CHICAGO AND AVALANCHE.   PHILIP AND NERO.
RIDERS—JOHN CARROLL, Purple.   AL THOMPSON, White.   JOE HOMER, Red.

SIXTH EVENT.—Clowns' Race. Shetland Ponies to Sulky. (Once around the track.)
ERNEST MILVO, J. PLAMONDON, W. PLAMONDON, Contestants.

SEVENTH EVENT.—Shetland Pony against Thoroughbred Horse. (Once around the track.)
HORSE—NAPOLEON, ridden by JOHN AGEE.   PONY—SPIDER, ridden by MASTER PHILIP ST. LEON.

EIGHTH EVENT.—Dog Race. English Whippet Hounds. (Once around the track.)

NINTH EVENT.—Terrific Four-Horse Roman Chariot Race. (Three times around the track.)
HORSES { BATTLE AXE—TROOPER—SAMPSON—SHERIDAN.   DRIVERS { MR. JOHN CARROLL, Red.
HARRISON—CYCLONE—MERMAID—ZENOBIA.   MR. JOHN SLATER, White.

APPENDIX II
The Ringling Family

The Ringling family, circa 1895. Standing, left to right: Al, Alf T., Gus, Charles, and Otto. Seated: John, Salome, August, Ida, and Henry. PRINT COLLECTION, CWM

August Frederich Rungeling (Ringling)

Born: 11/24/1826, Hanover, Germany
Died: 2/16/1898, Baraboo, Wisconsin. Buried at Walnut Hill Cemetery, Baraboo
Married: Salome Marie Juliar, 2/16/1852, Milwaukee, Wisconsin

Salome Marie Juliar

Born: 7/25/1833, Ostheim, Alsace, France
Died: 1/27/1907, Baraboo, Wisconsin. Buried at Walnut Hill Cemetery, Baraboo, Wisconsin
Married: August Frederich Rungeling (Ringling), 2/16/1852, Milwaukee, Wisconsin

Albert Charles "Al" Ringling

Born: 12/13/1852, Chicago, Illinois
Died: 1/1/1916, Baraboo, Wisconsin. Buried at Walnut Hill Cemetery, Baraboo, Wisconsin
Married: Eliza "Lou" Morris, 12/19/1883

August Albert "A. G." "Gus" Ringling

Born: 7/20/1854, Milwaukee, Wisconsin
Died: 12/18/1907, New Orleans, Louisiana. Buried at St. Joseph's Catholic Cemetery, Baraboo, Wisconsin
Married: Anna G. "Annie" Hurley, 11/21/1883

George G. Ringling

Born: 1857(?)
Died: February 19, 1857, Baraboo, Wisconsin. Buried at Walnut Hill Cemetery, Baraboo, Wisconsin

William Henry Otto "Otto" Ringling

Born: 6/28/1858, Baraboo, Wisconsin
Died: 3/31/1911, New York. Buried at Walnut Hill Cemetery, Baraboo, Wisconsin
Never married

Baby Boy/Girl

Born: Circa 1860, birthplace unknown
Died: Circa 1860, burial place unknown

Alfred Theodore "Alf T." Ringling

Born: 11/6/1863, McGregor, Iowa
Died: 10/21/1919, Oak Ridge, New Jersey. Buried at Kensico Cemetery, Valhalla, New York
Married: Adella Mae "Della" Andrews, 7/8/1890
Divorced: September–October 1913, Madison, Wisconsin
Married: Elizabeth Shuttleworth, date unknown

Carl Edward "Charles" Ringling

Born: 12/2/1864, McGregor, Iowa
Died: 12/3/1926, Evanston, Illinois. Buried at Manasota Memorial Park, Sarasota, Florida
Married: Edith Conway, 10/23/1889, Baraboo, Wisconsin

John Nicholas Ringling

Born: 5/31/1866, McGregor, Iowa
Died: 12/2/1936, New York. Buried at Ringling Museum Grounds, Sarasota, Florida
Married: Mable Burton, 1905 (Mable died 6/8/1929)
Married: Emily Haag Buck, 12/19/1930
Divorced: 7/6/1936

Henry William George Ringling

Born: 10/27/1868, McGregor, Iowa
Died: 10/10/1918, Baraboo, Wisconsin. Buried at Walnut Hill Cemetery, Baraboo,
    Wisconsin
Married: Ida Belle Palmer, 12/31/1902

Baby Boy/Girl

Born: Circa 1871, birthplace unknown
Died: Circa 1871, burial place unknown

Ida Lorina Wilhemina Ringling

Born: 2/2/1874, Prairie du Chien, Wisconsin
Died: 12/21/1950, Sarasota, Florida. Buried at Ringling Museum Grounds, Sarasota,
    Florida
Married: Henry Whitestone "Harry" North, 8/11/1902

Based on data compiled by Fred Dahlinger Jr. and Donald Heflin. Not all primary documents are available.

Appendix III

Ringling Homes in Baraboo and Vicinity

Several Ringling homes still exist in and around Baraboo. Perhaps the most elegant and stunning is Al Ringling's former home, which was built in 1900 and is one block off the Court House Square on Broadway. The house is now owned by the Elks Club, which has worked toward restoring the mansion.

August Ringling's home is located at 210 Second Avenue. Gus Ringling's home, now privately owned, stands at the northeast corner of Eighth Avenue and Birch Street.

Alfred T. Ringling's first wife, Della, donated his spacious downtown home to the Catholic Church, and it became Ringling St. Mary's Hospital. The home, formerly located at 103 Tenth Street, has since been razed.

Alf T.'s country chalet, located on his former farm between Baraboo and Portage, was demolished in 2002. The 350-acre farm, which is currently owned by the Aldo Leopold Foundation, now comprises a large carriage shop, a concrete swimming pool (likely built by a later owner), a barn, and other farm buildings. At one time the fields grew hay that was hauled to Ringlingville and fed to the circus's several hundred horses and other hay-eating animals.

Charles Ringling's Colonial Revival home on the corner of Ash and Eighth Streets was sold to Henry Ringling after Charles's death. It boasts a nearby carriage house and servant quarters with spacious lawns. All the buildings were once white. A Ringling descendent still lives in the house.

The Ringling farm, on Lynn Avenue, includes a modest house and one of the Ringling horse barns. Most of the land has been sold and developed for other purposes.

All of these properties are privately owned and not open to the public, but several can be viewed from the street.[1]

Notes

Preface and Introduction

1. Henry Ringling North and Alden Hatch, *Circus Kings* (New York: Doubleday, 1960). Throughout this book, *Brothers,* upper case, is used to denote the five Ringling partners; *brothers,* lower case, is used when talking about the seven boys in general.

2. Fred Dahlinger Jr. and Stuart Thayer, *Badger State Showman* (Baraboo, WI: Circus World Museum, 1998); Dean Jensen, *The Biggest, the Smallest, the Longest, the Shortest* (Madison, WI: Wisconsin House, 1975); and Janet Davis, "Circuses," in *The Oxford Companion to U.S. History,* ed. Paul Boyer (New York: Oxford University Press, 2001), pp. 120–121.

Chapter 1

1. *North Iowa Times,* October 2, 1867.

2. Alfred T. Ringling in his book *Life Story of the Ringling Brothers* (Chicago: R. R. Donnelley & Sons, 1900) wrote that his father was twenty-one when he sailed to America. As August was born in 1826, he must have arrived in Canada in 1847. Alf T. also wrote that August spent "about a year" in Canada; thus he likely arrived in Milwaukee in 1848.

3. Ibid., p. 72.

4. J. J. Schlicher, "On the Trail of the Ringlings," *Wisconsin Magazine of History* 26, no. 1 (September 1942): 9.

5. Quoted in Schlicher, "On the Trail of the Ringlings," p. 10.

6. Richard Current, *The History of Wisconsin,* vol. 2, *The Civil War Era, 1848–1873* (Madison: State Historical Society of Wisconsin, 1976), p. 237.

7. Schlicher, "On the Trail of the Ringlings," p. 11.

8. *North Iowa Times,* December 10, 1862.

9. Marian Carroll Rischmueller, "The Ringlings of McGregor," *Palimpsest* (State Historical Society of Iowa), June 1944, p. 182.

10. *North Iowa Times,* October 2, 1867.

11. *North Iowa Times,* May 25, 1870.

12. Rischmueller, "Ringlings of McGregor," p. 184.

13. Consolidation Circus, Mike Lipman's Colossal Combination of Circus and Trained Animals, and Dan Castello's Great Show, Moral Exhibition and Wonderful Wild Animals. Rischmueller, "Ringlings of McGregor," p. 185.

14. Ibid.

15. *North Iowa Times,* May 18, 1870, and May 25, 1870.

16. Alfred T. Ringling, *Life Story of the Ringling Brothers,* p. 21.

17. Stuart Thayer, "The Circus That Inspired the Ringlings," *Bandwagon,* May–June 1996, p. 25.

18. Ibid., p. 24.

19. James D. Allen, "McGregor and the Ringlings," *Annals of Iowa,* October 1952, p. 458.

20. *North Iowa Times,* [1967?].

21. Sally Veit Scarff, interview by the author, McGregor, Iowa, July 2, 2002.

22. Schlicher, "On the Trail of the Ringlings," pp. 17–18.

23. Frances Burt, "Brodhead Claims Beginning of the 'Greatest Show on Earth,'" *White Tops,* November–December 1955, p. 37.

24. Ibid., p. 37.

25. Alvin F. Harlow, *Ringlings, Wizards of the Circus* (New York: Julian Messner, 1951), p. 47.

26. Stillwater, Minnesota, May 1, 1875, Minnesota Census.

27. *Town and Country Business Directory, Sauk County, Wisconsin* (Baraboo, WI: Woodman and Powers, 1881).

28. Ibid.

29. Schlicher, "On the Trail of the Ringlings," pp. 18–19.

30. Jerry Apps, *Cheese: The Making of a Wisconsin Tradition* (Amherst, WI: Amherst Press, 1998).

31. Charles Bernard, "Old-Time Showmen," *Billboard,* July 12, 1930, pp. 54, 83. In 1881 (and perhaps in 1882) Al Ringling was with the Parson and Roy Circus out of Darlington, Wisconsin.

Chapter 2

1. *Richland Center (Wisconsin) Republican-Observer,* December 7, 1882.

2. Schlicher, "On the Trail of the Ringlings," p. 21.

3. Robert C. Nesbit, *The History of Wisconsin: Urbanization and Industrialization, 1873–1893,* vol. 3 (Madison: State Historical Society of Wisconsin, 1985), p. 280.

4. Ibid., pp. 476–477.

5. Alfred T. Ringling, *Life Story of the Ringling Brothers,* p. 88.

6. Ibid., p. 92.

7. *The Route Book of Ringling Bros. Shows: 1882–1914,* Circus World Museum Robert L. Parkinson Library and Research Center (hereafter referred to as CWM Library), p. 1; and Charles E. Ringling, unpublished notes, ca. 1925, CWM Library. Trinkhouse was variously spelled Trinkhaus and Trinkaus.

8. Ringling Concert Company Program, ca. 1882, Circus World Museum, Baraboo, Wisconsin (hereafter referred to as CWM).

9. Alfred T. Ringling, *Life Story of the Ringling Brothers,* p. 94.

10. Ibid., p. 95.

11. *The Route Book of Ringling Bros. Shows: 1882–1914,* pp. 1–4.

12. *Spring Green (Wisconsin) News,* November 30, 1882.

13. *New York Clipper,* August 11, 1883; Route Book of J. H. LaPearl's Shows, p. 5, CWM Library.

14. *Sauk County (Wisconsin) Democrat,* August 25, 1883.

15. *Sauk County (Wisconsin) Democrat,* June 23, 1883.

16. Charles E. Ringling, unpublished notes.

17. Alfred T. Ringling, *Life Story of the Ringling Brothers,* pp. 133–134.

18. Charles E. Ringling, unpublished notes.

19. Schlicher, "On the Trail of the Ringlings," p. 22.

20. *The Route Book of Ringling Bros. Shows: 1882–1914,* pp. 5–10.

21. *New York Clipper,* February 9, 1884, p. 807.

22. According to circus historian Richard J. Reynolds III, the Yankee Robinson name had enough attraction that circus owner Fred Buchanan used it for his circus as late as 1920. Richard J. Reynolds III, correspondence with the author, November 27, 2002.

23. Gene Plowden, *Those Amazing Ringlings and Their Circus* (Caldwell, ID: Caxton Printers, 1967), p. 44.

24. Alfred T. Ringling, *Life Story of the Ringling Brothers,* p. 172.

25. Ibid., pp. 173–178.

26. *Baraboo (Wisconsin) Republic,* April 16, 1884.

27. *Sauk County (Wisconsin) Democrat,* May 3, 1884.

28. *Baraboo (Wisconsin) Republic,* May 14, 1884.

29. J. T. Walker, Baraboo City Clerk, to C. P. Fox, June 3, 1960, CWM Library.

30. North and Hatch, *Circus Kings,* pp. 79–80.

31. Charles Philip Fox, *A Ticket to the Circus* (Seattle, WA: Superior, 1959), p. 21.

32. Ibid.

33. *Sauk County (Wisconsin) Democrat,* May 24, 1884.

34. W. C. Coup, quoted in Stuart Thayer, *Traveling Showmen: The American Circus before the Civil War* (Detroit: Astley and Ricketts, 1997), p. 48.

35. *Darlington (Wisconsin) Republican,* June 13, 1884.

36. *Dodgeville (Wisconsin) Star,* June 1884.

37. *Route Book of the Ringling Brothers, 1882–1914,* pp. 11–14.

38. W. C. Coup, quoted in Thayer, *Traveling Showmen,* p. 49.

39. Frank Parkinson to Circus World Museum, CWM Library, ca. 1954.

40. Alfred T. Ringling, *Life Story of the Ringling Brothers,* p. 204.

41. Charles E. Ringling, unpublished notes, CWM Library.

42. *Route Book of the Ringling Brothers, 1882–1914,* pp. 11–14.

43. Ibid., pp. 15–17.

Chapter 3

1. Otto Ringling to the Bank of Baraboo, May 15, 1888, CWM Library.

2. *The Route Book of Ringling Bros. Shows: 1882–1914.*

3. *Waterford (Wisconsin) Post,* September 17, 1885.

4. *Richland (Wisconsin) Rustic,* May 30, 1885.

5. 1885 advertising poster, CWM.

6. Alfred T. Ringling, *Life Story of the Ringling Brothers,* p. 210.

7. The November 24, 1886, *Baraboo (Wisconsin) Republic* reported Evansville, Indiana, as the source for the animals, but Evansville, Wisconsin, would have been more likely, as it was much closer to Baraboo and a circus was located there.

8. *The Route Book of Ringling Bros. Shows: 1882–1914,* pp. 28–31.

9. *Shullsburg (Wisconsin) Pick and Gad,* October 7, 1886.

10. *Darlington (Wisconsin) Republican,* October 8, 1886.

11. *The Route Book of Ringling Bros. Shows: 1882–1914,* pp. 32–33.

12. *Fond du Lac (Wisconsin) Daily Reporter,* May 23, 1887; *Juneau (Wisconsin) Telephone,* May 27, 1887; *Stoughton (Wisconsin) Hub,* May 20, 1887. The Interstate Commerce Act became effective February 4, 1887, and was supposed to stabilize rates and eliminate price discrimination. American Source Documents, http://www.multied.com/documents.

13. *The Route Book of Ringling Bros. Shows: 1882–1914,* pp. 34–38.

14. Ibid., pp. 39–48.

15. Reynolds, correspondence with the author, November 27, 2002.

16. *The Route Book of Ringling Bros. Shows: 1882–1914,* p. 45.

17. Otto Ringling to Bank of Baraboo, May 15, 1888 (on Mason House [a Waukon, Iowa, hotel] stationery). Courtesy of John Ringling North II. Copy at CWM.

18. Bank of Baraboo Loan Records, 1880–1919. Courtesy of Baraboo National Bank. Abstract at CWM.

19. Ibid.

20. Otto Ringling to Bank of Baraboo, May 25, 1888 (on Plainview [Minnesota] Hotel stationery). Courtesy of John Ringling North II. Copy at CWM.

21. Otto Ringling to Bank of Baraboo, June 14, 1888. Courtesy of John Ringling North II. Copy at CWM.

22. Otto Ringling to J. Van Orden, Bank of Baraboo, August 8, 1888 (on Boyd Hotel [Wayne, Nebraska] stationery). Courtesy of John Ringling North II. Copy at CWM.

23. *The Route Book of Ringling Bros. Shows: 1882–1914,* p. 44.

24. *Prairie du Chien (Wisconsin) Courier,* October 2, 1888.

25. *Sauk County (Wisconsin) News,* October 1888.

26. Sauk County Register of Deeds Office, Baraboo, Wisconsin, November 25, 1887, bk. 56, p. 561.

27. *The Route Book of Ringling Bros. Shows: 1882–1914,* p. 48; *Sauk County (Wisconsin) Democrat,* October 18, 1888, and November 29, 1888.

28. Handbill reprinted in Fox, *Ticket to the Circus,* p. 32.

29. *Hartford (Wisconsin) Press,* May 17, 1889.

30. *Columbus (Wisconsin) Democrat* [May 1889?].

31. *Brodhead (Wisconsin) Independent,* June 21, 1889.

32. Reynolds, correspondence with the author, November 27, 2002; Fred D. Pfening III, correspondence with the author, December 1, 2002.

33. *New York Clipper,* November 16, 1889.

34. Richard E. Conover, "Notes on the Early Ringling Railer," *Bandwagon,* March–April 1967, pp. 4–8.

35. *Sauk County (Wisconsin) Democrat,* October 10, 1889.

36. *Sauk County (Wisconsin) Democrat,* December 12, 1889.

37. *Baraboo (Wisconsin) Republic,* January 29, 1890.

Chapter 4

1. Part of a clothing store ad that offered free tickets, with a $5.00 purchase, for the Ringling circus opening in Baraboo. *Baraboo (Wisconsin) Republic,* April 23, 1890.

2. *The Route Book of Ringling Bros. Shows: 1882–1914,* p. 54.

3. William Grant and Ken Dvorak, "The American 1890s: A Chronology," Bowling Green University, http://www.bgsu.edu/departments/acs/1890s/chronology.html.

4. Information Please, "Inventions and Discoveries," http://www.infoplease.com/ipa/A0004636.html.

5. *Baraboo (Wisconsin) Republic,* April 16, 1890.

6. H. D. Barretta, *Route Book, Season of 1890* (Cincinnati, OH: Donaldson Lith. Co., 1890), p. 6.

7. *Baraboo (Wisconsin) Republic,* April 23, 1890. According to circus historian Richard Reynolds III, the elephant was really Asian and had been acquired from the Forepaugh show, where she was named Juliet. Calling the elephant "umbrella-eared (African)" was likely carelessness on the part of the circus press. Richard Reynolds III, correspondence with the author, November 29, 2002.

8. *Baraboo (Wisconsin) Republic,* April 23, 1890.

9. *Baraboo (Wisconsin) Republic,* May 7, 1890.

10. "The Late James E. Cooper," *New York Clipper,* January 9, 1892, p. 730.

11. Barretta, *Route Book, Season of 1890,* p. 12.

12. Ibid., p. 22.

13. Ibid., p. 17.

14. Ibid., p. 19.

15. Ibid., pp. 11–15.

16. *The Route Book of Ringling Bros. Shows: 1882–1914,* p. 64.

17. Barretta, *Route Book, Season of 1890,* p. 21.

18. *Baraboo (Wisconsin) Republic,* August 29, 1890.

19. Barretta, *Route Book, Season of 1890,* p. 29.

20. *Baraboo (Wisconsin) Republic,* October 15, 1890.

21. Sverre O. Braathen to Chappie Fox, November 7, 1964, Fred Pfening III, private collection, Columbus, Ohio (hereafter referred to as Pfening collection).

22. "Ringling Bros. Circus Car Shops," Car shops, Reference Docs, CWM.

23. Fred D. Pfening Jr., "Ringling Bros. World's Greatest Railroad Shows: The 1890–1891 Seasons," *Bandwagon,* July–August, 1993, p. 11.

24. *Sauk County (Wisconsin) Democrat,* November 13, 1890.

25. *Baraboo (Wisconsin) Republic,* December 24, 1890.

26. *Baraboo (Wisconsin) Republic,* April 8, 1891.

27. *The Route Book of Ringling Bros. Shows: 1882–1914,* p. 59.

28. H. D. Barretta, *Official Route Book of Ringling Bros. World's Greatest Railroad Shows: Season of 1891* (Buffalo, NY: Courier, 1891), pp. 27–43.

29. From the *Grand Forks (North Dakota) Daily Plaindealer,* quoted in the *Baraboo (Wisconsin) Republic,* October 15, 1891.

30. From the *Galesburg (Illinois) Daily Mail,* quoted in the *Baraboo (Wisconsin) Republic,* October 15, 1891.

31. Ringling Daily Ledger, 1891, Pfening collection. Data compiled by Fred Pfening III.

32. Ibid.

33. Ringling Salary Ledger, 1895, Ringling business records, CWM.

34. Thayer, *Traveling Showmen,* pp. 20–21.

35. *Baraboo (Wisconsin) Republic,* November 26, 1891.

36. Best known as the Malayan tapir. It has striking white saddle markings on a black body and is also called a saddle-backed tapir. It is found in Sumatra, Thailand, and Indonesia, as well as Malaysia. Mature Malayan tapirs will grow from three to three and a half feet tall and weigh from 551 to 1,100 pounds. Sheryl Todd, "Tapirback Homepage," http://www.tapirback.com; Richard J. Reynolds, correspondence with the author, December 1, 2002.

37. *Baraboo (Wisconsin) Republic,* October 29, 1891.

38. *Baraboo (Wisconsin) Republic,* February 4, 1892.

39. *Sauk County (Wisconsin) Democrat,* March 24, 1892.

40. Ibid.

41. The bell wagon is now on display at Circus World Museum in Baraboo, on loan from Kenneth Feld and Ringling Bros. and Barnum & Bailey Circus.

42. O. H. Kurtz, *Official Route Book of Ringling Brothers: Season of 1892* (Buffalo, NY: Courier, 1892).

43. *Baraboo (Wisconsin) Republic,* April 28, 1892.

44. Ibid.

45. *Duluth (Minnesota) Herald,* June 27, 1892.

46. *Waupaca (Wisconsin) Post,* July 14, 1892.

47. Kurtz, *Official Route Book of Ringling Brothers: Season of 1892,* p. 90.

48. Ringling Ledger, 1892, Pfening collection. Material compiled by Fred Pfening III.

49. Fred Pfening III and Richard Reynolds III, conversation with the author, July 10, 2001.

50. *The Route Book of Ringling Bros. Shows: 1882–1914,* p. 71.

51. Reynolds, correspondence with the author, December 1, 2002.

52. *Baraboo (Wisconsin) Republic,* January 26, 1893.

53. *Sauk County (Wisconsin) Democrat,* January 1893.

54. Gary B. Nash, John R. Howe, Allen F. Davis, Julie Roy Jeffrey, Peter J. Frederick, and Allan M. Winkler, eds., *The American People: Creating a Nation and a Society* (New York: HarperCollins, 1996), pp. 427–428.

55. Ibid.

56. According to Richard J. Reynolds III, the Panic of 1893 ultimately forced the Adam Forepaugh Circus out of existence. It lost heavily in 1893, went out as a small twenty-one-car, one-ring show in 1894, and was off the road in 1895. Its name reappeared in 1896 as the Forepaugh-Sells show, which was mostly the Sells Circus with some Forepaugh animals and equipment added. Reynolds, correspondence with the author, December 1, 2002.

57. Display ad in *Columbus (Ohio) Dispatch,* September 9, 1893.

58. *Route Book of Ringling Brothers, Season of 1893* (Buffalo, NY: Courier, 1893).

59. Ibid., pp. 44, 50, 54.

60. Ringling Bros. Daily Ledger, 1893, Pfening collection.

61. John D. Buenker, *The History of Wisconsin,* vol. 4, *The Progressive Era, 1893–1914* (Madison: State Historical Society of Wisconsin, 1998), p. 10.

62. *Route Book of Ringling Brothers, Season of 1893,* p. 62.

63. Ringling Bros. Daily Ledger, 1893.

64. *Route Book of Ringling Brothers, Season of 1893,* p. 76.

65. Farewell dinner menu, "Farewell Dinner: Tendered to the Employees of Ringling Bros. World's Greatest Shows. Havanna, Illinois, October 10, 1993. By E. C. Haley," CWM Library.

66. Ringling Bros. Daily Ledger, 1893. Data complied by Fred Pfening III.

67. Alf T. Ringling, *Beneath White Tents: Route Book of Ringling Brothers, 1894 Season,* p. 144.

68. Ibid.

69. Ibid., p. 155.

70. Ringling Bros. Daily Ledgers, 1894, Pfening collection. Data compiled by Fred Pfening III.

71. Data from 1891, 1892, 1893, and 1894 Ringling Bros. daily ledgers, Pfening collection. Income includes matinee and evening performances, concert, sideshow, reserved seats, and privileges. Data compiled by Fred Pfening III.

72. Ringling Bros. Daily Ledgers, 1894.

73. *Sauk County (Wisconsin) Democrat,* November 22, 1894.

Chapter 5

1. Alf T. Ringling, *With the Circus: A Route Book of Ringling Bros. World's Greatest Shows, Seasons of 1895 and 1896* (St. Louis: Great Western Printing, 1896), p. 131.

2. Ibid., pp. 128–129.

3. *The Route Book of Ringling Bros. Shows: 1882–1914,* p. 83.

4. Alf T. Ringling, *With the Circus,* p. 129.

5. Ibid., p. 129.

6. *Chicago InterOcean,* April 28, 1895.

7. Ringling Brothers Receipt Book, 1895, Pfening collection.

8. Alf T. Ringling, *With the Circus,* p. 131.

9. Ringling Brothers Receipt Book, 1895. Data compiled by Fred Pfening III.

10. Alf T. Ringling, *With the Circus,* p. 137.

11. Quoted in Alf T. Ringling, *With the Circus,* p. 137.

12. Ringling Brothers Receipt Book, 1895. Data compiled by Fred Pfening III.

13. Quoted in Alf T. Ringling, *With the Circus,* p. 33.

14. *Chicago InterOcean,* May 2, 1896.

15. Alf T. Ringling, *With the Circus,* p. 33.

16. George L. Chindahl, "The W. B. Reynolds Circus," *White Tops,* July–August 1950, pp. 7–8, 18.

17. Alf T. Ringling, *With the Circus,* p. 71.

18. *The Route Book of Ringling Bros. Shows, 1882–1914,* p. 91.

19. Alf T. Ringling, *With the Circus,* pp. 29–30.

20. Ringling Receipt Book, 1896, Pfening collection. Data compiled by Fred Pfening III.

21. *Berlin (Wisconsin) Journal,* July 16, 1896.

22. Chang Reynolds, "The Ringling Elephants 1888–1967," *Bandwagon,* September–October 1968, pp. 3–12.

23. Ringling Receipt Book, 1895, 1896, and 1897, Pfening collection.

24. Ibid.

25. *The Circus Annual: A Route Book of Ringling Brothers World's Greatest Shows, Season of 1897* (Buffalo, NY: Courier, 1897), p. 107.

26. Ibid.

27. *Janesville (Wisconsin) Daily Gazette,* July 16, 1897.

28. *The Circus Annual: A Route Book of Ringling Brothers World's Greatest Shows, Season of 1897,* p. 103.

29. Ibid., pp. 121, 133.

30. Ringling Receipt Book, 1897, Pfening collection. Data compiled by Fred Pfening III.

31. Henry Casson, "A Ringling Item," *Circus Scrap Book* 8 (October 1930): 50.

32. *Baraboo (Wisconsin) Republic,* Wednesday, April 6, 1898.

33. *Route Book of Ringling Bros. Shows: 1882–1914,* p. 103.

34. Ibid., p. 97.

35. *Red Wagon: Route Book of The Ringing Bros. World's Greatest Show, Season 1898* (Chicago: Central Printing and Engraving, 1898), p. 37.

36. Ringling Receipt Book, 1898, Pfening collection.

37. *Red Wagon: Route Book of The Ringing Bros. World's Greatest Show, Season 1898,* p. 37.

38. Ibid.

39. Ibid., p. 39.

40. Ibid., p. 45.

41. Ibid., p. 47.

42. Ibid., p. 58.

43. Ibid., p. 59.

44. Ibid., p. 45.

45. Ibid., p. 75.

46. *The Route Book of Ringling Bros. Shows: 1882–1914,* p. 102.

47. For more information, see Fred Dahlinger Jr. and Stuart Thayer, "The Ringling Cottage Cages," *Bandwagon,* November–December 1998.

48. Baraboo, Wisconsin, Register of Deeds Office, October 24, 1898, bk. 73, p. 627.

49. *Sauk County (Wisconsin) Democrat,* October 6, 1898, and October 12, 1898.

50. Martindale Mercantile Agency to Strobridge Litho Company, August 19, 1899, Pfening collection.

51. *Red Wagon: Route Book of The Ringing Bros. World's Greatest Show, Season 1899* (Chicago: Central Printing and Engraving, 1899), p. 3.

52. Ibid.

Chapter 6

1. *Route Book: Ringling Bros.' World's Greatest Shows, Season 1900.*

2. Kingwood College Library, "American Cultural History, 1900–1909," http://kclibrary.nhmccd.edu/decade00.html.

3. Ibid.

4. *Baraboo (Wisconsin) Evening News,* January 3, 1900.

5. Hagenbeck's (Hamburg, Germany) to Ringling Brothers, January 14, 1900, Pfening collection.

6. Otto was likely well aware of the problems involved in caring for a walrus. They require a very specialized diet of heavy cream and clams on ground herring—not readily available to a circus on tour. Richard J. Reynolds III, correspondence with the author, December 4, 2002.

7. E. D. Colvin (Hagenbeck's U.S. agent) to Otto Ringling, February 6, 1900, Pfening collection.

8. *Route Book, Ringling Bros. World's Greatest Shows, Season 1900,* p. 9.

9. *Columbus (Ohio) Dispatch,* May 26, 1900.

10. *Route Book, Ringling Bros. World's Greatest Shows, Season 1900,* p. 8.

11. Ibid.

12. *Richland (Wisconsin) Rustic,* July 1900.

13. *Appleton (Wisconsin) Crescent,* July 28, 1900.

14. *Columbus (Ohio) Dispatch,* June 4, 1900.

15. *Chicago Tribune,* April 14, 1901.

16. Alf T. Ringling, *The Circus Annual: A Route Book of Ringling Brothers, Season 1901* (Chicago: Central Printing and Engraving, 1901), p. 33.

17. Ibid., p. 48.

18. Ibid., p. 51.

19. Ibid., p. 54.

20. Ibid., p. 63.

21. Ibid., pp. 69–73.

22. Ibid., pp. 81–82.

23. Quoted in Alf T. Ringling, *The Circus Annual: A Route Book of Ringling Brothers, Season 1901,* p. 81.

24. *Sauk County (Wisconsin) Democrat,* November 7, 1901.

Chapter 7

1. *Canton (Ohio) News Democrat,* May 1, 1902.

2. Fred Dahlinger Jr., correspondence with the author, May 1, 2001.

3. *The Circus: A Route Book of Ringling Bros.' World's Greatest Shows, Season 1902* (Chicago: Central Printing and Engraving, 1902), p. 15.

4. *Baraboo (Wisconsin) Republic,* April 30, 1902.

5. *The Circus: A Route Book of Ringling Bros.' World's Greatest Shows, Season 1902,* p. 17.

6. Ibid.

7. Ibid., p. 21.

8. Ibid., p. 23.

9. Ibid., p. 25.

10. Ibid.

11. Dahlinger, correspondence with the author, May 1, 2001.

12. *The Circus: A Route Book of Ringling Bros.' World's Greatest Shows, Season 1902,* p. 17.

13. Fred Dahlinger Jr., "The History of the Golden Age of Chivalry," *Bandwagon,* March–April 1997, pp. 24–31.

14. Hagenbeck's to Ringling Brothers, August 5, 1902; Hagenbeck's agent, C. L. Williams, to Ringling Brothers, November 12, 1902, Pfening collection.

15. Mammoth spectacles were not a new idea in the circus world. The Barnum show put on "Nero and the Destruction of Rome" in 1890–1891. In 1893 Forepaugh presented "1776." John Robinson did "Solomon and Sheba" in the 1890s and early 1900s. Fred Pfening III, correspondence with the author, December 1, 2002.

16. *The Circus Annual: A Route Book of Ringling Brothers' World's Greatest Shows, Season 1903,* p. 57.

17. Ibid.

18. *Canton (Ohio) News-Democrat,* May 14, 1903.

19. *The Circus Annual: A Route Book of Ringling Brothers' World's Greatest Shows, Season 1903,* p. 64.

20. Ibid.

21. Ibid., p. 65.

22. Ibid.

23. *Canton (Ohio) News-Democrat,* May 22, 1903.

24. *The Circus Annual: A Route Book of Ringling Brothers' World's Greatest Shows, Season 1903,* p. 66.

25. *Detroit Free Press,* June 20, 1903.

26. *The Circus Annual: A Route Book of Ringling Brothers' World's Greatest Shows, Season 1903,* p. 68.

27. "Thirty Years Ago Today," *Baraboo (Wisconsin) News Republic,* December 20, 1933.

28. Dahlinger, correspondence with the author, May 1, 2001.

29. *Baraboo (Wisconsin) Evening News,* November 4, 1903.

30. Richard J. Reynolds III, correspondence with the author, December 17, 2002.

Chapter 8

1. *Duluth (Minnesota) Herald,* January 14, 1905.

2. *Columbus (Ohio) Post Press,* May 1, 1904.

3. *Newark (Ohio) American Tribune,* April 21, 1904, and April 23, 1904. According to Richard Reynolds III, the huge spectacles mounted by both the Ringling and Barnum & Bailey shows required removing part of the grandstand on the side of the tent opposite the center ring, where they would install a stage with overhead canopy, scenic backdrop, and other features necessary for an elaborate production. Reynolds, correspondence with the author, December 17, 2002.

4. *Columbus (Ohio) Post Press,* May 1, 1904.

5. *Newark (Ohio) American Tribune,* May 5, 1904.

6. *Chicago Evening Post,* March 29, 1904.

7. Ibid.

8. *Columbus (Ohio) Dispatch,* May 1, 1904.

9. *Duluth (Minnesota) Herald,* July 2, 1904.

10. *Sauk County (Wisconsin) Democrat,* September 1, 1904, and January 12, 1905.

11. *Duluth (Minnesota) Herald,* January 14, 1905.

12. Ibid.

13. Article of Agreement between Barnum and Bailey Shows and Ringling Brothers Shows, November 1, 1904, CWM.

14. Al Ringling to Henry Ringling, March 1905, Pfening collection.

15. Otto Ringling to Henry Ringling, March 13, 1905, Pfening collection.

16. Ibid.

17. Otto Ringling to Henry Ringling, March 20, 1905, Pfening collection.

18. Otto Ringling to Henry Ringling, March 25, 1905, Pfening collection.

19. Bank of Baraboo Loans, Discount Register A, January 5, 1880, to April 7, 1906, CWM.

20. *Canton (Ohio) Morning News,* May 5, 1905.

21. *Sauk County (Wisconsin) Democrat,* September 22, 1905.

22. Fred Pfening III, correspondence with the author, December 1, 2002.

Chapter 9

1. *Show World,* November 9, 1907, p. 20.

2. Agreement, Barnum & Bailey Show and Ringling Brothers Show, December 2, 1905, CWM.

3. *Appleton (Wisconsin) Crescent,* August 18, 1906.

4. Ringling Brothers Receipts Ledger Summary, 1906, Pfening collection.

5. Legal agreement between Ruth Louisa Bailey and Ringling Brothers, June 5, 1906, Milner Library collection, Illinois State University, Normal, Illinois.

6. *Appleton (Wisconsin) Crescent,* August 28, 1906.

7. *Newark (Ohio) American Tribune,* April 21, 1906.

8. Candy Stand Book, Ringling Bros. Show, Season of 1906, Frank Parson, CWM.

9. *Van Wert (Ohio) Times Democrat,* June 29, 1906.

10. Candy Stand Book, p. 150.

11. Ibid., p. 178.

12. *Baraboo (Wisconsin) News,* November 28, 1906.

13. *Duluth (Minnesota) Evening Herald,* July 10, 1906.

14. Ibid.

15. *Duluth (Minnesota) Evening Herald,* July 11, 1906.

16. *Baraboo (Wisconsin) News,* November 28, 1906.

17. Ibid.

18. Ibid.

19. Ringling Brothers Receipts Ledger Summary, 1906, Pfening collection.

20. *Baraboo (Wisconsin) News,* November 7, 1906.

21. *Baraboo (Wisconsin) Republic,* November 6, 1907.

22. Allen Paschen, interview by the author, Baraboo, Wisconsin, January 2, 2002.

23. The purchase took place in stages, with the October date culminating the deal.

24. Otto Ringling to Ringling Brothers, October 26, 1907, Pfening collection.

25. *Baraboo (Wisconsin) Republic,* October 30, 1907.

26. *Billboard,* 1907, p. 22.

27. Glenn Shirley, *Pawnee Bill: A Biography of Major Gordon W. Lillie* (Albuquerque: University of New Mexico Press, 1958), pp. 162–163, 180.

28. *Show World,* November 9, 1907, p. 20.

29. Otto Ringling to Ringling Brothers, October 26, 1907, Pfening collection.

30. Otto was probably referring to elephants that were a part of Forepaugh-Sells show, as Barnum & Bailey had no African elephants. Richard J. Reynolds III, correspondence with the author, December 14, 2002.

31. By this time some circuses were having difficulties mounting a parade on city streets clogged with automobile, truck, and streetcar traffic. Barnum & Bailey had already eliminated parades by the time of the Ringling purchase.

32. Otto Ringling to Ringling Brothers, October 26, 1907, Pfening collection.

33. *Baraboo (Wisconsin) Republic,* December 25, 1907.

Chapter 10

1. *Racine (Wisconsin) Daily Times,* July 31, 1908.

2. *Van Wert (Ohio) Daily Times,* July 26, 1908.

3. *Duluth (Minnesota) Herald,* June 13, 1908.

4. *Show World,* December 21, 1907, p. 140.

5. *Racine (Wisconsin) Daily Times,* July 31, 1908.

6. *Duluth (Minnesota) Herald,* June 25, 1908.

7. Fred Dahlinger Jr., correspondence with the author, November 13, 2002.

8. Otto Ringling to Charles Ringling, October 28, 1908, Pfening collection.

9. Ibid.

10. "With the White Tops," *Show World,* March 28, 1908, p. 16.

11. H. L. S., Letter, *Boys' World,* June 20, 1908.

12. "With the White Tops: Free Zoo at Baraboo, Wis.," *Show World,* February 1, 1908, p. 8.

13. "One hundred fifty years of Masonry in Baraboo: Program of Celebration," CWM.

14. Allen Paschen, interview by the author, Baraboo, Wisconsin, March 5, 2001.

15. John Ringling to the Ringling Brothers, winter 1908, Pfening collection.

16. John L. Sullivan to the Ringling Brothers, October 31, 1908, Milner Library collection, Illinois State University, Normal, Illinois.

17. Reynolds, correspondence with the author, December 17, 2002.

18. Shirley, *Pawnee Bill,* p. 197.

19. Ibid., pp. 162–163, 197–198.

20. "With the White Tops," *Show World,* December 28, 1908.

21. Reynolds, correspondence with the author, December 18, 2002.

22. "With the White Tops," *Show World,* January 15, 1910, p. 17.

23. Ibid.

24. Ibid., October 16, 1909, p. 22

25. Ibid., January 15, 1910, p. 17.

26. By the 1910 season the Ringling Brothers' train comprised three advertising cars, twenty-six stockcars, forty flatcars, and fifteen passenger cars. Havirland list, Circuses on Tour, Season 1910, CWM.

27. *Baraboo (Wisconsin) News,* October 7, 1909.

28. *Baraboo (Wisconsin) News,* November 4, 1909.

29. The Ringlings bought their first railcars used and later purchased new ones from Barney and Smith of Dayton, Ohio; "Ringling Bros. Circus Car Shops," CWM.

Chapter 11

1. *Show World,* August 6, 1910, p. 1.

2. Havirland list, Circuses on Tour, Season 1910, CWM.

3. "With the White Tops," *Show World,* January 15, 1910, p. 17.

4. John M. Staudenmaier, "Henry Ford," in *The Oxford Companion to United States History,* ed. Paul Boyer (New York: Oxford University Press, 2001), p. 275.

5. Timothy E. Scheurer, "Irving Berlin (1888–1989)," in *The Oxford Companion to United States History,* ed. Paul Boyer (New York: Oxford University Press, 2001), p. 70.

6. Havirland list, Circuses on Tour, Season 1910.

7. Ringling Brothers to E. Allen Frost, January 7, 1910, Pfening collection.

8. Otto Ringling to Al Ringling, February 21, 1910, CWM.

9. Fred Pfening III, correspondence with the author, December 1, 2002.

10. "With the White Tops," *Show World,* July 2, 1910.

11. *Janesville (Wisconsin) Daily Gazette,* August 13, 1910.

12. 1910 reviews file, Decatur (Illinois) newspaper, August 7, 1910, CWM.

13. *Janesville (Wisconsin) Daily Gazette,* August 13, 1910.

14. 1910 reviews file, Decatur (Illinois) newspaper, August 7, 1910, CWM.

15. *Columbus (Ohio) Dispatch,* May 19, 1910.

16. Richard J. Reynolds III, correspondence with the author, December 22, 2002.

17. Internal memorandum, Circus World Museum, December 23, 1998.

18. *Sauk County (Wisconsin) Democrat,* October 13, 1910.

19. *Baraboo (Wisconsin) Weekly News,* November 14, 1912.

20. Jan and Duane Neuman, interview with the author, Baraboo, Wisconsin, December 10, 2001.

21. Sauk County, Wisconsin, Register of Deeds, vol. 94, p. 366.

22. *Sauk County (Wisconsin) Democrat,* February 2, 1911.

23. *Chicago Sunday Record-Herald,* April 16, 1911.

24. Otto Ringling to his brothers, January 18, 1910. Copy from original owned by Sally Clayton Jones, CWM.

25. Purchase agreement for Forepaugh-Sells drafted November 1911, Pfening collection.

26. County Court of Sauk County, Wisconsin, Estate of Otto Ringling, Summary of Inventory with Appraised Values. March 31, 1911.

27. *Baraboo (Wisconsin) Weekly News,* May 29, 1913.

28. Release, dated June 23, 1913, and signed by the three nieces. Copy from original owned by Sally Clayton Jones, CWM.

29. Reynolds, correspondence with the author, December 22, 2002; cables and telegrams between Jordon and Ringling in September and October 1910, Milner; and *Baraboo (Wisconsin) News,* April 6, 1911, and May 4, 1911.

30. Ringling Brothers Road Ledger, 1911, CWM

31. Ringling Brothers Standard Daily Journal, 1911, Pfening collection.

32. Ibid.

33. Richard J. Reynolds III, correspondence with the author, December 19, 2002.

34. Ringling Brothers Road Ledger, 1911, CWM.

35. *Baraboo (Wisconsin) News,* November 9, 1911.

36. Fred Pfening III, correspondence with the author, December 1, 2002; sales agreement for Adam Forepaugh and Sells Brothers Circus, 1911, Milner Library collection, Illinois State University, Normal, Illinois.

Chapter 12

1. *Baraboo (Wisconsin) Republic,* November 16, 1911.

2. Buenker, *The History of Wisconsin,* vol. 4, *The Progressive Era, 1893–1914,* pp. 553–554.

3. Reprinted in *Baraboo (Wisconsin) Weekly News,* May 30, 1912.

4. Ibid.

5. *Milwaukee Sentinel,* February 5, 1888.

6. Fred Pfening III, correspondence with the author, December 1, 2002.

7. *Sauk County (Wisconsin) Democrat,* September 16, 1897.

8. *Baraboo (Wisconsin) Weekly News,* March 7, 1912.

9. *Baraboo (Wisconsin) Republic,* April 18, 1912.

10. Al Ringling to Charles Ringling, March 6, 1912, Pfening collection.

11. Summary of information in regard to winter quarters at Chicago office, July 1, 1912, Pfening collection.

12. *Necedah (Wisconsin) Republic,* April 18, 1912.

13. "With the White Tops," *Show World,* January 15, 1910, p. 17.

14. *Sauk County (Wisconsin) Democrat,* April 25, 1912.

15. *Baraboo (Wisconsin) Weekly News,* May 30, 1912.

16. *Baraboo (Wisconsin) Weekly News,* April 25, 1912.

17. Ibid.

18. John Ringling to Al Ringling, January 27, 1912, Pfening collection.

19. Al Ringling to John Ringling, February 1, 1912, CWM.

20. John Ringling to Al Ringling, March 4, 1912, CWM.

21. Charles Ringling to John Ringling, March 12, 1912, CWM.

22. Ibid.

23. *Toledo (Ohio) Blade,* June 14, 1912; *Duluth (Minnesota) Herald,* July 17, 1912.

24. Ad in *Toledo (Ohio) Blade,* June 25, 1912.

25. *Toledo (Ohio) Blade,* June 25, 1912.

26. *Duluth (Minnesota) Herald,* July 17, 1912.

27. Unidentified writer, Coliseum Building, Chicago, to John Ringling, April 10, 1912, Pfening collection.

28. *Baraboo (Wisconsin) Weekly News,* April 18, 1912.

29. *Findley (Ohio) Courier,* August 23, 1912.

30. Charles Ringling to Al Ringling, August 8, 1912, Pfening collection.

31. Ibid.

32. *Baraboo (Wisconsin) Weekly News,* December 26, 1912.

33. Ibid.

34. Ringling Brothers, Baraboo, to various suppliers, January 24, 1912, November 8, 1912, November 13, 1912, Pfening collection.

35. John H. Snellen to Al Ringling, December 12, 1912, Pfening collection.

36. Display ad published by the News Publishing Co., Baraboo, Wisconsin, November 1, 1912, Pfening collection.

37. Harry Humphrey to Ringling Brothers, December 30, 1912, Pfening collection.

38. Al Ringling to Charles Ringling, February 6, 1913, Pfening collection.

39. Contract between Ringling Brothers and Thomas Zingaro, November 9, 1911, Pfening collection.

40. Thomas Zingaro to Al Ringling, December 9, 1912, Pfening collection.

41. Al Ringling to Thomas Zingaro, December 12, 1912, Pfening collection.

42. Al Ringling to John Ringling, December 16, 1912, Pfening collection.

43. George Rapp to Al Ringling, February 3, 1913, Pfening collection.

44. Al Ringling to C. W. and Geo. L. Rapp, February 5, 1913, Pfening collection.

45. *Baraboo (Wisconsin) Weekly News,* April 24, 1913.

46. Ibid.

47. Wisconsin was the first state to pass a Workmen's Compensation Act (1911). Before the law, a worker who was injured had to sue his employer for compensation and prove that the employer was negligent. Under the new law no such proof was needed, and an injured worker could be promptly compensated, although with financial limits. Employers could choose whether to comply with the act. State of Wisconsin Office of the Commissioner of Insurance, http://oci.wi.gov/.

48. *Duluth (Minnesota) Labor World,* December 28, 1912.

49. Charles Ringling to Al Ringling, August 14, 1913, Pfening collection.

50. See Fred D. Pfening Jr., "Ringling Bros. World's Greatest Show: The 1913 Season," *Bandwagon,* March–April 1993, pp. 6–7, for an extended discussion of the electric generator.

51. *Billboard,* June 6, 1914, p. 22; *Baraboo (Wisconsin) Weekly News,* May 28, 1914; *Sauk County (Wisconsin) Democrat,* May 28, 1914; *Cleveland (Ohio) Leader,* May 26, 27, 1914.

52. Three contracts between the Ringling Brothers (signed by Henry Ringling) and the Barney & Smith Car Company, May 29, 1914, CWM.

53. Correspondence between Ringling Brothers and Barney & Smith Car Company, June 18, 1914, and June 22, 1914, CWM.

Chapter 13

1. "Deaths," *New York Clipper,* January 8, 1916.

2. Ringling Brothers to Eretto Trio, December 17, 1914, Pfening collection.

3. Richard J. Reynolds III, correspondence with the author, December 29, 2002.

4. *New York Clipper,* May 1, 1915.

5. Fred Bradna, *The Big Top* (New York: Simon and Schuster, 1952), p. 306.

6. Havirland list of railroad shows, 1915, CWM.

7. Daily Receipts, Ringling Bros.' World's Greatest Shows, Season 1915, Pfening collection.

8. *Volksblatt,* September 10, 1915, translation from German by Jon Romelton.

9. Winter Quarters Ledger, 1915–1916, CWM.

10. Sauk County, Wisconsin, Register of Deeds, recorded December 1, 1914, vol. 104, p. 301.

11. "From Mud to the Field of the Cloth of Gold," *Show World,* September 17, 1910, p. 12.

12. North and Hatch, *Circus Kings,* p. 169.

13. Charles Ringling to Fred Warrell (a Ringling employee), February 7, 1916, Pfening collection.

14. *Columbus Citizen,* May 16, 1916.

15. Charles Philip Fox, *A Tribute to the Percheron Horse* (Boulder, CO: Pruett, 1983), pp. 168–169.

16. Ringling Brothers Receipts Book, 1916, Pfening collection.

17. Official Route: Ringling Brothers World's Greatest Shows, Season 1916, CWM.

18. *Sauk County (Wisconsin) Democrat,* November 8, 1916.

19. Thomas J. Knock, "World War I," in Paul S. Boyer (ed.), *The Oxford Companion to United States History,* (New York: Oxford University Press, 2001), p. 844; Nash, Howe, Davis, Jeffrey, Frederick, and Winkler, *American People,* pp. 485–494; and Oscar Handlin, *The History of the United States* (New York: Holt, Rinehart and Winston, 1968), pp. 329–340.

20. Bradna, *Big Top,* p. 93.

21. *Chicago Herald and Examiner,* April 5, 1917.

22. Artist's contract and release, The Clarkonians (three Clarke Brothers), April 7, 1917, Pfening collection.

23. Havirland list of railroad shows, 1917, CWM.

24. Official Route: Ringling Brothers World's Greatest Shows, Season 1917, CWM.

25. Daily Receipts: Ringling Bros. World's Greatest Shows, Season 1917, CWM.

26. Charles Ringling to the Strobridge Lithographing Company (Cincinnati, Ohio), July 20, 1917, Pfening collection.

27. W. W. Dunkle, "Ringlings Ready to Ramble," *Billboard,* March 23, 1918, p. 16.

28. Havirland list of railroad shows, 1918, CWM.

29. Dunkle, "Ringlings Ready to Ramble," p. 16.

30. The American Experience, "Influenza, 1918," Public Broadcasting System, http://www.pbs.org/wgbh/amex/influenza/.

31. World Almanac, *The World Almanac and Book of Facts* (Mahwah, NJ: World Almanac Books, 2001), p. 448.

32. "Circus Season Virtually Brought to Close," *Billboard,* October 19, 1918, p. 26.

33. Daily Receipts, Ringling Bros. World's Greatest Shows 1918, Pfening collection.

34. Richard Thomas, *John Ringling* (New York: Pageant Press, 1960), p. 126.

35. "Still a Question: Nothing Definite as to Barnum & Bailey Wintering in Baraboo," *Billboard,* May 25, 1918.

36. *Baraboo (Wisconsin) Weekly News,* October 17, 1918.

37. C. P. "Chappie" Fox, interview by the author, Baraboo, Wisconsin, December 10, 2001.

38. "Ringling Circus: To Winter at Bridgeport?" *Billboard,* October 5, 1918.

39. "Circus Season Virtually Brought to Close," *Billboard,* October 19, 1918, p. 54.

40. North and Hatch, *Circus Kings,* p. 171.

41. "Circus Season Virtually Brought to Close," *Billboard,* October 19, 1918.

42. Railroads and other seized carriers were returned to private control on March 1, 1920. See www.archives.gov/research_room/federal_records_guide/us_railroad_administration_rg014.html.

43. Richard J. Reynolds III, correspondence with the author, July 21, 2001, and December 29, 2002.

44. Thomas, *John Ringling,* pp. 125–126.

45. According to the 1917 Barnum & Bailey Route Book, they showed in Toledo, Ohio, on June 13, 1917. 1917 Barnum & Bailey Route Book, CWM.

46. Bradna, *Big Top,* p. 95.

47. Fred Dahlinger Jr., correspondence with the author, February 10, 2004.

48. Robert Barnes, interview with author, Madison, January 2002.

Epilogue

1. North and Hatch, *Circus Kings,* p. 174.

2. Thomas, *John Ringling,* pp. 122–123.

3. Havirland list of railroad shows, 1920, 1921, 1927, 1928, CWM.

4. North and Hatch, *Circus Kings,* pp. 194–195.

5. Sarasota Government homepage, "John Ringling, Dreamer," http://www.co.sarasota.fl.us/.

6. Jane Bancroft Cook Library, "The Charles Ringling Estate," http://www.ncf.edu/library/speccoll/CREstate.htm.

7. *Peoria (Illinois) Journal Star,* September 29, 1991.

8. *Chicago Tribune,* October 11, 1987.

9. Will of Charles E. Ringling, dated September 1, 1926, Sauk County, Baraboo, Wisconsin, Register of Deeds, vol. 140, p. 545.

10. Richard J. Reynolds III, correspondence with the author, December 30, 2002.

11. John & Mable Ringling Museum of Art, http://www.ringling.org/.

12. Havirland list of railroad shows, 1929, CWM.

13. North and Hatch, *Circus Kings,* p. 220.

14. Ibid., pp. 222–226.

15. Ibid., p. 251.

16. David Lewis Hammarstrom, *Big Top Boss: John Ringling North and the Circus* (Urbana and Chicago: University of Illinois Press, 1992), pp. 38–39.

17. *White Tops,* May–June 1962, p. 23.

18. John & Mable Ringling Museum of Art, http://www.ringling.org/.

19. Reynolds, correspondence with the author, July 21, 2001.

20. Fred Dahlinger Jr., correspondence with the author, February 11, 2004.

21. Reynolds, correspondence with the author, July 21, 2001.

22. Robert Barnes, interview with the author, Madison, January 2002.

23. *Baraboo (Wisconsin) News,* March 2, 1939.

24. Ibid.

25. *Baraboo (Wisconsin) Weekly News,* June 15, 1939.

Appendixes

1. See Bob Dewel, "The Opulent Ringling Bros. Homes," *Baraboo (Wisconsin) News Republic,* April 14, 1999, for a description of Ringling homes. Paul Wolter, Wisconsin Dells, Wisconsin, also provided information.

Index